Good But Not Perfect

Good But Not Perfect

A Case Study of Managed Care

Maxine W. Epstein
University of Houston

Patti Aldredge
University of Houston

Allyn and Bacon
Boston • London • Toronto • Sydney • Tokyo • Singapore

Senior Series Editor: Judy Fifer
Editorial Assistant: Julianna Cancio
Composition Buyer: Linda Cox
Manufacturing Buyer: Megan Cochran
Marketing Manager: Jackie Aaron
Editorial-Production Service: P. M. Gordon Associates
Production Administrator: Deborah Brown
Cover Administrator: Jenny Hart

A Pearson Education Company
160 Gould Street
Needham Heights, Massachusetts 02494

Internet: www.abacon.com

Library of Congress Cataloging-in-Publication Data

Epstein, Maxine W.
Good but not perfect : a case study of managed care / Maxine W. Epstein, Patti Aldredge.
p. cm.
Includes bibliographical references and index.
ISBN 0-321-02467-2
1. Managed care plans (Medical care)—United States. 2. Health maintenance organizations—United States. I. Aldredge, Patti. II. Title.
RA413.E66 2000
362.1′04258′0873—dc21 99-37898
CIP

Printed in the United States of America

10 9 8 7 6 5 4 3 2 1 04 03 02 01 00 99

To the memory of my beloved father, Charles Rosenberg, a good and kind person; a storyteller.

Maxine Weinman Epstein

To Dawn Arnold, my brave companion in this extraordinary world.

Patti Aldredge

Contents

Preface

You are about to embark on a new and innovative approach to social work practice. In the following six chapters you will be able to identify and begin to resolve the complexities of managed care environments as they affect the interdisciplinary treatment team and the patient. These chapters are presented through characterizations rather than being presented in didactic form.

The process of learning skill-based practice unfolds in the Introduction, which provides an overview of the issues of managed care and sets the stage for each chapter—the narrative, the analysis of the narrative, and practice skills to help you discuss the issues in the classroom.

We hope you will be enticed to read more about managed care in general. It is our intention to provide a synthesis of why it came into being and the inherent conflicts for social workers who must assess when managed care strategies conflict with individual rights. Our intention is to combine scholarship, art, and analysis in a way to make managed care information accessible to you.

In essence, this is a book about critical thinking. Our experiences in teaching and talking with students have made us realize that social workers and students like to hear and tell stories. Much of what we do as social workers is to listen to people's stories and to reframe these experiences in the context of case assessments. Therefore, this book offers the student a way of capturing the patient's view in the context of being in a changing health care system. The characters are based on personalities we have encountered in our professional lives and represent various dilemmas and challenges that we have struggled with. As authors, we found the best way to describe these situations was to put the words in the mouths of characters.

Thus, we began this endeavor by hours of storytelling to each other. We then analyzed the critical issues in our stories. We believed this was an effective way to share information. The book was written for students with this in mind. You will begin by learning about the *issues* surrounding managed care; you will then read about how these issues affect the delivery of health care as seen through the eyes of the patient and the health care team. You will be given the skills to *analyze* these situations, and finally, you will be encouraged to *apply* those skills in practice exercises. Some of the characters represent stereotypes. We have done this on purpose so that you might find ways you would like to see them change. In other words, we would like you, the reader, to write your own epilogue.

This book can be used as a recommended text for health care practice and policy as well as for micro/macro and interdisciplinary practice courses. The case study method was chosen because the mode of the book is to provide a developmental framework for understanding the growth of managed care and the parallel growth of the patient and the interdisciplinary team as they struggle through a changing health care system.

In Chapter 1, The Event: The Rules Are Changing, you are exposed to a managed care environment and how it affects interdisciplinary practice. In Chapter 2, Diagnosis: Facing the Limits of Change, you are exposed to traditional role conflicts and professional turf issues. In Chapter 3, Disability: The Patient and the Team Deny Change, you learn about attempts professionals make to strengthen team-building skills and some of the current problems with the changing nature of professional practice. In Chapter 4, Change: Crisis, Conflict, Opportunities, and Rehabilitation, you can explore the process skills necessary for collaboration. In Chapter 5, Seeking Wholeness: Hearing, Accepting, Adjusting, and Advocating, you see how the team as a whole works to advocate for the patient's rights. Finally, in Chapter 6, Compromise: Good But Not Perfect, you are presented with a model for good interdisciplinary teamwork. Throughout the chapters, you are exposed to the components of good patient assessment, treatment planning, and discharge planning, as well as listening skills and quality-of-life issues. The patient's voice will be heard throughout the text as you get to know her and her family, her strengths and weaknesses, and her struggle to function as someone who is good but not perfect.

In order to examine the content of the chapters, a few conceptual issues about managed care systems are provided. Social workers tend to have a negative view of managed care because they are not familiar with its development and feel isolated from policy changes. The Introduction provides a general discussion of issues every social worker should be aware of. Before you can critique a system, you must be familiar with its elements. The term *managed care* is confusing because there is no one particular system of managed care. Rather, managed care is a system that in varying degrees integrates financing and delivery of medical care through contracts with health care providers, hospitals, and other health care institutions, such as nursing homes and rehabilitation units. All forms of managed care represent attempts to control costs by modifying the behaviors of physicians, consumers, and other providers. The term *managed care* refers to health maintenance organizations (HMOs), preferred provider organizations (PPOs), and point-of-service (POS) financing and delivery systems. The rapid growth of managed care reflects the need for more organized delivery of comprehensive health care and the determination of employers to constrain health care costs by limiting their employees' options through some form of managed care (Inglehart 1994a). When physicians sign on with managed health care plans, they are demonstrating a greater willingness to accept some financial risk in making clinical decisions and to adapt to health care plans that by definition seek to curtail their independence. These plans affect practice through clinical rules that include quality assurance procedures, treatment protocols, practice guidelines, and utilization reviews.

Managed care organizations can also negotiate for a discounted rate of payment to physicians and hospitals in exchange for a larger volume of patients. The American Medical Association estimated in 1993 that 75 percent of physicians had signed a contract with a managed care plan (Inglehart 1994a). Managed care plans, although threatening to the independence of health care professionals, are by no means incongruous with good health care. In fact, a review of the literature suggests that compared with indemnity plans, HMO plans exhibit significantly lower utilization of hospital services and expensive procedures and tests. They also increase use of preventive services and office visits. Some HMO plan enrollees accept the trade-off of less satisfaction with care in return for lower out-of-pocket premiums and service costs (Miller and Luft 1994).

It is estimated that by the year 2000, 40 to 65 percent of Americans will be receiving their health care through managed care plans, and the supply of physicians, especially specialists, will outstrip demand by 30 percent (Weiner 1994). Inglehart (1994b) suggests that physician practice is managed in managed care plans because when physicians sign managed care contracts, by definition they are curtailing their independence. The selection of network physicians is the starting point for such arrangements and the single most important feature that distinguishes managed care plans from fee-for-service plans. According to Kern (1995), the lack of control over practice and the refusal of physicians to believe that managed care could compete with the practitioner's care and concern were oversights by physicians who did not recognize the economic pressures created by business and industry. These pressures were far more powerful than government's attempt to control the costs of health care. Additionally, managed care organizations have excellent public relations programs that are aimed at selling the benefits of managed care. While managed care suggests outside interference, there is opportunity for health care professionals to provide effective medical care and be efficient as well. This philosophy may not be trusted by interdisciplinary teams because some may view managed care as an anathema to good practice. Kern (1995) states, however, that because physicians have been paid according to the amount of care rendered, rather than their efficiency, managed care threatens their power. As such, physicians have paid insufficient attention to the economic consideration of prescribing a costly medication over a less expensive one, or using laboratory and radiological tests on a selective rather than on a global basis. In summary, managed care systems have developed and grown because of a variety of pressures to regulate and control the costs of health care. Health care professionals who are critical of managed care need to be educated about its delivery before they can effectively propose a better system.

Acknowledgments

We wish to thank the following people who have helped us during the course of writing this book.

Howard Karger, professor, Graduate School of Social Work, provided us with the encouragement to pursue this endeavor when we were not sure this type of textbook could be written. We appreciate his many suggestions and comments as we tried to create this highly innovative text.

Dr. Victor Rivera, MD, professor of neurology, Baylor College of Medicine, gave us much needed information about stroke patients and believed in our efforts in educating students in new and creative ways.

Wini Breitbach, RN, Department of Neurology, Baylor College of Medicine, gave us insight into the struggles of patients and medical staff during managed care changes.

Janice Wiggins Clarke, our former editor at Addison-Wesley Longman, was with us from the very beginning and offered both excellent suggestions (which we used) as well as support, interest, and enthusiasm.

Carolyn Brooks, secretary, Graduate School of Social Work, typed endless revisions and corrections, worked with narrative and text, notes, and produced our final copy with detailed attention and caring to all our final editing.

Maxine Silberstein, dance coordinator, Jewish Community Center, provided us with details about the daily routine of ballet dancers and encouraged us in our efforts to combine art and scholarship.

Margie Kalhorn, ballet instructor, Jewish Community Center, teacher extraordinaire, brought to life the essence of always striving for perfecting aspirations and achievements.

Rena Bond and Jean Kapulski, adult ballet students at the Jewish Community Center, demonstrated that ballet can be a lifetime pursuit as well as lots of fun.

We gratefully acknowledge the efforts of the following people who reviewed this manuscript: Terry Mizrahi, Hunter College; Letitia Bratton, Southern Illinois University at Carbondale; Scott Miyake Geron, Boston University; Diane Byington, University of Denver; Mark Frenzel, University of Minnesota; Maria C. Bartlett, Humboldt State University; Margaret Christopher, California University of Pennsylvania; Patricia Kolar, University of Pittsburgh; Carol A. Heintzelman, Millersville University; and K. Jean Peterson, University of Kansas.

I would also like to thank my family for their love and support during the years I worked on this book: my husband Henry, my daughter Jennifer and her husband Craig, my daughter Veronica and her husband Stuart, my sons Daniel and Adam, my grandchildren Holden, Brady, Abarrane, and Cormac, and my mother Hana Rosenberg, the first of three generations of social workers in our family.

—Maxine Weinman Epstein

I would not have been driven to write this book were it not for the patients of managed care systems, each with a unique story, who allowed me to be a part of their lives in trying times. Their needs constantly challenge me to embrace the role of change agent with urgency and integrity.

My parents, C. G. and Evelyn Pearcy, impressed upon me the importance of education and teaching—I hope I've done them proud.

My brother, Jerry Aldredge, has always told me I was smart, and my sister, Kay Carrigan, has always told me I could write—I hope I've done them proud.

My partner, and friend, and champion, Dawn Arnold, believed in me long before I did. For richer, for poorer, in health and in sickness, she has always been my greatest inspiration. I would never have finished this book without her love and encouragement.

—Patti Aldredge

Good But Not Perfect

Introduction: Overview to Managed Care

Many social workers, and other health care professionals as well, state they do not like managed care. However, much of this dislike stems from uncertainty about what managed care is all about. This is understandable because managed care organizations literally sprung into being and overwhelmed health care professionals with changes in structure of their work environments, new terminologies, and new ways of providing care. Every day there are articles in newspapers and magazines about managed care. Some of the articles are confusing unless you know a lot about managed care and how it works. Some articles evoke strong feelings of anger, especially when they discuss people who have been neglected or who have not gotten needed services because of managed care. Some articles make managed care organizations look like villains. Can you imagine how confusing it is to the public and to patients who are trying to understand why a system that has tried to control costs and provide quality care has not worked as well as it should? Therefore, it is important that social workers understand the basic tenets of managed care so that they, as a profession, can understand the impact it has on society, participate in change-making strategies, advocate for patients' rights, and deliver problem-based solutions. Social workers in particular are distrustful of large bureaucracies with endless paperwork. They prefer direct services to individuals, families, and communities. Therefore, while it is easier to blame a system rather than critique and analyze it, social workers must nevertheless educate themselves about managed care. Then they may thoughtfully and critically evaluate professional concerns about managed care organizations.

As Dennis L. Poole (1996) points out in a recent editorial in *Health and Social Work,* "managed care has thrown us off balance—and rightfully so. Who would have predicted 10 years ago that nearly all Americans would be covered under a managed care plan by the turn of the century" (163). A major issue is whether social workers can adjust quickly to the complex field of managed competition which includes understanding the system of cost containment which includes the profit motive. Health care expenditures in the United States will approach the $2 trillion mark by the year 2000, 20 percent of the nation's gross national product (GNP). Managed care began with the passage of the Health Maintenance Organization Act of 1973 (P.L. #93-222) and accelerated during the Reagan administration with the Deficit Reduction Act of 1984 (P.L. #98-369). This act implemented the prospective payment system to control Medicare cost by removing payment from the federal government to health care insurance companies. The defeat of Clinton's Health Security Act of 1993 (S. 1757 and H.R. 3600) hastened reforms in state government as well and for managed care for Medicaid programs (Poole 1996). According to a recent report by Levit, Lazenby, Braden, and the National Health Accounts Team (1998) while spending for personal health care services is higher in the United States than any other industrialized country, in the past five years the spending increases have slowed dramatically due to the growth of managed care, the low general inflation of medical care, and discounts negotiated by managed care companies with providers. Managed care enrollment increased to 60 percent of the population in 1996, up from 36 percent in 1992. The shift from fee-for-service to managed care attracted purchasers interested in lower premiums, thus slowing growth in health care expenses, especially as consumers got less services. However, there is some indication that premiums will go up again in order for managed care companies to maintain their profits.

Hospital social work departments have been feeling the effects of changes in the health care field. The Society for Social Work Administrators in Health Care (now called the Society of Social Work Leaders in Health Care) and NASW (the National Association of Social Workers) recently collaborated on a national study of recent changes in social work departments and the impact of those changes on social work (Berger, Cayner, Jensen, Mizrahi, Scesny, and Trachtenberg 1996). Using a sample of 340 hospitals drawn from membership in the American Hospital Association, the authors found that while most hospitals continued to have a centralized social work department, the trend was decreasing. Social work departments were reporting changes that were also similar to other departments and personnel. Thus, changes affecting social work departments reflected changes in the health care industry. There was a decrease in bed occupancy, average daily census, and average length of stay. Hospitals are responding to this changing environment through the use of care maps and case management approaches which manage the utilization of resources while maintaining quality of care. Restructuring and resizing are also occurring. Restructuring includes combining departments and eliminating management levels. The growth of community-based care, which is less costly, is growing, and although social work enrollment is increasing in this area, it is not commensurate with the dramatic increase in these services. Nursing personnel within social work departments is increasing and social work administrative personnel is declining. Change in health care systems is a constant part of the professional lives of social workers. Change requires education and, in today's health care environment, understanding the influence of managed care is an important part of social work career development.

In the following section, managed care organizations are further defined and the particular issues for health professionals and social workers are presented. This will provide to the reader an understanding of the setting in which the patient and team issues will be depicted. The Introduction is meant as an adjunct to major texts and references on managed care. It is presented to the student as a synthesis of the current knowledge base that is necessary in order to critically evaluate the managed care literature. It also forms the basis of the issues that will be presented in the narrative that follows. While the patient care issues in the narrative can be read and appreciated by any social work student, the hidden meanings related to managed care organizations will have a greater impact once this Introduction is read.

History and Growth of Managed Care Organizations

The health insurance sector has been transformed in the past fifteen years with managed care replacing fee-for-service insurance as the norm. This transformation was intended to change the nature of competition in health care by allowing market forces to control costs. For example, in physician-dominated markets of the past, in which insurance companies did not restrict beneficiaries' choice of physician or hospital or the care patients received, physicians had control over when and where to admit patients and how to use hospital resources. Therefore, hospitals competed for patients through physicians while insurers played a passive role. Physicians were insensitive to the cost of care at different facilities because fee-for-service insurance insulated both them and their patients from these costs. In managed care environments, before attracting physicians, hospitals must first compete for inclusion in insurers' networks, and the better they control their costs, the more attractive they are to network contracts (Zwanziger and Melnick 1996).

With managed care plans, hospitals and insurers are more complexly involved. Thus, providers are reimbursed according to a contract negotiated with insurers and these insurers decide whether a treatment or service is appropriate (Wilkerson, Devers, and Given 1997). In simpler terms, managed care is the application of business principles to the delivery of medical care in that the insurer's goal is to maximize profit through control of consumer flexibility. Managed care was instituted to reduce the increasing cost of medical services and it was supposed to improve access to care while providing quality of care.

A managed care plan can be defined as an integrated delivery system that manages health care services, rather than simply financing or delivering them. The health maintenance organization (HMO) represents the prototype managed care plan. Health maintenance organizations have served as the model for a broad range of other health plans including preferred provider organizations (PPO) and point-of-service plans (POS) (Weiner 1994).

Managed care began to attract attention during the 1970s as government and industry became concerned about rising health costs. In 1973, President Nixon signed the Health Maintenance Organization Act to encourage the formation and expansion of prepaid health care plans. Although the act fell short of creating 1,700 HMOs serving forty million members by 1976 (only 174 HMOs had formed by 1976, serving six million Americans), the managed care industry began to expand during the 1980s when health care costs increased and economic growth had slowed. Rising health care costs became a concern for large corporations that included health care benefits in retirement packages and for small companies that already had difficulties in affording these benefits. For many businesses, managed care offered a less-expensive alternative. Between 1981 and 1987, HMO enrollment tripled from ten million to almost thirty million. As of 1994, according to the Group Health Association of America, HMO enrollment was about forty-five million (Vitberg 1996). Between 1992 and 1995, HMO enrollment increased from thirty-six million to fifty-eight million Americans (Wilkerson, Devers, and Given 1997). The original intent of the HMO Act in 1973 was to stimulate consumers to select for themselves either a prepaid system for obtaining health services or the more traditional fee-for-service. However, Huntt and Growick (1997) state that the current paradigm of managed care allows few options for informed consumer input.

Most Americans began to be familiar with the term managed care quite recently. President Clinton's 1993 Health Security Act was an attempt to combine private market forces with government oversight to provide universal health care to all legal residents while at the same time control costs. The plan called for the government to regulate competition among private prepaid health plans for both private and publicly funded enrollees. While the legislation was defeated, policymakers hoped solutions lay with many large employers who were achieving cost savings through the increasing competition among managed care organizations. This increasing competition occurred as a result of the acceleration of managed care organizations' anticipation of national health care reform and their aggressive purchasing of health insurance plans (Wilkerson, Devers, and Given 1997).

What Is Managed Care?

It is almost impossible to describe the variety of types of managed care plans because they are changing so rapidly. Therefore, a few basic models are presented in order to provide a basis for understanding the growth of the generation types of health care plans.

Managed care models refer primarily to four different basic arrangements between health care plans and physicians (Katz and Cropp 1994; Miller and Luft 1994). They are as follows:

> *Staff Model HMO*: The health plan employs its physicians directly and such decisions need to be approved by the board of an HMO.
>
> *Group Model HMO*: The health plan contracts for the exclusive services of one or more large physician group practices that devote a substantial percent of their practices to an HMO. This usually means the group has administrative functions and is involved in compensation, benefits, and contracting negotiations.
>
> *Network Model HMO*: The plan contracts with one or more large groups of independent practitioners, but the relationship is not exclusive.
>
> *Independent Practice Association (IPA)*: The HMO negotiates contracts with individual practitioners or small group practices through an intermediary.

While these models provide a general description of managed care plans, the largest growth in recent years, both in terms of plans and enrollment, has been in mixed plans that offer the enrollee the option of seeing an out-of-network provider, although the consumer will have to pay more for that option. Between 1990 and 1994, enrollment in mixed plans grew from 10 to 30 percent of all managed care enrollees, while enrollment in IPA plans declined from 40 to 38 percent, and enrollment in traditional group and staff model HMOs declined from 50 to 32 percent. Much of this dramatic increase resulted from traditional managed care organizations being reclassified into the mixed category with their addition of an out-of-network option (Wilkerson, Devers, and Given 1997).

Under managed care, the financing and delivery of health care are organized by a single entity. Managed care plans are classified as health maintenance organizations (HMOs) and preferred provider organizations (PPOs) or various mixtures of the two. There are two major forms of HMO: group model or staff model, and network or independent practice association (IPA) HMOs. Both types are usually at risk for the costs of care and therefore often control costs by requiring patients to be referred to specialists by primary care doctors. The doctors in the network of IPA HMOs are usually in independent practice. A PPO, in contrast, consists of a group of doctors who agree to provide services to the plan's patients for discounted fees (Gold, Hurley, Lake, Ensor, and Berenson 1995). Although there is more known about group or staff HMOs than newer types such as IPA HMOs, little is known about how managed care plans recruit, pay, and monitor physicians. In their 1994 study, the authors surveyed by telephone HMOs and PPOs in twenty metropolitan areas nationwide. This consisted of 138 managed care plans. Of the 108 who responded, twenty-nine were group or staff model HMOs, fifty were network or independent practice associations (IPAs), and twenty-nine were preferred provider organizations (PPOs). Managed care respondents emphasized careful selection of physicians, although group or staff HMOs tended to have more demanding requirements such as board certification or eligibility. Sixty-one percent of the plans said physicians' previous patterns of costs or utilization of resources had little influence on the selection. Risk sharing was typical in HMOs but rare in PPOs. About half of network IPA HMOs used capitation as the major payment for primary care physicians. More than half of the HMOs adjusted payment based on utilization or cost patterns, patient complaints or quality of care. Ninety-two percent of network or IPA HMOs and 61 percent of group or staff HMOs required patients to select a primary care physician who was responible for most referrals. Seventy-five percent of HMOs and 31 percent of PPOs reported using studies of outcomes for medical care as part of their quality-improvement programs (Gold et al. 1995). Physician practices have greatly changed over the past five years. Between 1990 and 1996, physicians' use of managed care contracts grew from 61 percent to 88 percent, and their revenues from managed care contracts grew from 28 percent to 44 percent during the same time period. They also increased their direct contracting with employers as they tried to gain back independence in their practice of medicine. This growth will continue. In 1996, 31 percent of physicians in practices with twenty-five or more physicians were engaged in direct-contracting activities with employers (Levit, Lazenby, Braden, and the National Health Accounts Team 1998).

As a rule, physicians who work an IPA or network HMO generally are paid on a fee-for-service or capitation basis in which payment is a set dollar amount per month or year for each HMO member under their care (Katz and Cropp 1994). Teamwork is an essential part of practice since most HMOs use nurse practitioners and/or physicians' assistants quite extensively. The role of gatekeeper is often assigned to the primary care physician and means that tighter control over utilization of services can be maintained by placing the primary care physician as manager of services. According to Katz and Cropp (1994) "from a physician's perspective this places them in the role of advocate for both the patient and the organization" (19). HMO physicians consciously manage service determining the need for outside consulting, proper use of technology, pharmaceuticals, and nursing care while at the same time providing the best care for the patient. Physicians also have administrative duties which include quality improvement, data analysis, clinic guidelines, and utilization management. On the other hand, multidisciplinary collaboration is readily available and can be readily called. Katz and Cropp (1994) believe the regular and flexible hours in HMO practice afford physicians the luxury of time to pursue other interests, both personal and professional.

Managed care organizations (MCOs) monitor practice by using programs in quality assurance and utilization management, by contracting with regional referral facilities for high technology, and by holding individual physicians accountable for the amount of money they authorize (spend) per enrollee per month. According to LaPuma and Schidermayer (1994), managed care and managed competition recognize the dual concepts of appropriateness and scarcity. This requires primary physicians to be resource agents and assumes that physicians will be both patient and MCO advocates even when these roles seem to conflict. Managed care organizations (MCOs) are founded on at least three ethical assumptions and it is important that they abide by these principles. They are as follows:

> *Equality of access*: This concept of equality requires that MCO physicians be consistent decisionmakers, making the same decisions for individual patients as for groups of patients.
>
> *The doctor-patient relationship will be nonadversarial even when contractually based*: Physicians will advocate for the patients and the patients will trust their physicians to work with them within the system.
>
> *Quality assurance and utilization management is educational and confidential*: It is used to promote quality care rather than punish patients or physicians. (34–35)

How Do Managed Care Plans Contain Costs?

Managed care health plans shift their financial risks to the physicians and medical groups with whom they contract. This is usually done by capitation and withholding. Capitation (providers are paid a fixed amount to provide all the care that an enrollee may require) and withholding (physicians are given a financial incentive to limit referrals to specialists and hospitals) are becoming more common, particularly in areas where HMO penetration is high. Capitation removes the incentive to provide unnecessary services to increase revenues; however, the low monthly payment to provide all the care an enrollee may need also necessitates that physicians refer these patients to specialists, which can increase cost. Withholding and capitation, with which physicians are at risk for the cost of all medically necessary services, are two tactics used to deal with this cost escalation. In 1994, 57 percent of network and IPA HMOs reported having capitation arrangements with their primary physicians and nearly 80 percent of those also withheld funds (or offered bonuses) as an incentive to limit referrals (Wilkinson, Devers, and Given 1997). Mergers and purchasing coalitions have provided another way to control costs by cutting out intermediaries.

Recent changes in the health care industry are leading to an unprecedented volume of mergers among insurers, hospitals, physicians, and drug companies. Health care plans recognize that their attractiveness to large employers increasingly depends on their ability to offer a wide range of services over as large a geographic area as possible. Providers are also forming alliances. Hospitals and physicians recognize that forming large (even national) networks improves their negotiating positions with insurers and positions them to market their services directly to employers. The effect of these mergers in controlling costs is still unknown. Group purchasing in the managed care marketplace has become a rapidly evolving market phenomenon. This works when a number of types of groups purchase health insurance, such as businesses and health coalitions, health insurance purchasing cooperatives (HIPCS), and health alliances. These arrangements include a range of organizational structures and interventions intended to bring multiple buyers together to improve the quality and efficiency of health care. Some groups are sponsored by public entities, although most are privately controlled. While the majority are organized by and for private employers, others extend membership to public employers, labor unions, and even health care providers. Although diverse, purchasing groups tend to share one fundamental premise: Collective action is more likely to achieve their goals than fragmented, single-party efforts (Bergthold and Solomon 1997). While the majority of these groups focus on local markets and are controlled by businesses that are either based in or have a large number of employees in those communities, the last few years have witnessed the use of the superalliance purchasing groups whose reach extends across multiple markets.

Bergthold and Solomon (1997) describe these purchasing groups as the new trend in managed care. Purchasing cooperatives undertake a wide range of activities related to negotiating with health plans and providers on behalf of group members. These purchasing groups can contract directly with provider networks, design plan benefits and provide—directly or through contract—utilization review, managed pharmacy plans, and other cost-containment services. The Pacific Business Group on Health (PBGH) is typical of the collective-negotiation model of joint purchasing. PBGH is the largest business and health coalition in California and the first private coalition in that state to negotiate collectively on behalf of its member companies. The group does not actually contract with plans on its members' behalf. The contracts are written directly between the health plans and PBGH members. PBGH does, however, serve as a negotiating agent for eleven of its members' companies which represent 400,000 people and $400 million a year in premiums. In that role, PBGH negotiates the premiums from the HMO that will serve the eleven companies. Each company decides which HMOs to offer, but all HMO plans must offer the same standardized benefit package to the group. All PBGH members are large, self-insured firms—a factor that contributes to individual member's need for autonomy within the purchasing arrangement. In general, health plans submit data to the purchasing group which reviews and debates premium increases.

Zwanziger and Melnick's 1996 review suggests that HMO penetration will reduce fees. Hospitals in highly competitive markets are forced to accept concessions, discounts in exchange for inclusion in the plan's provider network. Payers that could threaten to move their beneficiaries to another provider are better able to negotiate lower prices. To do this, there must be other hospitals in the area and those hospitals must have excess capacity. Thus, managed care plans have reduced the growth of health care costs where the government has not. They have done this through price competition that forces cost down. They also suggest that some aspects of redesigning health care will be painful and unpopular. They believe that the public must accept hospital closures, restrictions on access to providers, and limitations on covered services. "Government legislation requiring managed care to enroll 'any willing' provider may be required but will undermine their ability to control costs. It is unclear whether the health care system as restructured to control costs will be able to provide acceptable access and quality" (197).

Additionally, the government will have to monitor advertising claims and prevent anticompetitive mergers. Antitrust enforcement is left with the difficult task of deciding when vertical and horizontal mergers no longer benefit the public. Selection processes of physicians is another element of managed care systems. For example, in PPOs, an insurer or other third-party payer contracts with selected physicians, hospitals, or other providers to deliver services at discounted rates. Since financial incentives are provided for enrollees to use these preferred providers, providers will accept discounted fees in exchange for patient volume; payers then hope to control costs, and enrollees save money by choosing a contract provider although they are free to go to other providers at an increased cost. In 1981, there were fewer than ten PPOs to serve enrollees. By 1987, there were one hundred. In 1994, there were over seven hundred plans. Physician participation increased from 45 percent in 1988 to 64 percent in 1993. Overall, physicians receive about one-fifth of their revenues from PPOs and the predominant form of payment was FFS (fee for service) (Verrilli and Zuckerman 1996).

Blumenthal (1996) notes that as a result of these complex changes, the public is receiving information through the media on mergers, acquisitions, antitrust actions, ownership, and financing of managed health care organizations at least superficially like other sectors of the U.S. economy. Physicians are joining these organizations to attract patients. Physicians are hearing from marketing strategies that health care is a commodity to be exchanged in the marketplace. Practicing medicine is becoming an economic transaction, not a professional calling. In a 1994 survey of a national sample of managed care organizations, the Physician Payment Review Commission (PPRC) found that 63 percent of these organizations held primary care physicians responsible for referrals to specialists (gatekeeping), 95 percent used some type of utilization management, 63 percent used practice guides, 74 percent used physician profiling, and 83 percent did focused studies of quality of care. Administrative interventions were judged just as important or more important than physician payment in assuring organization success. However, in his review Blumenthal found that the evidence of the effectiveness of these techniques in reducing costs or improving quality is scant and the effect on clinical decision making and on physician/patient interactions is sparser still. While gatekeeping may reduce the intensity of services and focus on primary care, little is known about the effect of gatekeeping on quality of care. On the other hand, gatekeeping can strain the physician/patient interaction by putting the primary care physician in the position of denying patients access to specialty care and emergency services especially to the chronically ill who are accustomed to using such services. Utilization management or review of costs by third parties who can influence clinical decisions is still unclear, and its relationship to quality is hard to find. Physicians are extremely hostile toward utilization management since they view it as interfering with patient-physician relationships and they believe it is not sensitive to individual patient's needs.

Vitberg (1996), a health care consultant, describes managed care as a "war zone characterized by battles between and among payers, physicians, and hospitals for enrollees, patients and health care dollars" (4). In fact, he states that those payers and providers who understand that they are fighting a war and act accordingly stand the best chance of short-term survival and long-term prosperity. The growth of managed care has been phenomenal and it is affecting the way customers perceive and purchase health insurance. It has created sophisticated buyers demanding quality outcomes at reasonable prices and has spanned the need for sophisticated information systems. Thomasma (1996) defines managed care as

> *an interventionist health care system that emphasizes social control through organized competition. The idea is to push providers and hospitals into networks such that the old fee for services providers will be far down the food chain. . . . Accountability will be required from doctors, hospitals, pharmaceutical companies, and manufacturers of medical devices. Accountability will tend to eliminate every aspect of a system that does not provide quality care. Consumers will look for the best deal in getting quality of care for the least expense. Prevention becomes a primary value for all providers since it is the least costly alternative to providing care (233).*

He furthermore believes that if health care is viewed as a commodity, then this business approach is feasible. However, similar to other critics, he questions whether organized competition is the best way to deliver an equitable and sound health care system because some health care services are not cost-effective. Managed care penetration by states varies from 0 percent for Alaska, West Virginia, Wyoming, Vermont, and Mississippi to more than 30 percent for Colorado, Minnesota, California, Maryland, Oregon, and Massachusetts (Vitberg 1996).

Managed care plans are held accountable by the National Committee for Quality Assurance (NCQA) and the Joint Commission on Accreditation of Healthcare Organizations (JCAHO). The predominant accrediting body in managed care today is the NCQA. It is an independent, nonprofit organization that measures, assesses, and reports on the quality of care and services in MCOs. An important component of NCAQ's mission is to provide the public with information about quality. This is accomplished via its Web site (http://www.ncqa.org) (Parisi 1997). Additionally, the Health Plan Employer Data and Information Set (HEDIS) contains more than sixty performance measures and is a renowned indicator of quality in managed care today. It was designed to provide MCOs a standardized reporting format for identifying quality performance indicators. MCOs have the option of selecting the Joint Commission or the NCQA for their accreditation performance improvement activities in managed care. These are heavily influenced by the requirements of the NCAQ, HEDIS, and JCAHO. Large employers are increasingly making demands for performance improvement and decreased costs (Parisi 1997).

O'Neil and Finocchio (1997) believe that the system of managed care that is emerging is bringing an increased emphasis on primary care, prevention, population-based practice, interdisciplinary teamwork, and clinical effectiveness research. The system that is emerging will be integrated through the delivery of primary care because it is less expensive. The model will not be dominated by physicians alone. Professional work in interdisciplinary teams will require that all health care practitioners be able to understand the values and functions of coordinated, comprehensive and continuous care, and practice within multiple-care-delivery services. There is also an emerging emphasis on ambulatory care in the community and at patients' homes. A further balance will be sought between treatment and prevention. All practitioners must be able to help individuals, families, and communities maintain and promote healthy behaviors. Future practitioners will have to possess a broad understanding of all the determinants of health such as the patient's physical environment, socioeconomic status, behavioral health care, and mental health and genetic backgrounds. Practitioners must be able to help patients and their families actively participate in health care decisions and be informed how cultural values affect health status and care. Practitioners must be able to frame their work in ethically sincere ways. Traditional quality improvement, continuous quality improvement, as well as newer best practices programs are growing in utilization and will be integrated in all levels of practice. For many years, staffing patterns within managed care organizations have been recognized as one standard for setting national physician requirement levels. Thus, overall physician labor supply will be greatly affected as HMOs and other similar plans grow. The education of health professionals will change and be challenged in the overall reform of health care. Educators will find themselves challenged to broaden their curricula beyond biomedical care and have greater understandings of epistemology and new systems of care, and better understandings of the relationship between mind and body and a more population-based approach to care. This includes understanding the increased complexity of patient needs, a better integration of skills across the professions, and effective team competencies.

It was not until the early 1990s that corporate payments for health insurance decelerated appreciably. The surplus capacity of hospitals and the weakening of the labor market for physicians enabled managed care companies to secure lower prices from providers in exchange for increases in referrals for patients and to retain for themselves and their stockholders a substantial margin of 20 to 30 percent of total revenues for profit and expansion (Ginzberg and Ostrow 1997). Currently, two-thirds of Americans working for medium-size and large-size firms belong to managed care plans. It took a decade of increasing enrollment in managed care plans before the decrease in national health expenditures became evident in the 1990s. The question remains whether this savings reflects a one-time 10 to 15 percent savings due to large enrollment shifts from higher-cost fee-for-service plans. The opposing view maintains that cost savings takes place because HMOs and MCOs use capitation, better educate patients, provide selective preventive services, and use clinical guidelines aimed at reducing waste or eliminating costly ineffective procedures. The authors believe that once the enrollees have shifted to less-costly plans, this savings is not likely to be replicated. There is a good likelihood of enrollment increases, especially with the recent trends in Medicare and Medicaid, although to date the Medicare beneficiaries who have chosen HMOs have disproportionately represented the healthier section of the eligible population. Whether managed care plans could accept the full one-third of the Medicaid population who are elderly, chronically ill or disabled, and blind is not known since together they account for two-thirds of all Medicaid outlays. Whether HMOs can treat these groups effectively at a cost that will be profitable to the plans and save the states money is also unknown. There is also a trend for purchasing groups of employers to bypass managed care and contract with larger provider units such as major teaching hositals and multispecialty groups of physicians which are growing nationally because of the desire of hospitals and physicians to regain some of the market power they lost. More legislative intervention and more public outcry is having an effect—as, for example, when managed care plans sought to limit new mothers to a one-day hospital stay after a normal delivery. Ginzberg and Ostrow believe "managed care is not the answer to Medicare depletion of the trust fund because the problem is more complex than managed care" (1019). Additionally, numerous large teaching hospitals, many of them affiliates of major academic health centers, and concentrated near the urban poor, are establishing their own HMOs to enroll the Medicaid population. These hospitals' and physicians' staffs are integrated to reassert their bargaining power and negotiate for services directly.

Medicaid and Managed Care

Sparer (1997) provides an analysis of Medicaid policies through three eras. The first Medicaid era, which lasted from the program's enactment in 1965 until around 1983, was characterized by giving states enormous discretion to set eligibility policy, benefit coverage policy, and reimbursement policy. While Medicaid was attached to AFDC (Aid to Families with Dependent Children), states themselves determined which persons received AFDC. States could also decide on options for covering optional medical services and had discretion in setting rates for physicians, nursing homes, and other providers. Thus, interstate variation was great. During the second era from 1984 to the early 1990s, the federal government significantly increased its control over state Medicaid policy. Congress mandated states to cover millions of new enrollees, mainly pregnant women and young children. Total program enrollment went from about twenty-two million in 1988 to well over thirty-three million in 1993. Congress expanded benefits to children even if such benefits were not available to adults and limited state control over reimbursement policy, requiring states to pay community health centers for all of their reasonable costs. Medicaid costs grew rapidly from $54.1 billion in 1988 to $131 billion in 1993. The federal mandates were not the only explanation for increased costs. One other factor was general health care inflation, and the other was a sicker Medicaid population (i.e., diseases such as AIDS or tuberculosis which are costly). A final factor was the recession of the late 1950s. The traditional options—cutting eligibility, benefits, or reimbursement—were unavailable; thus, the most plausible alternative was to promote managed care (Sparer 1997).

Medicaid managed care enrollment grew from 750,000 in 1983, 3 percent of all enrollees, to 11.6 million in 1995, 36 percent of all enrollees (Sparer 1997). Of the thirty-six million people covered by Medicaid, 4.9 million are children or adults who are blind or who have other significant disabilities. The 15 percent of Medicaid beneficiaries who are disabled accounted for over 39 percent of the expenditures in 1993 (Huntt and Growick 1997). Thus, they are the most expensive to serve of all Medicaid recipients. By 1994, all but six states had Medicaid managed care programs (Smith, Cotter, and Rossiter 1996). Seven states have expanded coverage for the poor through managed care initiatives. Medicaid is a national health insurance program for three distinct low-income populations: families with children, the blind and disabled, and the aged. There is continuing debate whether all three groups should be part of managed care plans. For example, no state requires managed care plans to provide every Medicaid-covered service. Some services remain part of the traditional fee-for-service plan. For example, managed care plans may not be able to offer certain services such as nursing home care, or some such as mental health or dental services may be better offered through fees for services or specialized managed care systems. Sparer believes this debate over the content of managed care benefit packages can be fierce. At the heart of the issue is the competition entering the Medicaid market. Traditionally, mainstream managed care organizations have ignored the Medicaid market, but are now pursuing it aggressively. Once in the market, HMOs discovered that enrolling Medicaid beneficiaries generates profits and that managed care plans that have large numbers of enrollees can negotiate with providers for discounts.

This trend of increased competition of managed care plans threatens the fiscal stability of the traditional Medicaid providers such as hospitals located in low-income communities, community health centers, and even individual providers with large numbers of Medicaid patients. According to Sparer

(1997), the fear is that mainstream health plans will attract the low-cost Medicaid client, and the safety net providers will be left with the high-cost Medicaid beneficiary and the uninsured [a "recipe for financial disaster," (244)]. Many HMOs, for example, prefer to contract with low-cost private hospitals rather than with generally high-cost public hospitals or academic medical centers. Sparer suggests that safety net providers themselves establish a plan which could be composed of a public hospital system, a group of community health centers, or simply a cadre of individual providers. It could compete primarily (or exclusively) in the Medicaid market, or it could seek Medicare and commercial businesses as well.

Safety net providers are especially threatened by the movement toward Medicaid managed care. These hospitals must cope with lower revenue (as Medicaid, Medicare, and the private sector all cut back), fewer staff as Congress threatens to scale back funding for graduate medical education, and a costlier and sicker patient population (as mainstream HMOs attract the low-cost Medicaid client but leave the hospital with the high-cost client and the uninsured). This outlook is bleak as well for community-based specialty clinics such as those that provide women's health services, mental health services, or substance abuse centers, since most HMOs often prefer not to contract with such clinics or to refer only the most difficult cases. HMOs often contract with the more primary care–oriented community health centers, but are generally unwilling to pay the 100 percent reimbursement that Congress mandates for Medicaid. Several states have filed 1,115 applications waivers [authorized by Section 1915(b) of the Social Security Act] to waive this requirement. In this environment, state officials must decide whether to develop a safety net protection program, or instead, let the market alone determine winners and losers (Sparer 1997). Some states, such as New York, created a new type of HMO that could enroll Medicaid and other publicly funded beneficiaries, but could not compete in the commercial market. Under the recently approved Two-Plan model by the federal government in California, Medicaid beneficiaries in twelve counties will have to choose between two managed care plans: a mainstream (or private sector) plan and a government-run plan which will feature the county-run public hospital system. Sparer notes that this will not only insure the survival of the public plan, it will also enable county hospitals to maintain most or all of their federal disproportionate-share income.

Medicaid managed care poses many new problems. Medicaid clients go on and off Medicaid rolls making it less likely that health care plans will focus on long-term health care or prevention. Given the culture of Medicaid clients using expensive local emergency rooms, Sparer (1997) questions whether patient education will be adequate to help clients understand their choices of options and whether there will be adequate quality control. Issues of quality control need to be addressed. Marketing and enrollment procedures, client questions, and client education were not adequately answered when California's infrastructure tried to convert 150,000 Sacramento beneficiaries in a few months (Sparer 1997). States such as Tennessee have little managed care experience or infrastructure, and rapid implementation was a problem. Incremental managed care, such as in Minnesota where it has taken 10 years to enroll 140,000 of its 400,000 Medicaid clients into managed care and it is slowly enrolling the rest, has been beneficial to beneficiaries and commercial health plans as they learn about the special needs and changes in enrollment procedures and delivery that would benefit both (Sparer 1997). Gold, Sparer, and Chu (1996) note that the transition to Medicaid is not easy. States such as Minnesota and Oregon had a smoother transition than Tennessee because of a well-designed program. For example, they note that Tennessee did not publish marketing policies during the first year and few policies or procedures were put in writing. California and New York, both large states, realized the complexity and length of such a transition. According to these authors, to ensure a good transition, beneficiaries must be informed about choices, help must be made available to understand these choices, and the administrative process must be handled in a timely and smooth manner. For example, Texas, with one of the most advanced medical centers, has some three million people without health insurance (10 percent of the national total), twenty-three couties without a primary care physician (eighteen with no physician whatsoever), and an 868-mile border with Mexico along which more than 180,000 people live within colonies in rural, unregulated subdivisions with poor drinking water, no sewage, and diseases associated with third-world poverty. Texas has a larger-than-average Medicaid population with 23.8 percent rural residents living below the poverty line. Texas is gradually entering the managed care Medicaid market with only limited contracts available to Medicaid recipients (Richardson 1994).

The movement toward managed care entails using commercial HMOs which have traditionally served a commercially insured middle-class population and are now competing to serve low-income populations; primary care physicians who have previously accepted few Medicaid clients are now pressured to expand their client base, and safety net providers which have traditionally cared for low-income populations are now learning to become insurers. Medicaid beneficiaries who are accustomed to relying for care on the local hospital emergency room are now sifting through various managed care plans. State (and sometimes) local officials must organize and supervise the entire initiative determining which beneficiaries are to be enrolled, developing benefit packages and enrollment and marketing plans, setting capitation rates, supervising quality of care, and ensuring that a medical safety net is not eliminated in the process (Sparer 1997).

In a review of the literature, Howell (1996) notes it is not clear how states will receive, review, and edit data that will be needed for Medicaid assessment. The Health Care Financing Administration (HCFA) Medicaid Bureau began to develop guidelines for quality assurance under Medicaid called Quality Assurance Reform Initiative (QARI). A 1994 survey by HCFA with thirty-two states responding showed that 90 percent were at least familiar with these guidelines and most were willing to use them. However, the increased growth raises concerns about how this accountability will actually occur and specifically whether quality of care will be adequately addressed (Smith, Cotter, and Rossiter 1996). According to a policy report for NASW, Warren (1994) recommends that NASW advocate for social workers to take the following stand in light of Medicaid waivers and managed care. This includes planning and implementing advisory groups to include consumers, culturally competent providers, and social workers. Social workers are especially crucial in managed care Medicaid organizations as they can be used to identify, assess, and refer patients through complex systems and ensure patient education and patient grievance procedures are put in place. Additionally, social workers should advocate for their own services especially in the treatment of mental health and addiction disorders. Perloff (1996) emphasizes the importance of social workers in settings in which Medicaid managed care eligibility is being established. This is important because without social workers, clients may not be able to sort through plan choices and enrollment, and they might automatically be enrolled in a state-mandated plan. The tasks of education and information will require that social workers be familiar with the rules and new care-seeking requirements of Medicaid managed care and be familiar with the policy developments of Medicaid in general. Additionally, as Huntt and Growick (1997) point out, people with disabilities, the largest segment of Medicaid reipients, especially need comprehensive services oriented to their frequent needs for health services and specific specialized services. Gatekeepers in managed care plans need to be particularly trained in the complexity of health care needs for this group and the importance of the independent living movement, which emphasizes choice and personal responsibility, including the opportunity to be involved in their own medical treatment. It may be precisely because of technical advances that the disabled can live and work independently.

Medicare and Managed Care

The federal government is a major purchaser of health care services and Medicare is the largest public payer for health care. In 1994, the Medicare and Medicaid programs alone accounted for nearly one-third of all health care spending in the United States and more than 17 percent of all spending by the federal government. Spending for Medicare continues to increase at a rate of 10 percent per year. As tens of millions of baby boomers begin to enter the program around 2010, the cost of the program will rise even more dramatically (Wilkerson 1997). Data from hospital expenses for fiscal year 1990 submitted to Medicare by 6,400 hospitals showed that nationwide administrative expenses averaged 24.8 percent of each hospital's spending and that these costs were similar in states with high and low rates of enrollment in HMOs. These costs are higher than previous estimates, twice as high as Canada's, and are not affected by competitive bidding by hospitals for managed care contracts (Woolhandler, Himmelstein, and Lewontin 1993). On an average day in 1968, U.S. hospitals employed 435,000 managers and clerks to assist in the care of 1,378,000 inpatients. By 1990, the average daily number of patients had fallen to 853,000, and the number of administrators and clerks had risen to 1,221,600.

In 1995, Medicare trustees reported that the hospital trust fund (Part A of Medicare) would run out of money by 2002. Medicare reform was proposed by Congressional Republicans to balance the federal budget. The reforms included $270 billion in projected savings which was to balance the federal budget in seven years while reducing taxes, rather than restoring the hospital trust fund to solvency ($90 billion). Reforms would introduce a wider range of private health plan options for enrollees. Any insurer that was willing to accept a fixed payment per enrollee from the government and meet state-mandated standards could offer its services to Medicare enrollees. Such insurers could also offer cash rebates to enrollees who chose limited coverage and could charge supplemental premiums for more comprehensive benefits (Wilkerson 1997).

Medicare provides health care coverage to approximately thirty-four million Americans 65 years or older, and approximately five million disabled younger Americans. The program is divided into two parts: hospital care (Part A) and outpatient physician services (Part B). Inpatient care accounts for about two-thirds of the $160 billion program. In the absence of reform, Medicare spending is expected to rise to about $340 billion in the year 2002. The two parts are financed differently. All workers are required to participate in Part A by contributing 1.45 percent of their wages to it; this contribution is matched by their employers. These contributions go into a trust fund that finances the program. Individuals can choose not to participate in Plan B. If they choose to (more than 90 percent do), they must pay a monthly premium while they are receiving benefits. By law this premium is currently set at 25 percent of the program's costs. Enrollee premiums currently cover about 31.5 percent of costs (in 1994, the monthly premium was $47.00). The remainder of Part B's costs are financed through general revenues (Wilkerson 1997). In addition, most enrollees (89 percent) now have private or public supplement insurance that expands their Part A and Part B benefits and reduces their out-of-the-pocket expenses even further. Medicare must absorb the medical costs of the baby-boom generation retiring after 2010. The number of Americans age sixty-five and older is projected to rise from thirty-two million in 1990 to sixty-eight million in 2040, and enrollment in Medicare is expected to increase from 14 percent of the population in 1995 to 22 percent by 2030 (Marmor and Oberlander 1998).

The Medicare reform that has been debated by the 104th Congress includes allowing insurers to market the services with few restrictions on the range of alternatives or prices they could charge. The government's payments would be fixed by law, but plans could compete on the basis of price (by offering cash rebates to enrollees) and on the basis of services (by offering more comprehensive benefits or provider choice). Medicare beneficiaries would be encouraged to enroll in private managed care plans which give insurers and providers a financial incentive to limit inappropriate utilizations and to open medical savings accounts (MSAs) which are thought to give individuals a financial incentive to consider the costs of their care. To achieve the cuts in spending and to achieve $270 billion savings, cuts would be targeted to reducing future payments to physicians, hospitals, and other facilities who are participating in fee-for-service Medicare. The Medicare Preservation Act was included in a much larger appropriations bill, the Balanced Budget Act of 1995 (H.R. 2491). These reforms would not increase beneficiaries' deductibles and would maintain Part B premiums at their current level of 31.5 percent for all but the wealthiest 3 percent of enrollees (H.R. 2491, Section 8511 and 8512) (Wilkerson 1997).

The new Medicare Plus Program (H.R. 2491, Section 8631) would offer a fixed or capitated payment to a private health plan in exchange for providing all covered services. Unlike existing Medicare HMO, the Medicare Plus Program would involve a much wider range of providers that would have to meet standards established by state insurance commissioners rather than the federal government. They could also charge supplemental premiums and offer cash rebates. These proposed reforms would gradually reduce regional differences and establish minimum monthly payments of $300 in 1997 and $350 in 1998. It is estimated that the savings proposed by these reforms is from reduced payment to fee-for-service providers rather than from increased competition among private managed care plans. Risk selection by insurance companies could be an effort used by these companies to attract healthy Medicare enrollees. In 1994, 10 percent of Medicare enrollees incurred about 70 percent of all Medicare costs. These enrollees cost the program more than $28,000 on the average compared to less than $1,500 for the other 90 percent of enrollees. When plans receive about $3,600 a year on the average, the bottom-line difference between attracting a healthy enrollee and an unhealthy one can be dramatic. Thus, overpayment could occur unless payment adjustment to plans with healthier enrollees receive less and sicker more (Wilkerson 1997). Medicare payments to managed care plans increased from 4.8 percent of total Medicare expenditures in 1990 to 10.1 percent in 1996 (Levit, Lazenby, Braden, and the National Health Accounts Team 1998).

Weil's (1996) review of empirical studies suggest that regional monopolies are growing and providers will often find that regions in which there is excess capacity, underused hospitals, or specialists will force "voluntary" alliances and mergers to become powerful, geographically linked regional health networks under one corporate umbrella. Weil notes that this may be more desirable and feasible than closing their doors (271). He believes that as immense health networks grow, with their monopolistic concerns about their bottom lines, they may begin to exhibit insensitivity about access, social equality, and comprehensive quality care and, along with disregard for lowering costs, they face the public's anger. The formation of these networks and expanded enrollment in HMOs will eventually require that most providers be associated with one of these dominant, geographically linked, vertical and horizontally diversified health alliances. As Medicare and Medicaid further limit reimbursement to providers, an area's fiscally weakest institutions and practitioners will seek the shelter of an affiliation or merger—or will be acquired—creating opportunities and new threats for the more aggressive regional networks (Weil 1996, 272). This may greatly affect the level of coverage that will be offered to recipients, especially as fewer contract options are available in individual locations.

Legislative Issues

Kassirer (1996) notes that the responsibility for regulating mergers and acquisitions in health care is determined by antitrust legislation at the federal level with the Federal Trade Commission and the Department of Justice. He believes the winners in these mergers are corporate executives, stockholders, lawyers who broke consolidations, and health care consultants. Additionally, as much as 2 to 3 percent of revenue goes to management consultants and these revenues are growing by 20 to 25 percent per year. Physicians are described as the losers, especially specialists and subspecialists. While some lose autonomy and financial authority, others lose jobs. When nonprofits are acquired by for-profits, with headquarters far from the site of care, long-term support of community services may be jeopardized. The accrediting bodies Joint Commission on Accreditation of Health Care Organizations and the National Committee for Quality Assurance are ill equipped to monitor new reorganized, complex systems of care. Kassirer (1996) believes there is no coherent national approach to the structure of delivery of care and that a comprehensive review of the adequacy of regulation and accreditation mechanisms is needed. More attention must be given to the consequences of mergers, consolidations, and acquisitions (723). In Kuttner's (1997b) review of antitrust guidelines, he noted that in August of 1996, the Federal Trade Commission (FTC) and the Department of Justice liberalized their joint antitrust guidelines on health care. The agencies agreed to review proposals for physician-operated networks case by case on the basis of their actual likely effects on competition rather than rigid formulas. This will allow doctors' groups to compete more effectively with HMOs and insurance companies, bypassing clinical intrusions and financial costs imposed by commercial intermediaries. In the 1970s, the FTC and the courts held that "learned" professions were not exempted from antitrust laws and challenged the AMA's ban on advertising and the efforts of organized medicine to bargain with insurers over the terms of cost-containment programs. As HMOs and other forms of managed care controlled by entrepreneurs grew and gained prominence in the market, doctors protested that antitrust guidelines systematically put doctors at a disadvantage while allowing the unfettered growth of health plans operated in the interest of corporate sponsors.

Kuttner's (1997b) analysis of recent antitrust legislation examines new trends in physician organization pertaining to managed care. He notes that in the past, since physicians in solo practice could not organize PPOs because of regulations on price fixing, some 93 percent of PPOs are owned by insurance companies and entrepreneurs. In the 104th Congress, the AMA sought legislation giving physician-operated plans broad exemptions from antitrust laws. The new guidelines issued by the FTC and the Justice Department gave organized medicine much of what it sought. The agencies will now subject physician-operated networks to a rule-of-reason test. This shift in policy opens the door to physician networks as long as there are no cartels. Some believe physician-operated networks will have a cost advantage over commercial managed care plans, which, according to the AMA, usually spend typically 20 to 30 cents of each dollar on marketing, administrative overhead, and shareholder dividends. Networks run by doctors will spend only 10 to 15 percent (from Kuttner's interview with Dr. Lonnie Bristow, immediate past president of the AMA, 388). The major question Kuttner poses is how they will be regulated and if they have the capital to grow. Start-up costs for a new network run about $5,000 per physician and $10,000 to $25,000 in capital contribution. Additionally, participating doctors contribute capital and bear substantial risk. Consumer advocates have called for direct regulation of managed care, as well as government-mandated disclosure to prevent abuses that competition and the application of antitrust regulations cannot correct.

To prevent some of the more flagrant abuses of managed care, at least 12 states have regulations on managed care practices that limit the right of allowing physicians to discuss treatment options with patients. The federal government has begun to regulate limitations on hospital stays by managed care plans, and the state of New York recently enacted the Comprehensive Managed Care Bill of Rights. Kttner believes these are at best partial solutions to complex issues of allowing the right of doctors to compete with managed care companies by creating their own networks. In Texas, consumer groups and the Texas Medical Association are urging Texas, legislators to codify protections recommended by a special committee Lieutenant Governor Bob Bullock appointed in 1996. The Senate Interim Committee on Managed Care issued its report in 1996, recommending that managed care companies be held accountable if they negligently deny medically necessary care that results in patient injury or if they use financial incentives to providers to limit medically necessary care (Jones 1997).

There has also been a change in the ERISA protection clause. In the past, managed care plans have escaped liability because of the federal law that regulates employee benefits, the Employee Retirement Income Security Act (ERISA), which Congress passed in 1974. ERISA established a set of uniform federal standards for employer-funded benefit plans. It was enacted when the standard kind of health insurance was fee-for-service plans in which decisions of whether to provide care was left to physicians and not to managed care utilization reviews. ERISA pre-empts state laws and mandates that employer-sponsored health plans cannot be sued on medical groups. Some sixty million Americans are enrolled in HMOs and another eighty-one million in other types of managed care, and about two-thirds of all employer-sponsored health plans are self-funded and covered by ERISA. Patients under such plans can only sue for their plan's denial of benefits and then only in federal courts which hold plaintiffs to higher burdens of proof and allow recovery for the cost of benefits denied, not for lost wages or pain or suffering (Jones 1997, 41). However, ERISA protection is eroding and most likely will be amended as malpractice cases against managed care companies grow. Jones notes that cases are more complex, public sentiment against managed care restrictions are growing, and the country wants physicians to advocate for their patients.

Managed Care and Social Work

Terry Mizrahi, the author of the column "National Health Line" in *Health and Social Work,* urges social workers to keep a broad perspective and open mind in terms of managed care and be open to innovations in health. She refers social workers to the NASW 1991, 1993 guidelines on managed care. Mizrahi (1993) makes the distinction between "managed care and health maintenance organizations" (86). She sees managed care as replacing the traditional HMO models such as the Kaiser-Permanente Medical Care Plan, the Health Insurance Plan of New York, and The Group Health Association, which began in the 1930s as consumer-oriented models and were nonprofit, prepaid group practices. These were progressive consumer-oriented models of comprehensive health services provided to members in exchange for a fixed monthly or yearly premium (capitation). These traditional HMOs were able to deliver care for a lower cost by lower hospitalization rates and they emphasized preventive and primary care. Until the 1970s, some state laws prohibited HMO development, but under Nixon, The Health Maintenance Organization Act of 1973 expanded the HMO concept to include profit-making and proprietary models as well as new types of organizational sponsorship known as independent practice associations (IPAs). Preferred provider organizations (PPOs) are networks of hospitals and doctors that have agreed to give the sponsoring organization discounted rates. Point-of-service models allow HMO members to opt out but use other providers at additional costs.

Mizrahi's (1993) concerns are that newer managed care models as well as profit-making HMOs will attempt to contain costs by obtaining discounts from providers by denying approval for care (regardless of whether physicians or patients think the care is necessary). This shifts costs elsewhere. These organizations also attempt to enroll healthy people. Managed competition relies on insurers and employers to control the direction of health care reform. The model assumes the market will control prices. Managed competition allows consumers and employees to be grouped into health insurance purchasing cooperatives (HIPCs) in which a government board establishes a basic standard package. Most managed competition plans are private and profit making although they vary quite a bit. Consumer choice requires out-of-pocket costs. Managed competition is an employer-based model of coverage. Since most Americans obtain their health insurance through their employment, benefits may be increasingly curtailed or a portion of the cost shifted to employees as premium deductibles or other coinsurance. The managed care administrative system is replete with paperwork because it handles differential eligibility, coverage, co-payments, and billing (Mizrahi 1993, 89). Thus, there is high overhead, lack of uniformity, and a lack of concern for long-term care and rehabilitation. This conflicts with the primary task of the interdisciplinary health care model which recognizes the complex social and medical needs of patients.

Cornelius (1994) in another social work article describes managed care as a strategy to contain the escalation of health care costs, but also as a way to represent strategies to insure more adequate health care for the poor and disadvantaged and as a way to insure quality health care by the closer scrutiny of care providers and users; it is a shift away from chronic illness toward prevention. He sees managed care as a cost-containment product that affects social work providers as well. Social workers are affected in the control of utilization either as an agency employee or as a private practitioner because managed care only succeeds if the routine practice of the provider is monitored carefully. Therefore, every client's case must be structured according to the protocols of the managed care firm. The social worker as the contractee must agree to these rules even before the client is seen. In essence, the social worker becomes an agent of managed care and agrees to serve the public within the corporate guidelines and not necessarily according to the assessed needs of the client. If the social workers practice outside their protocols, the case manager can deny coverage for both patient and social worker. Additionally, claims for managed care are paid only if they meet the preset needs of the company. Fee negotiation is no longer between social worker and client but is determined by the managed care contract. The social worker and managed care company are responsible for billing and fee collection. Thus, the perception solidifies the relationship that the provider social worker is an agent of managed care. Social workers, when accepting contracts (and discounts), have lost control over pricing services, thus decreasing professional autonomy.

Information control is another area of concern since providers and patients are not aware of what the standards are when a claim is being evaluated or treatment is being certified. Although the data is based on information given by the provider, neither the provider nor the patient has access to the way it is being used. For mental health services, managed care companies may specify short-term psychotherapy as an appropriate level of care for problems such as marital dysfunction and may dictate the length of treatment. These decisions are dictated by efficiency and may not be the most effective. The power of information is in the hands of the insurance industry and professionals are on the outside. The control of information solidifies the control of social work services under managed care. The social worker becomes both the collector of information about the client and the conduit of that data to the managed care case manager. Social workers who provide information have no way of knowing whether the information will be used for their clients' good or ill (Cornelius 1994).

In April 1993, the Board of the Society for Social Work Administrators in Health Care appointed a task force to review and assess managed care and its potential impact on social work in health care (Society for Social Work Administrators in Health Care 1994). The information from this report included definitions and issues to help social workers assess strategies to deal with managed care issues, especially in hospital practice. These guidelines familiarize social workers with the concept of cost-incentive functions and the need for intersystem knowledge, which includes limiting choices for patients but tracking care, choosing the best resources, understanding critical pathways, educating families, and evaluating outcomes. All this must be done within the broad range of contract requirements. There may be some loss of autonomy when case managers are directly involved in delivery care; policies need to be developed to insure collaboration. Social work skills of advocacy and negotiation become increasingly important and necessary. Social workers will focus more on managing overall costs and increasing educational services to patients and families especially as it relates to understanding contracts and models of care. Their value on the interdisciplinary team is emphasized. Social workers will need to increase their focus on tracking patient information across settings for optimal care and decreasing the need for high-cost utilization.

The report also stresses opportunities for social workers in managed care settings, which include being case managers, working in physician group practices to assist inpatient management, working within managed care systems to help coordinate patients, being flexible in service site location which may include the home, and helping clients get referrals to services when managed care doesn't cover needed areas. Attention should be given to helping clients integrate into their appropriate managed care system, helping clients to be compliant, preparing families for preadmission assessment, triangulating patients to appropriate services, providing psychosocial treatment affecting consumers' ability to participate in and benefit from treatment, developing consumer-focused delivery systems, working with and supervising professional extenders and volunteers, and expanding their roles in management utilization. The social worker should be involved in contract development by providing "the voice of the consumer" (Society for Social Work Administrators in Health Care 1994, 13) in examining contract development and its fit with existing consumer needs and community resources.

Strom-Gottfriend (1997) notes that social work has been slower in responding to managed care than other disciplines, perhaps due to ambivalence about the acceptability of the managed care system. She argues there is now a need to incorporate information into the social work educational curriculum. She notes that to practice in managed care environments, students will need knowledge in three key areas: how managed care practices have emerged and evolved; how services are redefined within managed care processes; and how research and outcome measures guide social work practice. Capitation represents a fundamental shift in service delivery and requires a knowledge about rate setting, risk assessment, and how these affect services. Students will also need to understand how employers, governmental and regulatory bodies, insurers, and providers shape managed care policies as well as how clients and service providers are affected. The philosophies differ as well in managed care. "Treatment is delivered by 'critical path models' where the most effective service plans are determined in advance for a given difficulty and psychosocial profile. Measurable and clear plans are desirable as a shift on social functioning to the current situation" (12). Research on outcomes will be emphasized. She further argues that since few social work texts address managed care concepts and effects, a fundamental first step is providing students with readings. If traditional social work resources are limited, educators may need to explore the health and business literature, both of which provide ongoing and extensive coverage of managed care developments. Notwithstanding all this, new ethical considerations have emerged. Shifting to managed care systems could lead to breaches of confidentiality as payers require and maintain data through electronic management systems, conflict between workers who are working for both the client and agencies, as well as issues of negligence that could arise through capitation. The social work profession is not alone in these concerns. With more and more social workers participating in managed care contracts, ethical concerns and practice guidelines have emerged as major issues. As discussed in the following section, all of the helping professions are voicing their concerns about professional conflict of interest.

Ethical Issues in Managed Care

The professions of medicine, nursing, and social work have been actively involved in providing policy statements on the ethics of managed care. A brief overview of these is provided. The major ethical issues that the 1990 statement by the Council on Ethical and Judicial Affairs (CEJA) of the American Medical Association focuses on how the financial incentives limit patient-physician relationship and provision of care on those in HMOs and IPAs (Council on Ethical and Judicial Affairs 1995). The Council recommends that disclosures about these incentives to plan members should be mandatory at the time of enrollment and at the time service is provided. Additionally, patient autonomy is limited by patients' choices of primary care physicians, specialists, and choice of treatment and the necessity of changing physicians to keep their health care benefits (Council 1995). According to the CEJA, the economic incentives may lead to two types of conflict of interest depending upon the economic incentives employed by the managed care plan. First, the physician may modify treatment recommendations to save money needed for the care of others; and second, the physician may modify his/her treatment recommendations to avoid personal economic loss. In either case, the interests of the patient are not necessarily placed first and, as such, the patient is no longer justified in trusting the physician (Brody 1997).

Halamka, Szolovits, Rind, and Safran (1997) are physicians who have developed at the Beth Israel Deaconess Medical Center, a proof-of-concept, Web-based, cross-institutional medical record called *CareWeb*, which meets the needs for security and confidentiality as recommended in 1995 by the National Research Council (NRC) of the National Academy of Sciences. They provide the Web address in their article in order to display the model. The address is http://freya.bidmc.harvard.edu/careweb.htm (458). In their article they note that although President Clinton recommended that every hospital be connected to the Internet so that doctors can share data about their patients with the best specialists in the field, the security and confidentiality implications of using the Internet are a major impediment to the goal. Thus, as more health information is available in electronics, there will be a need for security implementation. The National Research Council's report provides eight recommendations for immediate implementation and they include authentication of users and strict protocols for user access. It also recommends that systems be audited on a regular basis and patient-identifiable data transmitted over public networks be encrypted. The authors of the CareWeb site designed the clinical data at the Beth Israel Hospital to meet all the NRC recommendations including those suggested for future implementation. The authors stress the importance of providing critical health information that is available only to authorized users while at the same time allowing access to longitudinal patient record data distributed across multiple sites, providers, and institutions.

Although the use of nonphysician providers such as physicians' assistants, nurse midwives, and nurse practitioners will increase with more emphasis on primary care and managed care, physicians still outnumber nonphysician providers, and most Americans still receive their care from physicians. Additionally, there is much written on the ideal physician-patient relationship in books as well as discussed on television programs and in other media (Emanuel and Dubler 1995). Traits that were idealized decades ago, such as paternalism, have now been tempered by respect for patient autonomy. As such, Emanuel and Dubler (1995) suggest six Cs that describe the fundamental elements of the ideal physician-patient relationship and these embody ethical and legal standards of practice. They are choice of physician and treatment setting, competence of physician, communication, compassion, continuity of care, and (no) conflict of interest between provider and patient over financial interests.

Thus, *choice* may be limited by employers restricting patients' choices of managed care plans and physicians; *competence* may be limited by underutilization of specialists and specialized facilities; *communication* may be limited by access barriers to physicians' offices; *compassion* may be limited by less time with patients; *continuity* may be limited by forcing patient choice of continuity by deselecting physicians by managed care plans and frequent changes of managed care plans by employees; and *(no) conflict of interest* may be jeopardized by linking physician salary incentives and bonuses to reducing use of tests and procedures on patients (326–327).

Emanuel and Dubler (1995) suggest that some of these problems can be offset by the increased use of multidisciplinary teams which can improve patient care, communication, and satisfaction because several providers will be knowledgeable about the patient's condition and be available to the patient. By increasing the number of providers for a patient, the team approach may increase the chances that patients with different cultural backgrounds might establish rapport and understanding with a provider. Emanuel and Dubler (1995) also recommend prohibiting schemes that use salary incentives or bonuses tied to physicians using less care, involving patients and physicians on managed care boards to review and approve processes regarding length of office visits and telephone calls, and using an independent review board to assess the reliability and validity of quality indicators before they are used or required for use by managed care plans. Finally, they recommend insurance reform legislation to ensure mobility of insurance with job changes and purchasing of coverage by individuals.

Johnson and Derlet's (1996) review of emergency departments in California noted that managed care organizations have also begun to have ethical conflicts with hospital emergency rooms. This conflict stems from the fundamental differences in mission and philosophy that characterize these two systems. Emergency medicine focuses on episodic crises necessitating open access and standby readiness, whereas managed care organizations focus on primary and preventive care and the planned use of a valuable resource. Under federal law, hospital emergency departments have an ethical and legal obligation to examine all patients who present for care and to provide stabilizing treatment of patients with emergency medical conditions. This is authorized under the Emergency Medical Treatment and Active Labor Act (EMTALA), commonly known as COBRA (Consolidated Omnibus Budget Reconciliation Act). This entitlement to a medical screening examination by a qualified medical professional must be done regardless of a patient's ability to pay or technical competence to provide consent. Managed care organization gatekeepers are frequently unable to assess the need for emergency medical care over the telephone. They have denied preauthorizations for care for some patients who do present to emergency department and have retrospectively denied payment to those who do visit. Under COBRA, a medical emergency is a condition that poses an immediate threat to a patient's survival or may result in permanent loss of function of an organ or body part or severe pain. Managed care organizations use life-threatening definitions. Most patients who come to emergency departments are genuinely concerned for their safety and think their conditions are serious threats. As such, many managed care organizations have used various methods of gatekeeping to discourage costly emergency expenses. Some states have applied these strategies to Medicare and Medicaid programs. Thus, there have been reductions in census in some emergency rooms in heavily managed care markets. Some managed care organizations have required emergency room department registration personnel to place a telephone call for authorization to a gatekeeper before a service is provided. In many cases, that gatekeeper is not the patient's primary care physician or an on-call physician. Patients may be denied treatment authorization and have been told to go to the managed care clinic (even patients in severe pain, with ectopic pregnancies, myocardial infarction, and pulmonary emboli). Managed care organizations frequently reserve the right to deny a claim based on retrospective review even when prior authorization was given, despite the fact that a patient may require a medical screening examination to rule out ischemic heart disease when being evaluated for chest pain. The state of California recently (January 1995) made revisions to Section 1317.4 of The Health and Safety Code, commonly referred to as the Bergeson Bill, to allow emergency departments to provide initiating stabilizing care without first calling the managed care organization for authorization. The managed care organization is required to pay for services but may appeal following specific procedures. Although it is estimated on several retrospective diagnostic studies that between 40 to 55 percent of patients seen in emergency rooms have nonurgent problems, emergency room departments treat everyone. This has resulted in strained relations between managed care organizations that seek to contain costs by managing access and emergency departments that are required by law to provide evaluation and care.

An interesting parallel of nursing is summarized by Mitchell, Uehlinger, and Owen (1996). They state that nurses as members of a health care team view patient autonomy as a hallmark of their profession and that knowledge of the ethical concepts of autonomy, beneficence nonmalfeasance, and distributive justice should be a core competency for nursing. Nurses, when faced with ethical dilemmas, tend to rely on intuition and instinct to settle such issues quickly. Although able to identify the ethical issues quickly, they believe themselves powerless to initiate a formal ethical discussion because of a lack of ethical theoretical background and a lack of knowledge about quality improvement theory as well. Quality improvement, which uses research-based outcomes, empowers professionals to work together to improve patient outcome. Its success is due to the ability of multidisciplinary teams to work together. Ethics education and discussion, the author notes, should include other disciplines (e.g., social work, occupational therapy, medicine, physical therapy), as greater collaboration positively affects good patient care (17). Health care improvement teams should be interdisciplinary, short-term, and focused. Managed care consumers will use quality assessment measures of outcomes to choose among health care providers and plans. The authors suggest ethics and ethical behavior be included in these outcomes. As managed care, quality improvement, and ethics enter a common arena, integrating ethics and quality improvement will provide the strongest force for the patient, payer, and provider to grapple with. Integrating the need for outcome data and ethical standards will become the biggest challenge in managed care systems. The authors use the following quote as a clarion call: "Act to maintain the gain." It is the call for all health care professionals to work within ethical frameworks while improving patient-centered care (18).

There are a variety of articles that examine the ethics in managed care systems for mental health providers. These articles suggest the inherent economics of managed care has lowered mental health services to a level insufficient for effective treatment. There is mounting evidence that, as the focus of cost incentives, managed care has cut mental health services to the point that they have been unable to keep their commitment to quality services (Karon 1995; Fraser 1996; Miller 1996). Some psychologists have viewed the reduction of therapeutic services and the dominance of brief oriented services as not sufficient in providing adequate service, and the fact that these services are delivered by lower-level professionals undermines the value of psychotherapy (Cummings 1995). Psychologists are forming multimodel group practices and rushing to acquire skills in brief effective therapies. Cummings (1995) predicts by the year 2000, 50 percent of current psychotherapists will be out of business. Miller's (1996) review of psychologists' surveys in the literature found that 64 percent reported managed care had discontinued treatment when it was still indicated; as many as 72 percent of psychologists indicated their overall experience with managed care negatively affected the quality of treatment; 59 percent of clients were misled by false advertising; and 79 percent of professionals reported they were dissatisfied with utilization reviews including the reviewer's knowledge and expertise.

Miller's (1996) review of surveys about confidentiality shows a high concern among professionals about issues of confidentiality. A national survey of 718 responding psychologists reported that partially because of concerns about confidentiality, 38 percent had refused to sign contracts with managed care organizations. The 1987 National Medical Expenditure Survey indicated that the portion of mental health expenses paid out of pocket by the consumer is high, between 45 and 48 percent. Additionally, 95 percent of insurance policies had limitations on outpatient mental health services, 76 percent had a co-payment requirement, and 77 percent had limitations of

$1,000 or less. While this does control outpatient mental health expenses, and thus has restrained excessive outpatient mental health expenditures, instituting additional managed care cost controls runs the risk of cutting into psychologically necessary services (Miller 1996). In sum, many aspects of the managed care philosophy are conducive to undertreatment.

Karon's (1995) review suggests that, as the purchaser of care, the employer is usually more interested in cost than quality, and owners and managers of managed care systems are also primarily interested in cost containment as a route to profitability. Patient-consumer needs and preferences are secondary and lower yet are health professionals' concerns about quality and long-term outcome. Prevention efforts have been largely ignored by managed care since it is a long-term approach. Karon (1995) further postulates that most managed care contracts are sold on the basis of providing twenty sessions of psychotherapy a year although there is no rational basis for just twenty sessions. Medication is often relied on in managed care settings to obviate the need for more sessions, and therapists who do not "permit patients to tell them about real psychological problems can survive well in such as system, but ethical psychotherapists are demoralized" (6). Therapists are also told to get rid of patients in six sessions and patients think this means there is clinical improvement. The overall aim, then, is to provide as little psychological care as possible (6).

According to Vivian H. Jackson's (1995) NASW publication, "A Brief Look at Managed Mental Health Care," mental health and substance abuse services have been targeted for cost containment in managed care organizations because of the apparent growth of these services compared to other health care services, and the lack of stigma of mental illness which makes more people want them (consumer demand and the interest of employers in the well-being of their employees). Managed care companies use a variety of types of continuous quality improvement principles with the intent of improving performance. Social workers who are involved in managed care companies specializing in mental health need to be familiar with measures to promote quality improvement such as reviewing clinical criteria for type of source, the process of reviewing providers credentials, outcome measures, and compliance and utilization management which includes matching client to appropriate provider and treatment. In order to effectively question whether clients are getting what they need, social workers must first understand the system. This allows them to analyze questions such as, Does the system work for the client? How is quality defined and who defines it? What appeals are in place? What are the precautions for confidentiality? (Jackson 1995, 3).

Jackson (1995) notes that social workers are struggling like other provider groups to join managed care organizations. Some are full and others will not accept social workers. Managed care competition fares better with group practices because they can offer a diversity of skills and delivery models. Social workers, at a minimum, will need to be prepared for utilization review activities and with skills in group therapy, brief therapy, and alcohol and substance abuse. These skills are advantageous to managed care organizations. Contacts for and maintaining referrals are important. Social workers must also learn to market their skills, to provide unique specialized services, to be competent, and to be visible. They must know how their services are being assessed relative to competition. Social workers must continue to advocate for ethical and appropriate treatment and the values embodied in social work, yet recognize the fierce competition in the field. Managed care organizations must be viewed as catalysts for the social worker's role in the health delivery system, which includes the person-in-environment perspective and advocacy for ethical and appropriate client treatment, as well.

Hersch's (1995) review of psychologists' responses to managed care suggests that psychologists and other mental health professionals feel traumatized by the effects of managed care organizations. He describes psychologists as having symptoms of post-traumatic stress disorder, and this is a normal response to a professionally "traumatic set of events" known collectively as "managed care" (16). He views managed care as a problem-manifested area of health care reform similar to the economic downsizing of American business. On the other hand, he notes that "psychologists cannot engage in positive problem-solving if we view it as an 'evil' monolith that exists only to destroy our profession" (17). Rather, he suggests that managed care is a first-stage response in situations where there is a realistic need for cost cutting since, in the past fifteen years, mental health care costs have doubled as a percent of health care costs. He believes this is why mental health benefits have been so adversely affected by managed care aggressive control strategies. Although, case management has been used as a key tool in cost containment, part of the problem is a lack of easily quantifiable outcomes (lab values) in psychotherapists' work. In general, psychologists tend to be independent, self-motivated, and autonomy-minded and embrace the medical model (reimbursed through illness-disease) as a medical necessity (18). He believes there is a need to broaden the disease model into areas in which there can be relationships with primary care physicians on psychological factors that address the stress and behavioral contributions of disease and prevent full-blown mental illness. Psychologists who can screen and identify a psychoeducational model can be important members of a medical team. Psychologists can deal with new roles, such as working with first-time families, exploring safety issues of children, and dealing with lifestyle issues and the prevention of illness through behavioral programs which reduce smoking, increase relaxation, and promote exercise. These types of programs fit better with team practice. Psychologists can form single-specialty groups and offer a number of clinicians to purchasers or multispecialty groups which include other specialists across disciplines. Expanding the range of mental health practice into mental health networks or "horizontal diversification" offers comprehensive services and organizational structures. Hersch believes psychologists will have to broaden their practices to include involvement in outcome evaluation as well as providing more team-oriented services.

Shapiro (1995) makes the following points from a social work view about the downside of managed care. There are disincentives in providing care when utilization reviewers and case managers employed by reimbursers decide whether treatment recommendations are necessary and can thus ration care. Administrative issues such as cost factors, advertising, marketing and reviewing, and distribution of care are provided by reimbursers and not by healers who want to help people and give back to the community. Shapiro (1995) calls managed care "managed indifference"; in fact, the term "managed care" is really an oxymoron that no one notices, a euphemism for social control in the health care arena (443). Certain kinds of training may become obsolete not because they would not benefit the client, but because the insurance industry will not pay. She uses long-term psychodynamic therapy as an example. The client's privacy is diminished as in Employee Assistance Programs (EAP) when problems become the property of the employers.

Inglehart's (1996) review of mental health and managed care notes that clients may have to deal with psychological trauma raised by an insurance company's case manager who makes decisions about therapeutic services. Treatment of mental disorders and substance abuse has undergone dramatic change with the emergence of for-profit companies that provide managed "behavioral health care" (131). The anger felt by many psychiatrists and other mental health professionals is over decisions that were once within their province but are now made in tandem with these commercial companies (131). These professionals cannot advocate for patients but must satisfy multiple masters-payers, insurance plans, and other consumers. Americans spent 10 percent of all personal health care expenditures or $85.1 billion in 1990 for behavior health care disorders with 40 percent paid for by private insurance and out-of-pocket payments. Most managed care plans do not cover chronic mental health in their standard benefits packages. A typical benefit is a maximum twenty outpatient visits and thirty hospital days a year. Most case managers and reviewers are psychiatric nurses, social workers, and psychologists who authorize use of mental health services through toll-free telephone lines staffed twenty-four hours a day, seven days a week. They use computer databases to review patient problems or standard clinical protocols and assign patients to the least-expensive appropriate treatment. They then will consult with databases and authorize an appointment with a provider in the company's selective network. On the average, psychiatrists make up about 20 percent of any given provider network and psychologists and social workers constitute about 40 percent each. The approximate revenue as of 1995 for managed care behavioral health was $2.1 billion with the ten largest concerns generating 90 percent of the revenues. About 21.7 million people are enrolled in managed care behavioral health plans in which the average payment is $60.00 per capita annually to provide mental health and substance abuse services. Growing numbers of mergers and vertical integration have emerged combining the roles of providers and managers in one for-profit enterprise. Little is known about outcomes. As a result of less use of psychiatrists, psychiatric residency slots were filled with 78 percent American-trained physicians in 1990–1991 compared to 65 percent in 1994–1995 (Inglehart 1996).

Davidson and Davidson (1996) discuss the fact that many social workers providing services in their managed care systems are concerned about the quantity of information sought about the client, the sensitive nature of the information, and the necessity of disclosing that information if third-party reimbursement is desired. The negative effect that the loss of confidentiality has on the client-worker relationship is also of primary concern, and this also introduces the possibility of liability. Social work's mission may be at odds with the mission of managed care organizations which are concerned with capitate risks for groups of people, and therefore the individual's particular need is evaluated in the context of all the other covered lives. Thus, gatekeepers are in place who examine intimate details about a person usually from a distance and may use that information to deny/refuse services. In contrast, social workers' general aim is to work with all who request and need services. Within managed care, the mission is restrictive and generalized, whereas with social workers, service delivery is inclusive and individualized. While outcome studies should be used to deliver optimum treatment, in fact, they are flawed with poorly defined variables and could be used in ways to determine which populations are healthy and which could drain profits. Davidson and Davidson point out "the legitimate clinical principle of 'least-restrictive alternatives' has been transliterated by managed care to mean 'severely restricted alternatives,' 'stop-loss,' and 'hold harmless' and are fundamental operating procedures written into managed care contracts" (209). Stop-loss clauses require the government to step in when providing care for those who are needy proves too costly, and hold harmless clauses require providers to shoulder the burden of further treatment and liability when managed care companies discontinue payments because "it does not appear that a positive treatment outcome is cheap and imminent" (209). For social workers who have traditionally advocated for people who need service, it seems perverse to contribute client data to a system that uses information to figure out who should not get treatment or to indicate to the case reviewer that treatment should stop.

Davidson and Davidson (1996) state that regardless of the form of managed care, client information is now shared in a much less discriminate manner than what occurred in traditional fee-for-service delivery systems. This information includes telephone review, voicemail, faxes, and high use of unregulated computer systems. With the revolving system of unidentified case reviewers, social workers may not know who knows what or who will have access in the future to client disclosures. Clients must sign consent forms to release information from social workers to gatekeepers and, while it relinquishes rights to privacy, it is the only way to receive service. The NASW Code of Ethics (NASW 1996) expects social workers to uphold the ethical standards of confidentiality, privacy, and to only release information with appropriate valid consent. Clients must authorize disclosure to third-party payers. However, Davidson and Davidson (1996) note much of the information the social worker gives to managed care companies is outside the worker's control. Technical permission to disclose information does not solve the ethical problem of clients losing their right to confidentiality. The authors also suggest that social workers must ask themselves if more good extended to more people will justify the loss of confidentiality and to what extent are social workers colluding with managed care personnel to violate clients' civil rights. To what extent are forms valid if the degree of their use is not known? How can social workers, if necessary, withhold limits of confidentiality in the client's best interest and justify ignoring the duty to tell the truth? A major dilemma occurs when social workers must disclose information for clients to be covered. And finally, they point to the question of whether the advent of managed care abrades social work values and ethics. They raise the question of whether social workers and social service agencies have allowed professional honor to give way to expediency (212–214).

Davidson and Davidson (1996) recommend, as have other professionals, that a depersonalized coding system should eventually replace all permanent entries. Such systems can be used for outcome research and, in keeping with NASW guidelines, the computer software storing client data should maintain certain personal and confidentiality protocols. Providers should refuse managed care contracts that include nondisclosure clauses (clients and therapists discuss limits of managed care coverage). Clients should have access to review records that have been given by social workers to managed care companies, and personal information should be destroyed after service is concluded. Clients should be notified whether records go from one company to another and be allowed to veto access to data, recorded reviews should be done, and professional organizations should be obligated to refuse companies that contravene clients' rights. Social workers should resist the temptation to "go along to get along" (213).

In conclusion, Davidson and Davidson (1995) as well as others have suggested that insurance companies should not have direct access to case notes or files, and that files should be destroyed when service is completed. Clients should be informed about the use of data and the limits of confidentiality and have adequate recourse to file grievances if there is misuse. In sum, across professional groups there is concern for not only the loss of patient autonomy and confidentiality in relationships, but also the erosion of trust as the provider is thrust between the needs of the patient and the contractual agreement of the insurance company. Physicians, nurses, social workers, and psychologists are all expressing through their professional journals and societies a major concern that managed care organizations are redefining their roles and practice models. Their issues are becoming public and new responses and modifications are beginning to occur. This is a good time to be part of the professional groups that are actively involved in changing the nature of managed care practices. The degree of success will depend on the ability to advocate for and insist on professional practices that are consistent with philosophical and historical roots but are also amenable to change and compromise.

We have tried to give a brief picture of some of the most important and current issues about managed care. In the following chapters, you will see these issues enacted through both the client and provider systems. In the final chapter, a system of promoting change will be presented. We hope this chapter gives our readers the impetus to develop, create, and advocate a good system that changes as it strives toward perfection.

Cast of Characters

The Setting

Not-for-profit, 800-bed teaching hospital in a metropolitan area.

The Team

Sergio Oliviero, MD, neurologist in his thirtieth year of practice; highly respected, a researcher and a humanist. He has good bedside manners, a brilliant research mind, and longs for the days when medicine was an art.

Carolyn McPherson, head nurse in her fifties, has worked with Dr. Oliviero since he was a Fellow. She is divorced and married to her job. Her yardstick for the state of medicine is how full the staff parking lot is on Sundays.

Frank Pearman, 32, MBA with a specialization in health care; vice president for managed care contracts for the Texas Hospital Center. He believes in managed care with a passion.

Reenie Shandler, 40-something MSW with one foot in the activism of the 1960s, the other in the outcome measurement systems of the 1980s. The bottom line for her is always: "Did the client get what he or she needed."

Josh Pollan, 23, physical therapist. He does his job, does it well, and leaves it behind when he clocks out every afternoon.

The Client System

Violet Mason, 29, from a small town, now lives in a big city; principal with the Metropolitan Ballet Company; second wife of Jack Mason.

Jack Mason, 35, a computer wizard and self-made man. His silver-tongued storytelling has earned him a "must invite" on party lists; husband of Violet.

Steve Woodson, 46, a plumber; hard work and surviving by one's own wit are the closest things to a philosophy he holds; a Vietnam veteran who drives a 1957 pickup truck with the dusty tailgate always open.

The Support Group

Mrs. Luber, 75, Medicare HMO, in-patient with a stroke.

Mr. Shaw, 68, Medicare patient.

Ms. Brown, 60, indigent patient of Dr. Oliviero.

Mr. Marshall, 61, PPO patient.

Mrs. Spelling, 66, fee-for-service, indemnity insurance patient.

Violet, 29, HMO and private-pay patient.

1

The Event: The Rules Are Changing

For a flicker she was nothing. She almost disappeared, suspended as she was, not so much hanging in air as becoming a part of it. Yet she knew it was not the loss of herself, but the control that made those seconds possible. Her strength, that sheer control of her body, touched her silently to the ground once more. In those moments, her nature succumbed. Moments all too brief, for even as she tried to clutch them to her, the curtain would fall. The beauty of ballet, Violet knew, was no illusion. It was always tightly controlled by a sure body of muscle and energy, welded perfectly by willpower. At twenty-nine, the possibility that such a finely trained body could fail was not even a real thought. It performed flawlessly, no matter the pain or fatigue, simply upon her command. She loved ballet; more specifically, she loved her body in ballet.

Violet also liked privacy. Before she put on her toe shoes for class, alone in her little corner, she examined her toes, her wounded soldiers hidden under silk. They were her visible proof that what occurred was not due to chance, but the result of years of pushing the limit, pushing, building, numbing until her body could move beyond all reasonable limits. Although other company members shared the room, they hardly etched a line in her mind. She was focused, determined, aware of nothing but muscle and air, pain and gravity. She wasn't even aware that she was being watched, not that it would have mattered. She was going over and over the moves of her dance in her new repertoire. She repeated the motions, pounding the kinetics into muscle memory as she expended all her mental energy remembering to focus on the steps and her partner.

Jack Mason stood just inside the room, leaning on the door frame. He loved watching her. She played to him, though she never looked his way. Jack was fairly well-to-do, so-called new money. Not rich, just very comfortable. When she met him, he was thirty-something and a little bored and more than a little soft. She, on the other hand, was strong and physical. Once spotted, she focused on her personal prince while he was unaware that he was not controlling the dance. Violet clung to her husband until he felt like a rock rather than a weight. She kept a silly scrapbook of their courtship hidden under her mattress. When they married, she meant to throw it away, but she never had time to go through everything, after all. And sometimes now, late at night, falling asleep alone in her bed while Jack worked late at the company, she remembered her scrapbook, and smiled.

Usually Violet knew when he was there. She didn't so much see him come in, as sense his presence. But today she was distracted, slightly off, and that annoyed her. Irritated, she was not aware of Jack, or anyone else, for that matter. Just herself, the mirror, and the class. "This is an opportunity to point those toes," said Miss Leland, the company master teacher. "This is ballet," demonstrating a leg lift in second position perfectly. "This is a teapot," she joked while turning her leg in. Violet didn't laugh with the class. She doubled her legwork at the barre, movement after movement, seeking perfection. She just wasn't getting it. The headache that woke her was still nagging. She never liked headaches. They were beyond her understanding—a betrayal of the body she sculpted! Earlier, she made her way down the hall to the massage therapy room, looking for the right "fix-it." No one was around. Her body needed more help than usual today, another fact that she could not comprehend. She always refused to take any medicine that would make her fingers tremble. She would lose her edge. So she stayed with the pain, went back to the studio, let its annoyance challenge her. She pushed harder, lunging for the barrier between body and spirit, trying to break the spell. She grabbed the barre, preparing to do whatever she had to, take as long as it took.

The noise. The noise was bothering her today. Usually nothing penetrated her finely honed focus. There was nothing peripheral in her vision. But suddenly the other dancers had become so loud. She turned to them, screaming to them to please be quiet, to obey company protocol. She screamed and screamed, but the dancers just stared. It was as if they had not heard. She herself was not certain whether she was screaming, or merely contemplating screaming. They moved close, coming closer and closer. She knew she was screaming now. She was screaming so loud that it took the air away from her, commanding their attention. But there was something else, something cold? No, nothing. Something was nothing and they were coming closer, bending over her. She must have slipped to the floor, screaming as she was. Suddenly she was tired, nauseated, and exhausted from the shouting. She had a severe headache. She knew only that she must sleep. She closed her eyes and saw pairs of slippers.

Jack was frozen, unable to comprehend the scene unfolding before him. He patted his pocket, inside the jacket, fingering his pen, his appointment book. A picture shot through his brain of schema from his FORTRAN classes back at the university. He reached instinctively for a backpack but there was not one to be found. Around him now there was pandemonium. Shrill screams, deeper, firmer commands. He thought he heard something about 911 and wondered for a moment if Violet had hit someone. But he looked again, shaking his head for clarity, knowing that she lay alone on the floor. He tried to move but his feet were of stone. He could only watch from his doorway, staring disbelieving at the butterfly fallen to the earth. He stayed there, rooted, watching the scurrying, the cold rags, the whispered questions. He caught her eyes once, and just for a moment it seemed as is she were looking directly at him, questioning, begging almost. He looked away quickly, knowing he must have imagined it. Violet's eyes would not be capable of a look like that.

They slammed through the studio's double doors, loud and commanding, taking charge in spite of the fact they clearly didn't belong. Sweating, in cotton shirts with little patches on the sleeves. They continued their command, moving medical-looking instruments over her chest and neck, peering into her eyes with tiny flashlights, talking on their static-filled toy radios. They moved her onto a portable stretcher, carrying on the pretense that she could not move herself. Jack gave them his health plan card. They said he was lucky the Hospital Center was in his network. They started to the doorway toward him. He caught her eyes. That look was there, no question, pleading. And then she was gone, out the door with the paramedics and their machines, the doors knocking to a close behind them. The hum of the dancers continued. Jack realized suddenly that many of them were whispering, pointing in his direction as if he should do something. The disbelief in his stomach whirled into nausea. He lunged for the door, gasping for air, groping for the light of day. Why did this have to happen today? His mind flashed on the rules of computer language once again. He pushed his way out the door, knowing he would have to figure out what he was to do as he went along.

The doors to the ambulance swung closed. The siren wailed as the lights began their furtive search, and the ambulance pulled away from the curb. Jack ran behind it, screaming in his bid to get the attention of the people who had just stolen his wife from before his eyes. The ambulance stopped abruptly, the doors flung open again. Once of the men jumped out and ran toward Jack. "You a friend of hers?" the medical machine man asked. "I am her husband. Let me in there." "Come on," the medical machine man commanded. "I think she's asking for you. You can ride in the back with us." Jack looked up. He could tell her eyes were open. He turned away for just a second, then grabbed the door handle and swung his way in.

Violet was cloudy. Why had they told Jack he could ride with her? This was stupid anyway. She was perfectly fine, just a little tired. Having a little trouble thinking, but that's the price you pay for pushing the barrier. No one else had apparently worked, pushed against the constraints of nature the way she pushed her body. A little sleep, that's all she needed. She started to drift off, waking suddenly as she realized someone's hand was on her stomach. She tried to look around but her movements were constricted by the stretcher and the small space. She wanted the hand off her. She did not know these people. She tried to jerk it off, but it would not move. Finally, she grabbed the hand with her own right hand, flinging it away. There, that should tell them just exactly what her boundaries were. Then it was back. Someone picked the hand up and put it back on her. She glanced to the right. She had not seen the man move but he must have retrieved the hand. She grabbed it with her right hand and flung it again. The man did not move, but the hand came back. She screamed. The man said something about "left neglect." Must be some political movement she hadn't heard about. How could she be expected to converse intelligently about a movement she knew nothing about. This gentleman really needed a few lessons in etiquette. But then again, he didn't seem quite right. He kept pulling that hand on her, and talking to himself. Must be taking him to the hospital too?

• • • • •

For Reenie, social worker at the Hospital Center, the day was like any other day. Relentlessly like every other day had become. She leaned heavily against the wall in the stairwell for a moment, trying to collect her thoughts, as well as all the loose pieces of paper stuffed into her notebook. Prioritize, prioritize—that was the mantra of the month in the Social Work Department. Unfortunately nobody had an answer for what to do when every case was top priority. Gone were the days when Reenie had time to actually work with patients. Time not only to hand out resources as she shuffled clients out the door, but time to talk with them about the life impact of their hospitalization. Time to listen to their grief, offer guidance and support. And working with the team. The team approach—social worker, physician, nurse, therapists, everybody working toward one end: the betterment of the patient. The team barely had time to meet these days. Oh, and counseling. Reenie realized how much she missed really counseling people, not just throwing phone numbers in their direction. Those days were definitely gone. They had slipped away slowly at first, barely noticed. A position that wasn't filled when a colleague retired, a few more patients a month for Reenie to see. Then another coworker found greener pastures at the for-profit hospital down the street and Reenie had a few more patients, and so on. Little by little, it added up to this moment, today, when she really wondered if she could squeeze in one more thing. And it had taken so long for social workers to be valued and accepted as providers of useful services. So much hard work slipping down the drain. The wall felt good, cool, and solid against her back as she slipped the shoes off first one aching foot, then the other. She had almost gotten a grip on herself when she was jolted back to reality by the shrill beep of her pager. No rest for the weary. The page was to unit 10, where Reenie was headed for a new consult. She glanced at her watch. Gees, couldn't they just chill for one second, allow her one simple moment of peace? Rhetorical question, she thought, and trudged up the stairs once again to the work that beckoned.

Carolyn McPherson waited impatiently for Reenie to return her page. These days she envied the social worker's freedom to roam the hospital while she was chained to her Head Nurse desk on the unit. She paged again, drumming all the while on the counter. Administration had sent some forms to be completed before the afternoon meeting. Of course, the fact that she had not actually gotten them in her hands until ten o'clock meant nothing to administration. *Can't* was not a permissible word in a head nurse's vocabulary. And usually, Carolyn was the first to agree. No war was ever won by soldiers chanting "can't." She was proud of her unit, her systematic approach that kept things running, kept both patients and doctors happy. Organizations maintaining tight control was the key to success. But the job just kept getting harder and harder. She was moving twice as fast and still finding it more challenging to stay on top of things. Insurance companies—what a royal pain. They had entirely too much power and they were using it to drive her and her physicians absolutely nuts. Probably a bunch of frustrated medical school dropouts. Couldn't make the grade and decided if they couldn't practice medicine one way, they would practice it another. There had been a time when she had thought wistfully about what it would be like, what she would do, if she had an MD after her name. Not now. Now she felt sorry for her doctors and all that they put up with. She did everything she could to take the pressure off them. And right now, she needed Reenie's help in doing that.

Reenie could literally see the tension as she approached a pacing Carolyn at the nurse's station. She was more than a little irritated herself, having gotten three pages in the last five minutes. "You paged?"

"Got a call from administration. The managed care company wants an up-to-the-minute report on 333, 336, 342, 343, 348, 351. . . ."

"351? Who is that?" Reenie had given up trying to get the nurses to call patients by their names rather than room numbers. She finally decided that it was better than calling them "the hip" or "the liver" like some professionals did. And she had to admit, they managed to remember the patients remarkably well long after discharge, even if they could only identify them by numbers.

"New admit. Mason. Uh, what's her first name . . . Violet. Violet Mason."

"Oh, yes, I saw her husband in the ER when she came in," Reenie recalled.

Anyway, they want all these papers filled out. And not only that, the vice president of managed care is going to sit in team with us this morning. Wants to address our 'problem' patients."

"Problem? Which one of my delightful patients is bothering you little ladies this morning?" Dr. Oliviero caught just the tail of the conversation as he walked up.

"Oh, Doctor, you're here. Thank goodness. I wish it were one of your patients. Unfortunately it's Mr. Pearman. He's going to sit in on our team meeting," Carolyn tried not to cringe as she prepared for the tirade. She had known Dr. Oliviero long enough to understand his ventilations were not directed at her, yet still her insides always churned when he started on a roll. He worked so hard and she hated to see him work himself up so.

Sensing Carolyn's sincere distress, Reenie jumped in. "Maybe this will be a good thing. If he hears about these patients first hand maybe he won't be so quick to refuse our equipment and therapy requests."

Dr. Oliviero, puzzled, barely reacted as he flipped open a chart. "Who is Pearman?"

"The managed care vice president, in charge of all managed care contracts. Remember. . . ?"

Dr. Oliviero stiffened, hammering in before Carolyn could finish. "He's not sitting in my team meeting." He was not going to allow it. This was stepping over the last line. "I've already spent precious time this morning returning phone calls to every insurance company on God's green earth when I should have been rounding on my patients. They all wanted the same thing—'Why can't patient *x*, *y*, or *z* be discharged?' If I said no, they argued. 'Protocol hasn't shown additional hospital days to be effective in this type of case,' they would say, or 'There is no proven reason to repeat that diagnostic procedure, blah, blah, blah.' Nothing more than blowhard bullies, using precertification, recertification, second-opinion certification, all to limit specialty care and to cut patients off from the technology that could make a life-or-death difference for them. I can't even send lab results where I want. I have to send them to the 'No Frills Lab.' That means I'll get back ten results in ten days and five of the patients are not mine, and the other five got lost. Last week I called a lab for a report that I said I needed immediately. They said, 'Sorry, it took so long, it got crushed in transit.'"

"Dr. O., I know. I know exactly how you feel. But administration has made the arrangements already. They didn't call to ask permission. They called to make sure I would have the paperwork done, which I don't."

"Sending some suit up here to check on us doesn't scare me, mind you. This unit, my team here, runs like a well-oiled machine. Sure, let him come up. It will be a wasted trip. He'll take one look at us and head back to corporate paper pushing."

"I don't know, Dr. O.," Carolyn countered. "I've heard that these managed care companies can be a bear to deal with and he is directly responsible for all of their contracts here."

"Listen, this pip-squeak and his bottom-line mentality are not getting in the way of my patients and me."

"But Dr. O., I have heard administration say that since rehab is carved out specifically, we have to cooperate. It's financially in the best interest. . . ." Reenie tried to mediate but was quickly interrupted.

"Reenie, I don't have to do a blessed thing. They think they can fire me based on some excessive utilization bull? Well, go ahead, boys, if you think you're big enough. I'm not scared of this hospital or that managed care company. Never have been, never will be. I have a friend on the West Coast who is all in an uproar because some upstart managed care group terminated his service because his care 'exceeded the area average.' I say, so what? Somebody wants to fire me for taking better care of my patients than the next guy, go ahead. Put it in writing so I can frame it along with all my other accolades. Now, let's get a move on. We need to be worrying about not discharging these patients before they are ready, not about how much I'm costing the insurance company or what contract the hospital is going to lose because we're taking care of the people who come here for our help."

"It is pitiful what is happening in other parts of the country. I hope it doesn't happen here any time soon." Reenie concurred. "I've got a friend in California who says there is so much pressure to discharge ASAP that her job description should read 'Shipping and Receiving.' And who is standing up for the patients in all of this? The poor patients don't even have a say anymore."

"Speaking of discharges," Carolyn jumped in, nervously gesturing to a tall stack of papers on the counter, "Mr. Pearman faxed these patient status forms over for us to fill out before the meeting. Perhaps we should review them so we're prepared to advocate for an adequate treatment plan."

Dr. Oliviero picked up a form, eyeballed it, then sent it sailing into the trash. "I'm too busy saving people for this nonsense. Starting to think maybe the only thing I'm saving them from is the insurance nonsense. I spend two hours everyday on the telephone with insurance companies. I spend one hour a day in paperwork. I spend the next two hours taking care of my stomach. I complain about all the time it takes—the managed care guys say do it at home. If I argue about treatment, they say 'Read your contract.' If I argue about treatment goals, they say 'Okay, we will give you a speech but not rehab.' Those doctors who are reviewers for managed care don't know squat. Only way we provide such excellent care at the Texas Hospital Center is to argue. And stop looking at me like that, Miss Carolyn—I am not about to stop arguing now!"

"Well, you go on ahead. I'll get them filled out in a hurry. Be there in a minute." Carolyn was not about to push poor Dr. Oliviero to do one more thing. And besides, he was right. Her only problem was the need for a paycheck—she had to find a way to keep both the doctor and administration happy.

"Mrs. McPherson, we start now, we will never stop. Come on people, we have patients to treat."

Carolyn followed him reluctantly, turning to Reenie. "He doesn't understand. We've got to do this. It came down from corporate and the patient suffers if we refuse. Besides, he's not salaried like the rest of us."

"This form is ridiculous. 'Length of stay'—what difference does that make?" Reenie asked, perusing the form. "We know when it's time, when everything is in place. It depends on the needs of the individual."

"What needs of what individual?" Josh dashed to catch up to the group as they headed down the hall. He was always the last to arrive, waiting until the last possible second to leave his patients in the gym. He loved being a physical therapist—the patient part, working on functional goals, that is—all the meetings and paperwork he could do without. He didn't actually hate that stuff—he understood why it had to be done. It just did not get his juices flowing like helping somebody put weight on a reconstructed leg for the first time or watching patients finally make it up the practice stairs by themselves, looking every bit like Rocky when they arrived at the top.

Dr. Oliviero clapped Josh on the back. "Bunch of crap, that's all. Now, how are all my little folks doing in therapy, Josh?"

Carolyn fretted, "Twenty years ago stroke patients went home as soon as they could blink their eyes. There was nothing we could do for them. I guess now we'll go back to that. I miss the time when medicine was so much fun you couldn't wait to get here. Now, our staff garage is like a ghost town over the weekend. No one wants to be here unless they have to."

Josh countered. "Hey, the contract therapist's car is there every weekend, thank you. Ever since we had to add Saturday and Sunday therapy sessions."

Reenie was distracted for a moment. "Contract therapist? I thought you said you were working weekends now, Josh."

"I am, but as a contract therapist for New Age PhysiCare. They pay me big bucks to work weekends at Greater Region Memorial."

"Why don't you just work here?"

"They can't pay me as much because I'm staff. So, I work contract somewhere else, and a staff therapist from some other hospital works contract here. Everybody's happy."

"Except the patient, who doesn't know who's coming in the door next. And me. I'm so confused. The place is just turning into a mess." Reenie was genuinely perplexed.

"It's all about money, now. That's it." Carolyn summed up.

"Carolyn, you are preaching to the choir. I want to go back to the days when we were all proud of what we were doing. Remember all the hard work we put in to get to the point of smooth, collaborative teamwork?" Reenie shuddered to herself, remembering how long it had taken her to convince the other team members that social workers had value and provided useful services to patients. She felt a deep uneasiness as she thought of the pride they each had in the team they had built together—an interprofessional medical team; four members, four professions, one and a half hours per day, decisions by consensus. But not these days. These days, Reenie knew, one hospital representative from the managed care networks could do a whole lot of damage and future damage as well.

"What are you guys so worried about?" Josh was confused, vaguely aware that something was different with the team this morning.

"Mr. Pearman."

"Who is Mr. Pearman?" Josh was clueless.

"Mr. Pearman, vice president in charge of managed care contracts. He's going to sit in on our team conference this afternoon to see if we're doing this correctly." Carolyn explained, not altogether patiently.

"Oh, yeah, that guy. Like he could find his way out of a paper bag. You should hear the questions he asks me about why patients need certain modalities. But if he does make it, no skin off my nose. I put all this stuff in my weekly report anyway," Josh offered. "He can just read my progress notes."

Carolyn eyed him and concluded that he was just a baby chick in this profession, too young to know the types of battles that were fought to get insurance to cover the treatment and procedures that affect the quality of patient recovery, some of the very treatments he so loved to do with his patients. He should know. "Josh, you think managed care is just another insurance company. You'll be getting an unpleasant surprise when they deny our treatments one of these days."

"Whew, we're a little touchy today, aren't we?" Josh was accustomed to Carolyn's moods, but today seemed different somehow.

"Dr. Oliviero is right, you know, we are a well-oiled machine," Reenie said, still hoping to boost the team's and her own confidence. 'I'm an experienced social worker, always trying to cooperate with the team, advocate for the patient, put out fires. Are my skills outdated?' she wondered.

Carolyn took the cue. "Tell you what—let's all make an effort to get the latest on every patient before this afternoon. Then we'll discuss just as we always do—we'll just include all of the patients this week. Reenie, all of the discharge plans had better be crystal clear."

Carolyn hit a raw nerve. "Are you kidding?" shot back Reenie. "As sick as most of these patients are? How can I possibly know what they're going to need at discharge. And do you know how much time it takes to find a good personal-care home? I'm talking about one that doesn't have rats and serves actual meals the way it's supposed to? The UR nurse wanted to know if 336 could get to a personal-care home today—just had surgery the first of the week. I guess next they'll be doing drive-by lobotomies and I'll just stand at the second window. 'Your head is ready now, sir, drive to the next window for your destination of choice.' I am sick and tired. . . ."

Carolyn bristled in return. "Hold on now. We need to concentrate on our team skills. Let's try to focus on today and not what might happen at some future time."

"Yes, but . . . ," Reenie responded with sarcasm.

Josh was off on a tangent. "Maybe the team of the future won't even meet face to face. We'll meet on the Internet. Do our planning in virtual reality."

Reenie was not deterred long. "Oh, I know . . . Won't that be just great? What about the ethical issues of the Internet? I can't find enough current literature about ethical dilemmas between professionals now. And, definitely, there is nothing about all the telecommunication issues."

Carolyn had had it with all the stewing. It certainly wasn't going to make the team work better together, and it would not impress Mr. Pearman. "Reenie," Carolyn blurted, "Josh, go see your patients."

"Yeah, yeah, alright. Let's go, Josh. We've got a lot of folks to see before the meeting." Reenie and Josh headed down the hallway. They often evaluated new patients together. Some of the things they needed to ask were the same and talking took patients' minds off the pain of the evaluative movement Josh had to do. Their first stop was to see 351, a young woman admitted to the neurosensory floor a few days before from the ER, and the source of concern of the managed care company. Josh listened to the initial psychosocial evaluation done by Reenie in the ER:

> *Violet Mason is a 29-year-old female admitted through the ER with a diagnosis of right CVA with left hemiparesis. She was oriented to person, but not to time or place at time of attempted interview. She felt weakness of the left side of her body and was reported blind on the left side of visual field. ER report showed massive bleeding in right side, probably due to aneurysm. Her husband was seen by this*

social worker at the time of patient's admission and is the informant for this assessment. The patient's husband, Jack B. Mason, 35, indicates that he and patient have been married for almost four years. This is the second marriage for him, the first for the patient. Mr. Mason was calm, cooperative during the interview, especially in view of the treatment of his wife in the trauma room. He stated he could "do better by her" to remain outside the room and "out of the way" of the treatment team. He was able to clearly describe the event that brought his wife to the hospital. She was participating in a dance class—ballet is one of her hobbies. Mr. Mason had gone to the class to pick her up, arriving a few minutes early. As he watched, she began to scream for help and "sort of fainted" and fell to the floor. He claimed he phoned 911 immediately and accompanied his wife to the emergency room. At the time of the interview he was aware of the possibility that his wife "had a light stroke or seizure" but expressed confidence that she would "get through this unscathed." When asked if he and his wife had faced such a crisis prior to this event, he replied, "No, we've pretty much been on a nonstop honeymoon." He pulled several photographs of the patient from his wallet.

He describes their relationship as "top-notch" and expressed confidence that "with her grace and my brains we can tackle anything." In terms of finances, he states that "money is not a problem—whatever she needs, we'll have; it's as simple as that." Unable to get specific environmental data from husband, as he was paged to his office for an emergency. Will need to talk with patient to complete assessment, but at this point she appears to have a strong, supportive marriage. She will likely need rehabilitation after acute care. Uncertain at this point whether she will be able to return to her homemaker responsibilities, but finances may be adequate to hire personal and household assistance as needed. While patient and husband will no doubt require education about the impact of a CVA and short-term counseling regarding adjustment to this medical event, their basic coping appears intact. Anticipate uncomplicated course through hospitalization, rehabilitation, and eventual return home.

"Reenie, slow down so we can discuss this before we go in. Do you even remember this patient?"

"Sorry, Josh, I guess I am obsessing about being prepared to advocate for her in that meeting. She's got to have full rehab and a sound discharge plan. She's so young. And I didn't expect to do this all so quickly. But, you're right. Let's slow down and do it the way it's supposed to be done."

• • • • •

Inside her room, Violet drifted in and out of sleep. She was more exhausted than she thought. There was something different about the bed, but she could not quite put her finger on it. There was some sort of ornamental metal attached to it. Something unexpected from the decorator perhaps? She could not focus long enough to figure things out, dozing on and off as she was. Voices filtered through the haze. A man and a woman were talking. She shook the cobwebs, tried to stretch her limbs as she caught some of what was being said. She did not have time for gossip, really. She needed to get to the studio; it must be late, seemed to her. She flexed her muscles, still humming from yesterday's workout. They were talking so loudly outside the bedroom.

"A housewife," the woman said, "very interested in dance, especially ballet." Who isn't, Violet thought to herself. She had little time for small talk; she must get dressed. She was hampered by the metal. And her arm and leg were not up to par. She must have a strain. She laughed, proud to have a strain—it had been a while since she had pushed herself hard enough to strain the muscles this intensely. At least she thought she was laughing, but tears came, rolling down her cheeks and splashing the sheet. Good. She must be really on the edge now. The perfect time to push harder. She inched her way toward the bottom of the bed, as the conversation continued from somewhere.

"She had the event while in a class."

An event in class? That was totally inappropriate—class is for work and nothing else. "She got help right away. That is probably what saved her. Mr. Mason—her husband, was there."

Hmm. Could be a relative of Jack's. No, he would have told her about any relative into ballet.

"He is an accountant. Don't have the name of the employer yet. He's taking this amazingly well—able to answer all my questions even though she was in the trauma room."

The trauma room, huh? Bad news—must have torn a ligament or something. Violet was halfway down the bed now, her gown wadded at her waist as she continued to scoot.

"Said he didn't want to get in the way. Looked very calm, steady. He'll be a big help. If he hadn't gotten paged to work so suddenly, we could have gotten his work number. Let's see, they seem to be comfortable financially. That's good because she's probably going to need quite a bit of help at discharge, right?"

"Maybe independent at the wheelchair level. I think she has pretty severe left hemiparesis. Of course, her arm will be the last to come back. If it does."

Violet paused, out of breath, her legs dangling off the end of the bed. What the heck are they talking about now? Someone's arm gone. Maybe that was the one she found last night. Was it last night? In a car? Must have been a dream, she thought. This is probably even a dream. A dream about a dream. She laughed again, and was perplexed again by the tears on her face. She hated dreams like this, dreams where you have to go to the bathroom but can't ever seem to get there. It was so frustrating. She began wiggling again. Even if it was a dream, she was uncomfortable.

"Lives in an apartment in the southwest part of town. Elevators, so access should not be a problem. Don't know about the inside, though the doors are likely to be too narrow for the wheelchair."

Violet's eyes widened as the word sunk in. Wheelchair. Chair with wheels. She tried to picture it. Must be some kind of sculpture. Sculpture is so boring, she thought. It doesn't do anything, it just sits there. Especially a wheelchair! She began to laugh again, felt moisture not only on her face this time, but down her right leg. She must focus. She simply had to get to the bathroom before it was too late. She began to move again, hoping it would wake her from the dream.

"Came from a small town in East Texas. Probably very rooted in her family—small town folks usually are. So, they may be able to offer some help." Her family. Who, the sculptor or the dancer? And what happened to the accountant? Whoever this woman was, she could certainly gossip in high gear.

"She copes, he said, by working out."

"Who doesn't?"

"Let's go in and see her." A noise, like a car alarm, shrill, but not as loud. "Uh-oh. Stat page. We'll have to come back to see her. What's her first name again?"

The male voice. "Violet. Violet Mason." It took a moment to soak in, as she heard the sound of heels retreating, the quiet left in the wake of the voices. Violet . . . Violet? Wait just a damn minute. They were talking about her? She screamed after them. Or, at least she thought she was screaming. It was hard to tell again. But she gave it all she had, bellowing out as she slipped off the end of the bed, screaming from the cold floor. "That's not me, that's not me," she yelled after the clicking heels. "You've got it all wrong. That's not me!"

• • • • •

The treatment team convened for the afternoon patient care meeting much the way they came together in the morning. Reenie and Carolyn arrived at the conference room at the same time, both still a bit jumpy.

"They must have called me fifty times from administration today to see if everything is ready for our managed care guru," said Carolyn. "Like we don't take care of patients every day! What do they think we do around here anyway? All these companies checking every treatment decision. Dr. O is fit to be tied."

"The concept is good, but I'm tired of hearing 'the patient's plan doesn't cover it,'" Reenie told Carolyn.

Carolyn agreed. "Or, 'it's not in PDR so the drug is experimental.' I wonder if they can distinguish a patient from an orangutan."

"Oh, Carolyn, you know they don't know," Reenie answered in support of her coworker. "Been years since any of them were within one hundred yards of an actual patient." The laughter eased the tension a bit as the two women settled into the conference chairs.

"What kinds of things are they checking on?" Reenie asked.

"What aren't they checking on . . . shift coordinator came up here and hid our extra pens! Can you believe that—she actually said we had too many ballpoints on the unit. Today, Dr. Oliviero said they ran out of progress note pads. Mostly though, they're looking at the charts, the care plans, that sort of thing."

"Any comments?"

"Not really. Mr. Pearman supposedly is carrying some sort of printout with him from unit to unit. Says he is looking at length of stay data for patients."

Josh crashed through the doorway in his usual fashion. "The managed care guy was actually on a unit? How did he recognize it—did he have a picture of a prototype?" Laughter filled the room again as Dr. Oliviero made his usual late entry.

"Now this is what I like to see—my team having fun with what they're doing." Dr. Oliviero didn't even inquire as to the source of their mirth as he settled at the head of the table and began talking about patients. "What's the status on Mrs. Luber's skin?"

"333? Still some redness in the sacral area, but no further breakdown," Carolyn reported. "Do you think we should wait for our guest?"

"Time and doctors wait for no one. Is she being turned according to my orders?"

"Absolutely. I checked on her myself yesterday afternoon."

"Well, you know skin integrity is crucial. Requires diligent attention. Back when I was a resident there was a patient who . . ."

Dr. Oliviero was in his teaching mode at these weekly meetings, feeling it his duty to impart wisdom, to inspire his team.

Carolyn had heard the decubitus lecture many, many times but she was always glad her nursing interns had the advantage of the doctor's information. Today, however, she could not wait for the tale to end. When Dr. Oliviero stopped for a breath, she added, "Mrs. Luber is quite anxious to leave. She hasn't seen her cat for two months now, according to what Reenie just told me."

"Josh, how's she doing in therapy?" Dr. Oliviero returned to his role as director.

"She's independent in bed mobility, goes from supine to sit and from sit to stand with no assistance. She's walking 300 feet with her quad cane with standby for supervision and needs minimal assistance with her bathing."

"I think another ten days or so and she'll be ready to go home," Dr. Oliviero replied thoughtfully. "That sound right to you, Josh?"

"Sounds good. She should be independent with a straight cane by then and able to do all her ADLs without supervision."

"She wants to go right now," Reenie offered, "but I will talk with her about the absolute necessity of her staying longer."

"Nonsense. She's far past ready to go," an unfamiliar voice interjected. The team members turned to see the figure who had stood in the doorway unnoticed until that moment. Dr. Oliviero was the first to respond, and rather coldly. "And you are?"

"I am Frank Pearman," the man replied as he sat down in the conference chair directly opposite Dr. Oliviero. "Very nice to meet ya'll. I've heard you are a hard-working team. I've benchmarked your length of stay data with that from our comparable network holdings and you are way over the mark. This woman, Mrs. Luber, must go. Anyway, you said yourself she wants to go home. Next, we need to discuss Mrs. Mason's discharge plan. She's an HMO patient. She doesn't need to be in the hospital once she's stable. You've got to start jumping on them right from the start. Let's talk about how we may improve this."

Dr. Oliviero could feel his ears getting hot and knew his blood pressure was rising. But he forged ahead. "Mrs. Luber will be medically ready to return home in ten days. End of discussion."

"I'll talk to her. Maybe a visit from the cat . . ." Reenie's negotiation was abruptly interrupted by Mr. Pearman.

"She goes home now. Today."

One glance in Dr. Oliviero's direction told Reenie he was about to blow. She jumped in quickly, hoping to head off Mr. Pearman before Mrs. Luber and her discharge plan became the first casualty of the managed care wars at the hospital. "Now just a minute here, Mr. Pearman. You have not heard one thing about the care this patient requires. You don't know the first thing about patient care."

"I know she needs a little help with bathing. A case manager can set that up in her sleep. As I was saying, so how is Mrs. Mason doing? What is the discharge plan?" The team members watched Dr. Oliviero and Frank Pearman like they were watching a master game in which patients were toys and they were squares. Only they each knew, in the sick part of their stomachs, that there was more than a game at stake here. People's lives hung in the balance while this particular battle raged, a forbearer of all the battles that would inevitably follow.

Analysis

Two separate but related issues are presented in the preceding chapter. The first is the specter of managed care as it affects the treatment planning of an interdisciplinary rehabilitation team. The second is how managed care systems affect the communication among specific professional members of the interdisciplinary team—the social worker, the nurse, the physician, and the rehabilitation specialist. The patient in this chapter, Violet Mason, had a right cerebral stroke. Her confusion following the trauma is depicted as an inability to identify self. She experiences "left neglect," which means she cannot recognize her own body and views it as a foreign object. This lack of ability to see and recognize herself is presented as a mirror for the treatment team who feel professional role disintegration is occurring as a result of changes due to managed care.

The term *stroke* denotes acute vascular and brain tissue changes leading to rapid development of neurological deficits. Cerebrovascular disease continues to be the third most common cause of death in the United States (Rivera 1985).

Less than 5 percent of stroke cases occur in individuals younger than 45. Little is known about the etiology or the diverse causes of these occurrences. The most common causes of spontaneous intracerebral hemorrhage in children and young adults are intracranial vascular malformations, aneurysms, arterial hypertension, and abuse of illicit drugs. The focus of many studies is weighted heavily toward persons 55 years of age and older, making each case among the young more difficult to characterize (Love, Orencia, and Biller 1994; Biller 1994).

Why was the diagnosis of right cerebral stroke a good analogy for the breakdown of the health care system as mirrored by this patient? Stroke disables an individual's physical and emotional makeup and is catastrophic in that it occurs all of a sudden, like a crisis. On the patient level, this crisis interrupts the expression of Violet's sense of purpose in life, her ability to express her presence in the world, to perform the job she has prepared herself for. Her career as a ballet dancer should not be over, yet her skills, her training, her history no long matter. Although she may become something else, what she was is no longer viable. Her previous self is gone. This destruction of self is seen as an analogy for the health care crisis in which the movement from the individual practitioner, the fee-for-service model, and the ability of the practitioner to express individualism is changed, altered, shattered by the slow but eventually cataclysmic effect of managed care.

What are the realities for this treatment team as managed care systems encroach on its professional practice? Each member responds with varying degrees of disability. Dr. Oliviero, the neurologist, cannot believe that a traditional and stable, "well-oiled" machine such as an established medical center hospital needs to change. He is still in charge and dismisses the emerging changes. Dr. Oliviero expresses a growing concern among physicians that the traditional patient-physician relationship is threatened by managed care requirements. He believes that managed care systems are only concerned with efficiency and not good medicine. He will not make any concessions to their gatekeeping because he views them as limiting good care. The nurse, Carolyn McPherson, is angry that the medical environment is no longer a place for good patient care and intellectual stimulation. Reenie Shandler, the social worker, is trying to justify her professional role and at the same time protect her patients' interests. And finally, Josh Pollan, the rehabilitation specialist, is trying to figure out why he alone seems at ease with the coming changes. The energy of the team is focused on old conflicts and problems. They defuse their anger by jointly ganging up on the vice president of managed care contracts who embodies everything they hate about organizational change. Although not obvious, there is a refusal to work from a team basis because each is struggling with professional role breakdown. On the patient level, Violet Mason, the professional ballet dancer, faces role breakdown through trauma. Both the patient and the team focus their energy on denying the reality of change that they view as antagonistic to their professional goals. The team cannot view the approaching managed care system change as anything but an enemy that is invading its professional space. Violet's sense of invasion of her professional space is first depicted through her egocentric view of her "dance space" and then later as her inability to control her physical body.

Violet Mason is a professional dancer who has an aneurysm which causes a stroke. She is a representative of system trauma as well because her condition was not anticipated or predictable. Her ego identity will be altered by something that will leave nothing intact or the same as it once was. Who would predict that a young and physically fit 29-year-old dancer should have such an affront to her life? It is not in keeping with what anyone would expect of a focused and determined person. Dr. Oliviero uses those words to describe the current team's functioning. The patient is just as much a professional as her treatment team, yet it is obvious in the first chapter that no one sees her as such. She represents the latent content of interdisciplinary communication. Although the words of the team sound like interdisciplinary teamwork, team members are actually ignoring their feelings of despair and anguish over the changes that are affecting the hospital; as such, they sound like the conversations of parallel play between two-year-olds. Each team member is functioning solely on maintaining his or her professional role with little attention to the professional needs of other group members.

Violet Mason also serves as a reminder to the reader that a professional ballet dancer is a good analogy for a health care professional. Both roles require focus, energy, commitment to long hours of training and have strong historical and traditional roots. In ballet, teamwork brings coordination of movement while each individual dancer finds a unique and complementary niche. Health care professionals move through systems that stress coordination of case planning. Each unique professional role adds a needed dimension to optimal care. As you read this chapter, you should be able to identify the disintegration that occurs when professionals feel threatened by organizational change. As such, you can view Chapter 1 as an assessment of this trauma.

Reenie Shandler, the social worker in the narrative, views managed care as an anathema to good social work practice. She describes it as threatening to the way social workers make decisions and to the timing and pacing of her work. She views advocating for her patients as outside the goals of managed care. She blurts out to Mr. Pearman, "You have not heard one thing about the care this patient requires. You don't know the first thing about patient care." In fact, the whole team views Mr. Pearman as incompetent. At another point in the narrative, this lack of communication affects the patient, Violet Mason, as well. Upon overhearing a part of the psychosocial assessment, she blurts out "that's not me." This parallel is set up to show that not understanding another's view is a symptom of organizational stress. Violet's illness has affected her ability to connect to herself and the team's blind anger detaches it from its mission of effective care.

The lack of interdisciplinary communication also prevents an analysis of managed care as a response to organizational insufficiency. On the patient level, the social worker describes Violet as a housewife with an interest in dance rather than as a professional dancer. Role confusion is a common response to threat. Managed care systems require revisiting professional roles. The social worker needs to revisit his or her role to include outcome as well as process objectives since managed care is outcome oriented. This also includes "hearing" Mrs. Luber's request to go home from her point of view. Social work services need to focus on cost reduction, enhanced quality of care, and customer satisfaction. Outcomes such as decreased length of stay and reduced utilization of resources will be part of the evaluation of effective practice. Social workers need to expand their roles to consider utilization review as a necessary step in ensuring that care is provided at the appropriate level of intensity and in the appropriate setting. This social work perspective must include negotiating in contract development with managed care networks by being the "voice of the consumer" in discharge planning and length of stay information. This connotes an understanding of the objectives of managed care. Expanded roles will include enhanced abilities to move resources between one component of the system to another. Flexibility on the part of social workers entails accepting new models of community care for the prevention of readmission rates and cost containment. It is not merely sufficient to view new service sites as inevitable, they must also be viewed with acceptability (Society for Social Work Administrators in Health Care 1994). In the narrative, you see this enacted by the conflict between how Dr. Oliviero, Reenie Shandler, and Mr. Pearman view Mrs. Luber's discharge plan. It is an example of the pitfalls of poor communication by the interdisciplinary team and the lack of flexibility by all in considering a variety of ways a discharge plan can be sound.

The scenario presented with the patient, Mrs. Luber, is a view of patient care from traditional professional roles. The social worker and nurse each view managed care regulations as interfering with treatment goals. They are obeying the regulations only because "patient suffering will take place if we don't." Mr. Pearman, the vice president of managed care contracts, has a similar view of his role. He does not specifically voice the needs of the patient, but only discusses cost containment as his major goal. This battle-type atmosphere is expressed through the words of Carolyn McPherson, the nurse who chides Josh Pollan, the young rehabilitation specialist, for "viewing managed care as just another insurance company." This leads into the question posed at the end of the chapter of whether this is the way things will remain or whether there is possibility for compromise and growth by all involved in the narrative. Before this is presented in the following chapters, another important skill must be learned. Interdisciplinary communication must take place first before negotiation can happen with managed care companies. This is presented through the words of Reenie Shandler who ponders how managed care will affect the interdisciplinary team goals. She remembers how long it has taken for social workers to be valued and accepted as providers of useful services to patients. As Mizrahi and Abramson (1985) note, social workers present psychosocial information that complicates straightforward decision making. Social workers pay attention to process, caution, nondirectedness, and patient readiness. They devote time and energy to examine the dynamic processes within the patient's family and supportive relationships. Facilitation, especially of issues concerning patient autonomy, is a distinct approach of social work and differs from the traditional approach of a physician's perspective that discloses or withholds information according to the anticipated effect upon patient well-being. Additionally, over the years, social workers have been recognized as vital components of interdisciplinary planning because communication about patient management can facilitate physician effectiveness, especially in the area of discharge planning (Abramson and Mizrahi 1986). The complex problems that exist in resource systems must be viewed as a coalition of collaborative efforts between professionals. Thus, the importance of the psychosocial assessment to discharge planning involves coordinating discharge planning through weekly rounds with team members. This prevents social workers from being bombarded with referrals from all personnel on their assigned floors (Dane and Simon 1991).

The use of interdisciplinary teams to plan and deliver services means areas of competence and associated tasks are interplayed with the creation of mutual support and alliances. On a professional level, this is consistent with good patient care. Managed care systems require an interdisciplinary approach because it fosters the efficient use of resources. This creates a difficult dilemma because team members worry that the interdisciplinary approach will not only destroy what has taken years to accomplish, but will also entail role changes that might affect their professional identities. The end of the chapter presents the patient, Violet Mason, as facing a change in her professional identity. This change will greatly alter her perception of herself and what she perceives to be her entire identity. The same issue is presented to the treatment team with the question of professional identity threatened through the presence of a managed care representative who is present in their physical environment.

The following practice skills are provided in order to enable the social work student to begin acquiring skills in problem identification and patient and organizational assessment.

Practice Skills

Client

1. Based on the psychosocial assessment provided in the narrative, analyze how well the following were assessed. What additional information do you think is necessary to complete the assessment?
   a. The pre-illness social functioning of the patient (include psychological history, drugs/alcohol, lifestyle)
   b. The resources in the community for the patient
   c. The assessment of her family (medical, social, psychological functioning, and availability)
   d. The cultural environment of the patient (include county of origin, education, mobility, travel, type of residence)
   e. The patient's profession as it affects illness and adjustment
2. What role changes is this patient facing? How will these changes impact the "person-environment" fit in her life?

Social Worker

1. Evaluate the adequacy of the facilitation skills of the social worker using the following concepts:
   a. With whom did the social worker feel most comfortable discussing her concerns about managed care?
   b. Who on the team appeared to be most supportive of her view?
   c. Did the social worker try to model appropriate interdisciplinary interaction skills? Find the passage in the text which best describes the way she communicates her role to other members of the team.
   d. Describe the way she presents the psychosocial assessment to Josh Pollan, the rehabilitation specialist.
   e. Based on what you have read in the first chapter, what is the likelihood that this team would be able to use collaborative case management tools to anticipate and plan for problems with the patient and her family to predict outcome of the case and to provide an organized predictable time managed plan?

2. What role changes is the social worker facing? How will these changes impact the "person-environment" fit for her professionally?

Team

1. Thomas and Morrison (1977) postulate there are five skills that should be used by interdisciplinary team members to promote effective communication. They are as follows:
   a. Self-awareness (gaining insight into one's feelings and reactions to others)
   b. Perceptiveness (understanding awareness and understanding feelings of others)
   c. Sending and receiving messages (increasing one's ability to understand one's feelings and express them to others)
   d. Sensitivity (being able to tune into and be aware of others' perceptions)
   e. Group process (understanding the processes in which groups make decisions and accomplish objectives, and increasing effectiveness by being more sensitive to the needs of others)

2. Tuckman (1965) describes these developmental stages of teams:
   a. *Forming*—In the early stages of the group, groups are concerned with testing in order to identify the boundaries of both interpersonal and task behaviors. Ground rules related to appropriate ways of interacting are formulated and members learn how to address problems.

Members are most often concerned with where they fit in; they test leaders and question authority. There is much talking, very little listening, and the group is not yet comfortable in its own identity.

b. *Storming*—Frustration is at its highest as team members try to reach consensus on goals. Power struggles, arguments, defensiveness, and competition are prevalent. The team frequently sets unrealistic goals, and then members complain that the task requires too much time.
c. *Norming*—A more systematic approach to problem solving begins to emerge. More collaboration is seen as disagreements are negotiated successfully. Resistance is overcome, new standards evolve and new roles are adopted. Approaches to decision making are identified.
d. *Performing*—The team is performing well, producing results, and developing continually as a team. Members work together harmoniously for a common good. There is excitement about achievements as ground rules guide interactions. Roles become flexible and functional.

Using Tuckman's paradigm describe the following:

a. The forming stage of the group prior to the introduction of the vice president for managed care contracts—identify specific roles, perceptions, and ground rules
b. The storming event that takes place
c. The reaction of each professional to the storming event, and the resulting impact of these reactions on the developmental stage of the team

2

Diagnosis: Facing the Limits of Change

Dr. Oliviero stood at the end of the bed, staring over the top of his glasses and the chart at Violet, now settled back in her bed, propped up with the hospital pillows.

"You can't get out of bed without help," he chided his patient as he made furious notes in the chart. "This could have been very serious."

"That noise was so loud. I couldn't take it," Violet answered, somewhat indignant.

"Noise?"

"I think she means the bed alarm, Dr." Carolyn translated.

"The alarm is supposed to be loud, young lady. Now you stay put and you won't have to worry about it again." Dr. Oliviero snapped the chart shut, turned to stride out of the room.

"Not that sound. The voices. The voices were very loud and I had to get to them. That is why I had to get up. The voices."

"The voices? When did you hear voices, Mrs. Mason?" Carolyn asked.

Dr. Oliviero stopped in his tracks once his nurse's question penetrated his focus. He turned back to Violet. "Voices, you say?"

"Yes, voices."

"And what did these voices say?" Dr. Oliviero arched his eyebrow in Carolyn's direction.

"Voices in the hallway. Talking about me."

"Uh-huh, voices in the hallway talking to you. Go on." The doctor was once again making notes in the chart.

"Talking about me, not to me. They were talking about me." Violet's voice rose as she became visibly agitated, trying to swing her legs off the end of the bed.

"Uh-huh. Voices talking about you. Where did they seem to be coming from?"

Jack strode into the room just in time to hear the end of the question. "Someone coming?" Jack tried to catch up with the conversation.

"Someone was talking about me, Jack. In the hall. I got up to go see who it was and I tripped." Violet was shooting words like torpedoes at her husband.

"You tripped? You're kidding, of course. You are far too graceful to trip."

"She tried to get out of bed by herself, Mr. Mason," Carolyn filled Jack in. "She fell, but she is okay."

"She seems to be having some, uh, mental difficulty. Hearing voices and such. I may need to have Dr. Downstrom look at her."

"She fell? I don't believe that. Violet is as graceful as the day is long. . . ." Jack was clearly baffled. "You should see her dance. Well, yes, of course you *should* see her dance. I'll get tickets for you—I have connections, you know." Jack was as charming as usual, taking in Carolyn with his impish smile.

"Oh, a recital. How nice . . ." Carolyn tried to follow.

"She fell, Mr. Mason." Dr. Oliviero brought the group back to the subject at hand.

"The voices. I had to see who the voices were. They had it all wrong."

"With the hemiparesis, she is not going to be able to walk without an assistive device and attendant for a while, Mr. Mason." The doctor forged ahead. "You can tell Dr. Downstrom all about these voices, dear. He'll be along this afternoon." Dr. Oliviero patted Violet on the calf as he once again closed the chart and turned to go. "See that she doesn't get up without the therapists or nurses," he instructed Jack on his way out.

"Hem what? What are you talking about?" Jack struggled to comprehend.

"They said I was a homemaker."

"A home wrecker? Who said that?" Jack looked from his wife, to Carolyn, to Dr. Oliviero, hoping for someone to make sense of it all for him. "She is pretty messy, but the help follows her around to pick up," Jack attempted a weak joke as he struggled to comprehend.

"You read the stroke packet we left for you, right?" Carolyn underscored the written materials the team had given the patient and her husband.

"I, uh, may be just a tad behind on my homework, teach." Jack picked up an apple from the fruit basket on Violet's nightstand. Polishing it on his jacket, he asked sheepishly, "This get me out of trouble?"

"Hemiparesis. The flaccid leg." Dr. Oliviero threw back the sheet to demonstrate the paralysis of Violet's leg, as Carolyn gently placed the apple back in the basket.

"Homemaker. A homemaker who was taking dance lessons. And a woman said you were an accountant, Jack. She had it all wrong. I had to tell her."

"Oh my God. You're saying she can't move that leg at all? What the hell is wrong with it?" Jack was shocked.

"Part of the stroke, Mr. Mason." It was Carolyn's turn to arch her brow at Dr. Oliviero. "The stroke that Mrs. Mason has had."

"It will move again, right? She will dance again, of course."

"Of course, in time, she possibly can return to her lessons." Dr. Oliviero hedged the question. "I don't know about a recital."

"Lessons? Recital? What are you talking about? She's a principal with the Metropolitan Ballet Company," Jack was incredulous. They might be joking, but he was losing his sense of humor.

"A principal . . . I thought the name sounded familiar," Dr. Oliviero took in the new information. "Where did I get the idea she was taking some sort of lesson . . . ?"

"Reenie told us that, Dr. Oliviero" Carolyn rushed to the rescue. "So sorry, Mr. Mason. We were told she was a homemaker . . ."

"Reenie. Yes, that was her. The voice in the hallway. Reenie. She had it all wrong. I was trying to get to her to tell her she had it all wrong. That's when I tripped."

"You really did trip, sweetheart?" Jack entertained the possibility. "Did she trip?"

"She did have a fall, Mr. Mason." Carolyn answered as Dr. Oliviero edged toward the door. "She had been instructed on fall precautions but she got out of bed unattended . . ."

"I was trying to get to her. Don't you hear me? She had it all wrong."

"Who had what all wrong, sweetheart?"

"Reenie. The one they were talking about. She was telling a man in the hall about me, about us. Only she had everything all wrong. She doesn't even know who I am!"

"Reenie?" Jack directed his question to Carolyn.

"Our social worker. She must have talked with you, right, Mrs. Mason?"

"No. She talked to a man in the hall."

"I think I talked with a social worker in the emergency room when we came in. But it sounds like she did not listen. I want to know why my wife has to be subjected to this. I don't even know why a welfare person was talking to us . . ."

"It's okay, Mr. Mason. A social worker sees everyone in the emergency room. It is not about welfare . . ."

"It's her fault Violet fell. You heard my wife. This woman caused her to fall." Jack was standing his ground now that the enemy was palpable. "What are you going to do about this?"

"Now, now. Mrs. Mason is just fine. I checked her out thoroughly. No problems from the fall." Dr. Oliviero moved to try to pacify Jack. "You do understand, don't you, that Mrs. Mason cannot stand by herself?"

"I understand that you don't understand a thing about her or me. That I understand."

"Uh, Dr. Oliviero, what do you think about having a family conference?" Carolyn interceded, "Perhaps we could all sit down together and get a fresh start."

"Yes. Mr. Mason, I'll have the social worker get with you about a time for a family conference." Dr. Oliviero, clearly agitated, turned and left the room. Carolyn followed quickly on his heels.

• • • • •

The team gathering held noticeably more tension than usual. Dr. Oliviero was visibly upset, and Carolyn set the tone for him. "Reenie, the information you gave us is clearly wrong."

"I cannot explain the discrepancies, guys. But I know what the husband said in the ER."

"She's a principal with the ballet company, for God's sake. How can you miss that?"

"He said she was in class. In dance class."

"Well, clearly we need more accurate information to work from." Dr. Oliviero closed the subject with some authority. "Yes, and we need a response to him about the fall," Carolyn reminded.

"She's a major fall risk, alright," Josh piped up. "She so impulsive she almost fell in therapy this morning."

"Well, that may be. But she says that she fell because she overheard you talking about her in the hallway, Reenie. She was trying to get to you." Carolyn kept the pressure on the social worker.

"Heard me? She doesn't even know me—I haven't had time to meet with her. Has Dr. Downstrom seen her yet?"

"'Impulsivity and poor judgment evident, but no hallucinations noted. Seems to be describing actual events.'" Dr. Oliviero quoted from the psychiatrist's note in the chart.

"I met with her husband in the ER. I have not met with her." Reenie continued to protest.

"How did she know what was in your psychosocial?" Carolyn was like a dog with a bone.

"Maybe she heard you giving me the rundown on the psychosocial," Josh interjected.

"Josh, I think I've seen a hundred patients already this morning. What are you talking about?" Reenie was less able to ward off defensiveness when she was overwhelmed. And with the layoffs of several of the newer social work staff, she was definitely overwhelmed.

"When we were going to co-treat. Before you got paged, remember?" Josh chimed in, oblivious to the mounting tension. "We stood in the hallway outside the door and you read me your notes."

"You were standing in the hallway?" Dr. Oliviero made meaningful eye contact with Carolyn. "Outside her door?"

"Yeah, we were about to go in." Josh continued his clarification.

"Well, we have a problem, folks," Dr. Oliviero declared with a heavy sigh. "And you know I do not like problems on my watch".

"Reenie, what is going on? You know better than to break confidentiality like that. Now we don't just have an 'unusual fall incident,' we have an ethical issue. I hate to think of the paperwork Nursing Administration is going to make me fill out."

"I am so sorry. You are right, Josh is right. I did read the psychosocial right outside the door. I remember now. But I didn't know she was hearing us."

"How many times have we discussed this? Usually *you're* lecturing *us* in the elevator. What were you thinking, Reenie?" Carolyn was irritated. As if the team didn't have enough to worry about, now they had an incident report, an ethical violation, and an unhappy family. "Oh, and by the way, her husband is aware of all this."

"Her husband knows she fell?"

"Knows she fell and knows she was trying to get to the hallway to talk with you, as she heard you presenting inaccurate information." Carolyn was becoming increasingly accusatory.

"I am so sorry, guys. It's my fault. I take complete responsibility. We were in such a rush." Reenie became more distraught as she recalled the circumstance. "We're always in a hurry these days."

"Excellent! If you're in a hurry, you're on the right track." Frank Pearman joined the team, and the fray, at the worst possible moment. He was not enthusiastically received.

"What is the matter here, team? You look like you lost your best friend, or in this case, your best patient." Frank's weak attempt at a joke was met with silence, team members averting their eyes.

"We're problem solving, here, Mr. Pearman. Is there something we can do for you?" Dr. Oliviero had no patience for the administrator's interruption.

"Just checking on the troops. How are we coming with those discharges? Are we on target?"

"*We're* discussing an issue here." Dr. Oliviero's invitation for Frank to depart was clear, even if unspoken.

"Right up my alley. Give me the facts and we'll graph it out in a New York minute. Time is money, right, doc?" Frank was poised with dry eraser board marker in hand before Dr. Oliviero could respond.

"There are some things that can't be graphed, Mr. Pearman." Reenie did not feel like having her patient reduced to means on a graph, nor did she want to air her dirty laundry with the administrator.

"Patient fell. Family mad. Make nice. There, we're done!" Josh was half-kidding, half-proud of his succinct summary.

"Patient fell? Has anybody called Risk Management? We're not assuming responsibility, of course." Frank was quick to absolve the hospital of involvement.

"The patient is not hurt, thanks for asking." Carolyn was indignant at Frank's approach.

"They signed the fall precaution waiver, I presume. Not our fault." Frank held firm.

"I'm afraid it is not that simple, Mr. Pearman. She fell due to an error in judgment on my part." Reenie acknowledged her mistake.

"Why did a social worker assist a patient with mobilization? If we don't have enough social work for you to do, go home!" Frank tunneled ahead.

"I have more than enough to do, thank you. I was not mobilizing anybody. I was in the hallway."

"Did you leave her side rails down? Wheelchair seatbelt off? Somebody fill me in. We're talking money here, folks. Stop tiptoeing and start talking."

"The patient heard the social worker and the physical therapist talking in the hallway. She wanted to talk with them and she got out of bed without assistance to do so. Rails were up; bed alarm on. Period, end of story, that's it. Thank you for your time, Mr. Pearman." Dr. Oliviero was protective of his team with outsiders, demanding of them within the team.

"Fine. I'm satisfied. Therefore, you're satisfied. Case closed. Now hit the hallways, kids. Time is money, right, doc?" Frank left the room as abruptly as he came, clearly expecting the others to follow him. They did not.

"Does he get anything we're doing here?" Reenie wondered out loud.

"He doesn't understand ethics. And we clearly have an ethical problem, here, Reenie." Dr. Oliviero redirected the discussion.

"I don't know how I let this happen. I know better. Patient confidentiality is my mantra. Look, I'm sorry. I'll talk with this couple about what happened, own up to my mistake."

"You've been kind of distracted lately, Reenie," Carolyn softened a bit. "And while we certainly need to look at the confidentiality issue, I am also concerned that the information you gave us was so far off. Mr. Mason was fairly indignant that we did not know his wife was a principal in the ballet."

"I am seeing so many patients. I guess, I mean it's possible, that I just missed it. Our staff has been cut in half—I'm seeing inpatients, outpatients, home patients. I don't know if I'm coming or going anymore. I guess the good news is that I still have a job. At least, that used to be good news. Now . . ." Reenie trailed off with a shrug of her shoulders.

"Who do I need to talk to about this? I need you full-time, 100 percent. This incident with the Masons proves that. Just tell me who to call." Dr. Oliviero was clearly accustomed to taking charge. Administration was quite used to receiving his calls.

"Oh, Dr. Oliviero, I don't know what can be done. It's managed care."

"We got two new positions last week for the work-hardening program. No big deal," Josh had not felt the impact of managed care yet.

"Carolyn, call our friendly CEO as soon as we get back to the office this afternoon. I will not have this." Dr. Oliviero was firm. "Now, what do we do with this patient and her husband?"

"Sounds like we need a family conference, as soon as possible."

"I imagine you're right, Reenie. Set it up for tomorrow morning. Let's . . ." The team was interrupted by the sound of a bed alarm and a floor nurse running down the hall toward Violet's room.

• • • • •

Jack was surprised by the lack of movement in Violet's leg. And he was irritated that people were talking about them behind their backs. Not just talking about them—that he was used to. But they weren't getting it right. It was ludicrous that anyone could even think for one minute that Violet might be a housewife. A housewife. Please! He almost laughed out loud at the thought of it. Violet was so undomestic. He remembered the first night they spent together. His housekeeper was off for the day and he asked Violet to make him a cup of coffee while he showered. Looking back now, he couldn't believe that he even asked it of her. And that she tried! He had not been able to hold back the laughter when he had ventured into the kitchen, wrapped in his towel, only to behold Violet looking quizzically into his coffee cup. The coffeemaker was on, steam rose from the cup, but from the clear water in the pot, it was evident something had gone awry. Seems Violet, never having had to make her own cup of coffee, had taken the "coffeemaker" label a bit too seriously and had not put coffee in the filter! Jack had told that story many times over, embellishing with a new detail with each retelling. That was the moment he fell in love with her. He knew he was going to marry her the minute he saw her dance. But he fell in love the only time she made him coffee. And some idiot here had ignorance to think that she was a homemaker. Fortunately he didn't have the time to dwell on it. Violet was pestering him to help with her exercises. He was glad to see her anxious to get up and about so soon. The recovery time would be nothing, he guessed. Violet's body was a finely turned instrument. He was confident.

"I just need a little help with this side. I'm a little weak from being in bed too long," Violet directed her husband. In most things, Jack was the leader. Violet rarely even spoke, and when she did, it was in a small, almost a whisper, voice. The photos of them that showed up with some regularity on the society pages revealed a thin wisp of a woman hanging tightly onto the arm of a strapping Irishman with a mischievous smile. But when it came to the dancer's body, especially now, despite the headache that made her so weak, she took more control.

Jack sat on the side of the bed, his arm around Violet's waist. He could have just picked her up, but he would not. He would never do that. He knew that Violet understood something about physical movement that he would never know, and he followed her lead. "Do you want to just lean against me as you stand?"

"Yes, just give me a little support on the left. Once I'm up I'll be fine."

"Ready?"

"Ready. Let's go."

The pair stood up awkwardly and with more difficulty than Jack had expected. Violet had really lost some strength on that left side. Good thing she was stretching already. As soon as she seemed erect, he let his arm fall away. About the same time, the bed alarm began to screech. With a jerk, Violet began to fall toward the floor. Jack jumped to reach out for her, but he was too late. Her dancer's body hit the linoleum with a thud. Before Jack could respond, the nurses came hurtling through the door to rescue Violet.

"What happened here, Mrs. Mason?"

"I was about to do my exercises and that damned siren scared me half to death."

Jack was relieved to realize it was the alarm that had thrown off Violet's balance. "That thing is going to cause her to hurt herself. Isn't there some way to stop it from going off?"

The nurses were checking Violet over before lifting her back to bed. "Mr. Mason, she is not to get out of bed without a staff member helping right now. She cannot stand alone."

"Of course she can stand alone."

"I was standing up when that siren scared me."

"Mr. Mason, did you read your instruction packet? It clearly states that you must call for staff any time Mrs. Mason needs to get up," the nurse continued. Then, to her coworker, "OK, one, two, three, and up." Jack watched with disbelief as the two nurses literally hoisted his wife back to the bed. It was a sight he had never imagined he would see in their lifetime together. And he certainly did not expect it today.

"I'm busy, a busy man. The packet is at the top of my reading list. I have a company to run, a wife to take care of . . . but just as soon as I get a spare minute . . . oh, man, I need some fresh air. I'm sorry." Jack fought his way out the door and down the hospital corridor.

• • • • •

The team prepared for the Mason family conference as it had many conferences before. This time, however, the air seemed a little different. "How are you going to start this off?" Carolyn asked of Reenie as they set up the chairs.

"Like I've started the other two thousand conferences we've done together, Carolyn!" Reenie responded, slightly bemused.

"You know what I mean—we have a problem. How are you going to address it?"

"I talked with the Masons privately already. I apologized for the breach of confidentiality. I'm not sure how much she took in, but he certainly seemed to understand that mistakes can happen when you are overworked."

"You told him you were overworked?" Carolyn sounded surprised.

"Well, yes, I suppose I did, in the course of explaining how it occurred. I took full responsibility, of course."

"Nurses get fired for telling patients they are overworked, though goodness knows we have been for a long time now." The last phrase sounded a bit like a dig to Reenie.

"So what are you saying, Carolyn. That I should be fired?" Reenie laughed nervously. "I know I made a mistake, but, how many have I made in our time working together? Not many."

"I'm just saying that, for nurses, the hospital is being very clear that we are not to discuss our opinion of the working conditions with the patients."

"Social workers work just as hard as nurses, Carolyn," Reenie felt compelled to defend.

"But nobody works as hard as me," Josh sauntered in, adding his bit to the end of the conversation.

"Yeah, right," Reenie responded. "You have too many patients, you just gather them all in a group and call it a special modality. I wish I had time to do a group."

"My, my, my, there is a sharpness in the air," Josh did not know when to quit.

"Well, it is not coming from your direction," Carolyn countered.

"Ouch, that hurt! What's going on here? We are really fussy today."

"Josh is right. I'm sorry, guys. There's just so much to do. And I guess I am nervous about this family conference." Reenie apologized.

"I'm sorry, too. Guess we'd all be enemies if managed care had its way." Carolyn offered her apologies as well.

"Mr. Pearman is already working on that," Josh blurted out.

"What do you mean, Josh?"

"He was in the gym again around lunchtime. Asked me if I thought things were going smoothly up here. What would I change if I could, ya know."

"He did what? The nerve of that man. I have a notion to give him a good piece of my mind." Carolyn was indignant.

"What did you tell him?" Reenie was a little more tactful.

"Told him I would clone you guys," Josh answered with a smile, certain that this would dispel the bad humor of his colleagues.

"You told him that? Oh, Josh! Why did you say that?" Reenie's voice was a pitch or two higher.

"What's wrong with that. Sorry—I was trying to give you a compliment."

"Now, he'll think we're not getting the work done. And we're doing double—no, triple—time as it is."

"Reenie, maybe we're getting paranoid. Josh was just joking around, I'm sure." Josh wasn't sure if Carolyn had forgiven him or not, but she changed the subject at least.

"Yes, you're right, Carolyn. Maybe Mr. Pearman isn't out to get us. Now if we just don't get each other."

"Get each other what?" Dr. Oliviero quizzed as he strode into the room. "It's too early for drawing names for the holiday party, isn't it?" Reenie knew the Masons couldn't be far behind. The nurses on the floor had this timed perfectly after years of practice. The family was prepared, an escort ready to whisk them into the room within seconds after Dr. Oliviero's appearance. There was not a minute of the physician's time to waste.

• • • • •

A nurse wheeled Violet down the hall to the conference room, Jack trailing a step or two behind. Violet had pondered over what to wear, calling Jack several times with requests for various outfits. She was accustomed to meeting her audiences in tights or ball gowns, not much between. She hoped there would not be cameras there; she did not feel up to cameras. She knew Jack would take care of that, whatever he decided would be best. Violet knew how to be the center of attention, though she did not always know how to become the center nor understand the being of the center. She loved to dance, loved it more than life itself, she thought, and craved the attention given to her because she danced. Did she love dance more than Jack? She wondered this occasionally, not consciously, just a fleeting awareness of something frightening. If she had to choose, she would be hard pressed. Fortunately, that was not a choice that would have to be made. Jack loved her dance as much as she did, perhaps loved that more than he loved her. Whatever, he was certainly good at both. And because of that, he took care of both: He took care of Violet and he took care of her dancing. Which is why she noticed, perhaps, his peculiar lack of interest in what she would wear to this meeting. Jack was always concerned about image, always seemed, in a very gentle way, to be able to lead Violet to making just the right decision for herself. Only today, he seemed uninterested. Violet thought for a moment that perhaps it did not matter or he did not care. Same thing, in a way. But she shook that off. They were both struggling a bit with the inconvenience of her injury. Their routine was altered, and it was affecting them both.

Jack was anxious to get the show on the road. He was ready for this kind of meeting, though he wasn't sure Violet was. He was not certain that she understood the purpose of the meeting, but that was okay. Jack was the leader when it came to directing her career. Violet knew how to dance, Jack knew how to map things out. His wife was a dance genius, but she needed someone to guide her *marketing*, a savvy business partner and he was more than happy to be the one. He had big plans for her. He hoped to break new ground in endorsements, appearances, and the like. Jack was an entrepreneur and he loved the idea of breaking new ground. And he loved the fact that it took nothing more than clear, logical planning. And a little luck. He had always had plenty of skill at both. Jack had taken a start-up software company that he and his college buddy started in their dorm room over pizza one blurry night and turned it into one of the fastest-growing new kids on the block. Now he hoped to do the same for the world of ballet in general and for Violet in particular. And they had to get some information today about the state of Violet's injury and the estimated date of her return to performance level before he could move his plans forward.

"Ready to go?" the nurse started to help Violet up to her walker.

"What are you doing?" Violet was horrified. Surely this woman did not expect her to appear with that contraption. That was for exercise time. Like the barre. Now, Violet pictured herself being wheeled in as her audience waited for her. Distant images of Liz Taylor emerging from a hospital, being pushed by an attendant in crisp white, appearing wan but beautiful still. And going on to make many more successful movies, of course. No, she would not appear with that contraption.

"I'm getting you ready to go to the conference," the nurse answered.

"I'm ready. Push me."

"You need to use the walker. You must walk when you can, Mrs. Mason. That is an important part of your recovery."

"I will not be seen with that thing today."

"Doctor's orders."

"What does the doctor have to do with . . ."

"I believe she is tired," Jack intervened on Violet's behalf. "She's a bit different than the other patients. She knows her body. I believe we'll go on down like this." Jack gently took the handles of the chair from the nurse and began to push Violet forward.

"Well, she really should walk." Jack acknowledged the nurse with one of his charming shrugs as he passed her. He pushed Violet slowly, almost tenderly, feeling a bit odd driving Violet's movements. He had spent so many hours watching Violet move, a seemingly weightless spirit commanded by a hidden force deep within her that no man would ever know. It was strange, now, that she should require force on his part to move her forward. He felt compelled to move slowly, lest he make some wrong move. Finally, wordlessly, they arrived at the door to the conference room.

Jack and Violet entered the conference room where the team members awaited them. They were greeted by each one, then invited to sit down. Reenie was the first to speak.

"Thank you both for coming today. You know all of us, I know. We like to sit down with patients and families at some point and talk about how things are going, what we think your course will be like from here and what our plans are for your discharge. And, of course, we want to answer any questions you may have."

The voice. Violet had heard that voice before. Where was it? One of the fund-raisers for the ballet? No, she had not attended a fund-raiser for the hospital before. And she realized now, this meeting was with people from the hospital. It always nagged at her, this sort of thing. Being unable to remember a name, a snippet from a piece of music. Especially when it seemed right on the tip of her tongue.

"Mrs. Mason, Mr. Mason, thanks for being here. Mrs. Mason's course is going as we expected. No medical problems—she is completely stable. Josh?" Dr. Oliviera started the discussion.

Jack almost flinched at the phrase "no medical problems." Was this doctor crazy? That was just a ridiculous statement. If she had no medical problems, then why was she in the hospital? Anybody could look at her and see that she had medical problems. Her muscles were strained beyond belief, for goodness sake. She was so banged up she couldn't move her left side. No medical problems? Jack wished that could be true, but it certainly was not. He missed some of what was being said as he processed the absurdity of the doctor's declaration.

"She is progressing quite well with mobility. She is ambulating three hundred feet with the assistive device with minimal assistance," the therapist was saying. "She is independent with bed mobility, as I think we all know."

Josh's weak attempt at humor hit Reenie in the stomach like a punch. She was trying so hard to avoid the subject with the Masons and here he was joking about it. And he was using so much jargon. How many times had they discussed this, how many team in-services had they had?

Violet tried to follow the conversation, but could not make heads nor tails of what the young man was talking about. He would have made a good dancer. Good body for it. Very lean and muscular. He was very helpful with her exercises, though public speaking clearly was not his specialty.

Jack also tried to follow, making mental notes of things to ask. He was used to jargon, he could talk computerese with anybody from any country, but he hadn't a clue what some of this young man's remarks were about. He did hear what sounded like an off-color remark related to Violet and bed. Surely he had not heard him correctly.

"The occupational therapist reports that she is dressing her upper extremity with minimal assistance with everything except moderate assistance with her brassiere. Lower extremity dressing is mod to max assist but should improve with the use of a sock aid, shoe horn, and reacher."

"Thank you, Josh. How much longer do we think she needs to be in the hospital, Dr. Oliviero?" Reenie hoped to move things right along, avoiding discussion of past difficulties, moving this couple to look to the future.

"Mr. Mason, she needs to stay at least ten more days. By then, she will be using a quad cane, if not a straight cane, and be able to ambulate with supervision around the house. She is getting good return in that left leg. She will, of course, continue to need hands-on supervision for quite some time. You will need to discuss such arrangements with Reenie. Any questions?"

"Hmm. Yes, what did you all just say?" Jack knew how to interject just enough humor in situations to put anyone at ease. He was at ease with himself and felt most comfortable when those around him were loose. The team took in a quick breath, then, seeing Jack's grin, laughed with him. It was a moment of relief for everyone, if a short one.

"Do you have any questions, Violet?" Jack deferred to his wife. It was, after all, her body that was being discussed.

"No. Whatever you think, Jack. Whatever will get me back to the barre as quickly as possible."

Reenie, thinking Violet was attempting a joke somehow related to alcohol, chuckled. She stopped as the couple and the team looked at her questioningly. "Oh, the barre. The ballet thing. I'm sorry, I'm a little tired," Reenie noticed Carolyn's disapproval out of the corner of her eye. "I'm sorry, Mrs.

Mason. You'll have to help me become more cultured before you leave." The social worker carefully avoided any mention of her workload. The couple was quiet.

Violet eyed Reenie. Not much potential, but she would do her best.

"So, the two of you have no questions?" Reenie asked with some relief. Carolyn had obviously made too much of the situation.

"Well, now, I do have a question or two," Jack began his move to assert his control. "I'm a little like a duck out of water, so forgive me while I try to catch up to what you are saying. Now, young man, Josh, I believe it is?" Jack continued as Josh nodded his assent. "You mentioned something about everybody knowing about Violet and bed movement?" Jack was not going to let this kid get away with a crude remark, joke or not. This was a professional setting after all.

Reenie stiffened, again noting Carolyn's grimace in her peripheral vision. Well, at least the team was all together to deal with it once and for all, she thought. She hoped she could count on the team's support in discussing Mrs. Mason's falls. After all, she had fallen more than once, not just the time when Reenie was talking indiscretely in the hallway. In the past, Reenie would not have even questioned the team support, but these days she was less sure. She couldn't quite put her finger on it, but something was happening. A subtle shift away from attention to the team, and focus on the patient. It almost seemed to her like they had suddenly arrived at every person for him- or herself. She could not trace the trail, however. It came as a surprise to her. Hopefully, the team would remember its skill now, in this situation, when collaboration was crucial to everyone. Not to keep Reenie out of trouble, though that would be nice. No, Reenie was concerned that the patient and her husband were in deep denial about Violet's condition and would get sidetracked on blaming someone else for her decreased physical function. This was a common tendency when people were facing this kind of traumatic event. Grieving certainly does embrace blame at times. But usually the team was able to keep the focus on the patient and reality and help clients through the very real losses confronting them. Usually. But today, Reenie found her stomach churning.

"Yes, sir. Fortunately, Mrs. Mason is able to pull herself from side to side, and from supine to sit without assist," Josh responded, knowing when to be more direct.

"Supine?"

"Yes, Mr. Mason. What Josh means, by 'supine to sit' is that Mrs. Mason can sit up by herself in the bed."

"Of course I can sit up in the bed by myself. Jack, why are we talking about this?" Violet had no clue why it was of significance to these people that she could sit up by herself. Their rightful concern should be whether or not she could lift her leg.

"Hang on, sweetheart. Let's try to get a timeline on things." Jack was familiar with Violet's impatience with this sort of thing. "Now, I'm confused here."

Carolyn nodded, making a mental note of all the nursing education still to be done. These folks were not in a good place to integrate new information—education would be a challenge but she had a crackerjack staff that was up to it.

"A very nice gentleman . . . what was his name? Perriwinkle? A VP here, I believe, and a ballet fan," Jack grinned. He really did enjoy the doors that Violet's social status opened, liked the attention his business success and her art brought them both. He liked people, and he liked hobnobbing. Not much better than a good cigar over brandy shared with a rapt audience. "Mr. Perriwinkle says Violet is ready to go. Says she can get what she needs coming in everyday for exercises. Hell, she might be able to go to the studio for those, I don't know."

The team members took a collective breath, and looked at each other with disbelief. "That would be Mr. Pearman, our vice president. I'm afraid . . ." Carolyn prepared to set the record straight. Dr. Oliviero, however, beat her to it.

"The man's a bureaucrat, Mr. Mason. He knows his number crunching, I'm sure. But he does not know medicine. Mrs. Mason needs to be here another ten days, period. And even then, she will not be ready to go to the studio."

"Jack, you know I can't stay ten days. We open the season next week. I'm already so behind."

"Dr. Oliviero, with all due respect, my wife is not your typical patient. First of all, her body is in beautiful form. It will not take her the usual time to recover. She is in great shape, she is accustomed to performing through pain. And second, she does not have the time to languish about in your hospital. She has a career to get back to posthaste. I have to agree with Mr. Pearman on this one."

Carolyn noted the reddening of Dr. Oliviero's face and knew she had to jump in. "Mr. Pearman is off on this one, Mr. Mason. Let me explain to you some of what has happened to Mrs. Mason physically. She has had a stroke. She has permanent damage to her brain that interferes with her ability to move the left side of her body . . ."

"Her brain? Wait a second here . . . nothing has happened to her brain." Jack was adamant as he reached a protective arm around his wife. He flinched as he felt the cold of the wheelchair handle against his flesh, but forged ahead. "Dr. Oliviero, please tell her. Muscle, right? Not brain? We need to know when her muscles will heal. When will she be able to dance again?" The team members made eye contact with each other, then settled back into their chairs. This was going to be an extended conference.

• • • • •

"So, we'll start off with introductions," Reenie explained to the circle of patients in front of her. She had already given her standard recitation of the purpose of the group. The members were all stroke patients of Dr. Oliviero; he was a strong believer in helping people not only in the acute phase of medical need, but in trying to adjust once they left the hospital. This group, for newly diagnosed patients, met in his office once a week. The "old-timers" group met once a month in the office. Reenie was glad to be able to still do both, though she could see the time approaching when her supervisor would begin to question the time it took. She had already had to start recording the time, by minutes, on her productivity report. Reenie looked around the room at the new faces before her. They were each hungry for knowledge and angry that they needed it. She shook the thoughts of numbers and justifications and changes from her tired brain and jumped in with her new group. "Who would like to start?" As usual, she was met with silence. "Okay," she laughed, "it was worth a shot. How about if we start to my left?"

One by one, the group members introduced themselves. There were six members this time. Mrs. Luber, Mr. Shaw, Ms. Brown, Mr. Marshall, Mrs. Spelling, and Mrs. Mason. Reenie knew them all from their time in the hospital. All except Ms. Brown. She was an indigent patient of Dr. Oliviero's who had been hospitalized in the county hospital. Reenie knew her supervisor would have a conniption at this point if she knew Reenie was working with patients from the county, but Dr. Oliviero had always wanted all of his patients to have this opportunity. And he figured if he could see indigent patients, then Reenie could as well. The hospital was not hurting for money—it was the least they could do, and "you know they will do the least they can" Dr. Oliviero had always said. He was proud of the hospital, but he believed in going a little further outside of the walls to meet the needs of the people in the community. Reenie wondered now if that would have to stop also. She heard the talk, and she was sure Dr. Oliviero had, too. Talk that physicians would have less and less say not only about what their patients could have—that was already clearly happening. But also less say about what they themselves could do with their own practice, a sense that physicians, too, would become a commodity "owned" by some for-profit entity. Reenie had a hard time imagining Dr. O being owned by anyone. Still, these were strange times. Reenie was brought out of her reverie by an animated discussion ensuing between Mr. Shaw and Mrs. Luber.

"Of course you can get your therapy at home. Don't matter that your daughter brings you to the doctor every now and then. You're still mostly stuck at home." Mr. Shaw was saying.

"All I know is my case manager told me I couldn't get anybody to come out to the house. Said I just needed a custodian there and I could come here for therapy as an outpatient," Mrs. Luber protested.

"You may both be right," Reenie intervened. "It depends on what kind of insurance coverage you have."

"I have Medicare and she does, too," Mr. Shaw explained.

"Yes, but with a difference, I think. Mrs. Luber, don't you have Metroplus Gold?"

"Yes. I signed up with them—they add to your Medicare. Give you medicines along with hospital and stuff."

"Yes, well, Mrs. Luber, you have a case manager at Metroplus who decides what to pay for—she tried to, uh, extend your Medicare benefits. And Mr. Shaw, going strictly by the Medicare rules, you would be correct."

"You have to get your home health therapy from one of the companies listed in your book. Then they pay the whole thing," Mr. Marshall added to the discussion. "Of course, you can go with another company. I was thinking of using my cousin's neighbor's boy's company, but they would have only paid half or something like that."

"No, they pay the whole thing," Mr. Shaw was insistent.

"They only gave me one company I could use, and I didn't like the therapist that came out. She was quite snooty and did not know a thing about ballet," Violet added. "So Jack said just have anybody I want to come. I don't know who is paying for it."

"You can have anybody you want, Mr. Shaw, but you do have to pay the 20 percent they don't pay." Mrs. Spelling offered.

"I have to pay 20 percent?" Mrs. Luber was shocked. "I'm going to call them today and tell them not to come. I can't afford 20 percent for this nonsense. They only stay a minute or two anyway."

"They told me I couldn't have any therapy at home. Said I would have to come in to the old county hospital building, take the bus in if I wanted therapy." Ms. Brown was indignant.

Reenie tried desperately to break off the discussion before it got totally out of hand. She didn't quite make it! She finally shouted the group down. "Hold on, everybody. Time out! Hold on just a minute!" They all turned to her in midsentence, waiting expectantly.

"Okay. You're all correct in your own way." This did little to change the puzzled, chagrined faces. "You each have a different type of insurance, and each one is a little different in what it will pay for when you have an illness or injury. Mr. Shaw you have Medicare, plain old vanilla Medicare. It will pay for 100 percent of your home health as long as it is medically necessary. Mrs. Luber, you have a Medicare HMO. It manages your Medicare benefits for you and will review and must approve all services. Mr. Marshall, you were still working and you have your company's PPO policy, which will pay more if you use one of the companies that it has a special contract with. Mrs. Mason, you have an HMO. You can have home health therapy if your primary care physician orders it, but only through the HMO's home health company. I believe you and your husband decided to pay out of pocket for a different company, so your insurance is not paying anything. Mrs. Spelling, you have regular, old-fashioned insurance which lets you decide what company you want to use without any case management review, and it pays 80 percent of services you receive. Mrs. Brown, you get your medical care through the county hospital district. It does not have any home health therapies, but it does provide outpatient therapy at the facility you mentioned. There. Have I confused you all enough?" The faces had shifted subtly to perplexed grimaces.

"So, who do I call to get these therapies that everybody is talking about?" Mrs. Luber asked.

"I'll tell you what. Why don't I meet with you individually after the group today and we can talk about it. And each of you can make an appointment time if you need to discuss your particular situation." The group members clamored to be the first on Reenie's calendar. This was something the hospital didn't plan on when it was calculating social service "man hours" per inpatient stay—the countless hours it was going to take to explain to patients the benefits offered them under their various plans, which weren't paying the hospital enough for Reenie to have time to do it! 'Mind boggling,' Reenie thought to herself, 'my mind is definitely boggled.'

"Okay, I'll get my appointment book out after group and set up a time with each of you. First, let's talk some about how each of you are feeling, how you are coping. You each have had a stroke, and that can bring with it many changes, including having obstinate insurance people in your life! Can you each talk a little about how your lives have been changed by your stroke?"

"My biggest problem is my kids. Won't let me alone now. They want to do everything for me, want me to have somebody with me every minute." Mrs. Luber jumped right in.

"This sure isn't what I thought I would be doing in retirement" Mr. Shaw added.

"You've both pointed out important losses that can come with a stroke. Mrs. Luber, sounds like you've lost control, or you at least feel that your kids may be trying to take some of your control away from you," Reenie guided the group. "And Mr. Shaw, you've lost something very important, a dream—your dream of what you thought retirement would be. Anyone else?"

Violet shrugged her shoulders. "Mostly inconvenient for me. I'm losing valuable dance time. And I guess I am missing the opening of the season. The company may be two to three shows in before I can get back to form."

"Honey, who are you kidding? You're never gonna dance again," Mr. Marshall was brutally honest. He met Violet eye to eye as he made his declaration. She did not blink, but tears began to roll down her cheeks.

"I can't remember a time when I haven't danced," Violet said, her voice barely audible. "I was born dancing."

"Well, you better think of something else you know how to do. Could be time." Mrs. Spelling was only slightly more gentle.

"Again, you are all hitting on something that is true," Reenie intervened.

"Each of you, and perhaps your lives, will never be the same. Something serious and profound has happened to you. Things—your body—has changed."

The group members went on to discuss their thoughts and observations about life changes. They were at varying places in terms of acceptance of their medical event. But they each, regardless of their ability to verbalize it, knew that they would never be the same. And Reenie knew that in order for them to move forward, they would have to look back at how their lives were, remember the dreams that they had, and grieve the losses that having a stroke brought to their lives. As a way of facilitating the grief process, she made an assignment.

"Okay, thank you all for sharing with us today. You each have been very courageous today and I commend you. I'm going to ask you to do some homework for next week. Some very difficult homework. I want you to spend some time with your past. Use photographs, letters, yearbooks, scrapbooks—whatever you can find that puts you in touch with your life, from the day you were born until the day you had your stroke. Spend some time looking at these things, and bring them with you to group next week. We will be talking about your past, where you are today, and begin the journey toward tomorrow together. Thank you."

Reenie saw each of the group members out the door, and then headed back to her office to finish the last task of the day. After the family conference with the Masons, the team stayed to finish its discussion of the ethical issues involved in Mrs. Mason's first fall. Clearly, the patient was a fall risk and the nursing staff had taken all the appropriate precautions. There was no avoiding the fact, however, that Violet's desire to respond to Reenie's discussion of her in the hallway led to her attempts to get out of the bed unassisted. And the team had a long and proud history of sensitivity to patient confidentiality. Rennie respected and nurtured that commitment. She was torn in this case between the desire to acknowledge her responsibility and her desire to keep her job. Mr. Pearman had made it clear that he did not expect to see anything in the incident report of Mrs. Mason's fall other than information regarding the precautions that were in place and the unavoidable impulsivity of the patient. Reenie knew the team felt that all the circumstances including

Reenie's unprofessional discussion of patient information in the hallway should be included, even if that meant opening up the hospital to some liability. To report any less would be in essence, trying to "hush-hush" the incident. Nobody had directly said so to her, leaving the final decision up to her. But all the team members had agreed that, while the primary reason Mrs. Mason fell was due to her stroke, there was certainly some question about how the hallway discussion had influenced her to try something unsafe. And they all knew that the conversation that took place in the hallway should have occurred behind closed doors. Well, nobody ever said that ethics were easy. Reenie finished scribbling on the incident form and dashed up the stairs to turn it in to Carolyn. Carolyn glanced at the comments, a slow smile spreading over her face as she glanced back up at her colleague. Reenie was relieved to see the respect still there. She had included all the details about Mrs. Mason's fall. It was the right thing to do. Frank Pearman would just have to deal with it.

Analysis

This chapter focuses on identity and role issues of the patient and the team. Each is struggling with issues of professional and personal role identity and communicating the importance of their roles to each other. The chapter opens with a variety of conversations that are defensive and misinterpreted. Rather than call them conversations, what follows appears to be a series of monologues. At first glance, the reader might find this amusing. Violet is trying desperately to figure out why people were talking about her and why they were confused about her identity as a professional ballet dancer. Dr. Oliviero is not listening to her because he is focusing on her "hearing voices" as a symptom that needs medical attention. Even when she tells him the voices were "talking about me, not to me," he appears preoccupied with his notes. Her husband Jack is trying to act supportive but seems more concerned with her professional identity than her personal one. He expresses disbelief that she could "trip out of bed—you are far too graceful for that."

This confusion about personal and professional identity becomes the core of the content of the chapter since it affects the team-building process and the patient's well-being. The characters are still linked to their past ways of interacting and seem traumatized by the events around them. There is little empathy for the struggles each is having as he or she faces adjustment to new requirements of functioning. The first few pages of the chapter may be summarized with the following observations about the characters. Violet is left unable to effectively express to the treatment team and her husband what she is feeling. Her attempts at explanations are seen as demands. Dr. Oliviero does not hear what she is saying except for the word "voices" which puts him in an automatic referral mode for a psychiatric consultation. His major concern is to close his chart with orders for her physical safety. He remains kind if not paternalistic in his manner of dealing with his patient. His interactions with the team follow a similar pattern. Carolyn, the nurse, assumes the diagnosis of stroke is comprehended as she underscores the importance of the written material that was given. This lack of comprehension is depicted by Jack, who has no understanding about the disability of his wife, but is concerned about the team describing her as a homemaker.

As the confusion dies down, blame seems to be directed at Reenie, the social worker. Jack has no idea why a social worker is even involved in the case. In fact, when he remembers meeting the social worker in the emergency room, his first impression was she did not listen to him. Jack then begins to blame the social worker for Violet's fall. This becomes a pivotal scene in the chapter. The social worker becomes the scapegoat for the team and she handles this by accepting and acknowledging the frustrations she has been experiencing. This scene reinforces a parallel between the team members not clearly supporting each others' roles and their inability to accept and recognize the importance of those roles to both the patient and her husband.

The ethical dilemma that Reenie acknowledges as her fault is not discussed, rather it is danced around by the team members. They are more concerned about the paperwork that results from Violet's fall than the reason it occurred. Their discussion with Reenie takes on an accusatory tone. Why isn't Reenie defending her role? Why is she responding and accepting *complete responsibility*? She even feels obliged to explain her culpability to the managed care administrator, Frank Pearman. Reenie appears to want to foster collaboration at the cost of her authority as a professional. Dr. Oliviero appears sympathetic to Reenie's problems and pressures but responds with a quick-fix answer to call administration. Reenie, in turn, blames managed care for her problems. The interaction with the managed care representative provides a perfect foil for the team. He is depicted as not understanding ethical issues and being unwanted by the team. This is an interesting analogy because that is exactly how Violet and Jack view the medical team.

The tensions build up further as the team prepares for a family conference. Carolyn is surprised at Reenie's honesty in accepting blame and apologizing to her patient. Reenie is stunned that this is not enough to satisfy Carolyn. She is having difficulty understanding how a mistake can endanger their long-standing team relationship. Reenie and Carolyn begin to attack Josh, the rehabilitation specialist who has not yet experienced the frustrations of managed care. These interactions show the breakdown of trust that occurs when self-image is challenged. When trust erodes, the primary focus of comprehensive patient care is lost. Jack is horrified at the medical terminology that is presented to him because he cannot relate it to the impact that the stroke has had on Violet. There is more misinterpretation of the meaning of the word "independence" from a medical versus a patient perspective. The family conference ends up a play on words with each member thinking about him- or herself and the dissolution of the team process. Self-consciousness and self-absorption replace professionalism. The scene is ended with a humorous twist, when Jack believes the managed care representative Mr. Pearman is part of the treatment team who wants to enable the discharge of the patient. In this vein, the reality of the injury "brain" not "muscle" becomes clear to Jack for the first time.

The last scene centers on a patient support group for postdischarge stroke patients. The social worker ponders the fate of such types of services when physicians have less say about what can be done in a for-profit hospital. The support group's conversation is about various kinds of insurance policies rather than adjustment to stroke. Reenie understands that this is the most important issue on their minds because benefits will determine how they will be able to make adaptations. As such, more and more of the social worker's time is spent in teaching herself about health insurance. She resents this intrusion into her work and avoids the importance of patients' fears about service cutbacks; this is another analogy for the intrusion the team is also experiencing but has yet to verbalize.

The social worker, nurse, physician, and rehabilitation specialist are referred to as a team. Although they obviously are performing professional activities, they are not functioning as a team. Billups (1987) offers a few basic assumptions about interprofessional teams. He maintains that the successful achievement of desired outcomes from teams will "depend heavily on a cognitive grasp, sensitive understanding, and careful handling by human service professionals of a number of specific and complex dynamics conceptually grouped under the generic label of interprofessional team process" (147). This includes both the functions of the team, its tasks or functions, and its socioemotional or self-renewing functions. Another assumption is that well-prepared professionals are not threatened with the idea that their areas of specialization will be depreciated or lost. He believes it is this area of distinctiveness of diverse contributions that enable changes in highly complex organizations. A third assumption is that there are no absolute arbitrators of the way in which interprofessional team processes are shaped. Thus, the relationship between team members, the larger environment, and the people in whose behalf the team functions are interlocking and mutually interdependent. A final assumption is that the outcomes of a well-functioning team can be considered greater in scope and value than the cumulative effects of the performance of individual practitioners or educators working separately. Use these assumptions to examine how the team in Chapter 2 conceptualizes the team process. In what ways were the individual expertise of the team professionals used to effectively collaborate on patient goals?

Billups (1987) provides a model for the ideal type of interprofessional processes using six guidelines: (1) Achieving a sound professional identification through each team member's unique role, place, and function on a team. This achievement is contingent upon how well the person has achieved his or her professional identity and can ward off defensiveness. (2) Comprehending the influence of the environmental context on the team which includes the policies and procedures of the host setting. (3) Maintaining intercommunication and openly resolving intrateam conflict. This entails an openness to understanding the contributions of others without overemphasizing one's autonomy or professional ethnocentrism that overestimates the values of one's own professional perspective. (4) Identifying and assessing problems to be addressed, setting goals, and developing actions plans. This requires team members collect, integrate, and interpret the parts of a complex situation. The team must have the ability to examine a full range of alternatives and avoid groupthink which reflects a closed system and occurs when teams are under stress. (5) Negotiating and implementing the action plan and engaging in necessary follow-through. In complex organizations negotiated sets of social relationships are necessary because of the multiplicity of purposes and goals that must be met by many different practitioners. Some consumer-patients are also involved in the process of influencing health care. (6) Utilizing feedback and evaluating outcomes. This is a continuous, reflective reappraisal that facilitates the stop-correct actions. You may want to review this model as you think about how the professional team in this chapter perceived these steps (148–150). Achieving team consensus is difficult for professionals who have not been exposed to these theoretical concepts as part of their professional education. However Sands, Stafford, and McClelland (1990) argue that team conflict is a necessary part of the group decision-making process because it allows team members to examine issues from a variety of perspectives and separate interpersonal issues from substantive ones. By examining conflict, teams can determine whether conflict is mirroring the emotions of the clients and their families or contradictions at the systems level. Conflict in interdisciplinary teams comes from a variety of sources including differences in professional values, professional socialization, status, and personality traits. However, team members must use conflict for an opportunity to grow.

Lee (1980) reviewed the team-building process at a large hospital and noted that professional teams might think they are sharing a task such as providing comprehensive care yet they may not even agree on what constitutes primary care. Many times these differences emerge when the team meets together with the patient. This was shown to occur many times in

Chapter 2 when a team member's view of what was important in the rehabilitation of the patient was not viewed the same way by the patient and her family. In fact, the team did not as a whole have a consistent view on the basic adaptation needs of the patient. Lee's view of team development requires a working-through phase. This includes steps so that a social worker is trained in order to facilitate group members to meet even when everyone feels too pressed for time, to actively support all members for exchange of information and sharing of conflicts, to foster a safe environment for exploring concerns, and to help the group sort out and resolve conflict in the interest of problem solving. While each professional can contribute areas of expertise, the team as a whole must view the patient in a consistent manner.

Because social workers are primarily responsible for concrete services, before they can be recognized as clinicians, they must first provide competency in expected areas and then move on to expanding the nature of their work on the team. Lee (1980) suggests that social workers do the following in order to expand their role on the team: (1) Make themselves visible by interacting with staff, talking with patients, reviewing charts; and (2) listen, question, discuss, and offer a willingness to share the burden of managing difficult patients (240). This allows social workers to be recognized as needed members of the team. Once this occurs, the social worker can begin to expand his or her role to include psychosocial intervention as well as concrete services. Social workers can help other members of the team augment their capacity to understand the patient's feelings. Social workers must also be willing to learn more about the medical aspects of patient care. This shift in attitude allows a new flexibility around problem solving. The decision-making process is no longer a rigid system in which team members supply the physician with the new data and the physician makes all final decisions. This model suggests that the primary decision maker shifts, depending on the decision that has to be made.

In health care settings today, unlike the past, changes are rapid. This can cause conflict especially as competition among institutions means restructuring organizational systems and thereby creating new issues for professional staff. Taccetta-Chapnick (1996), a staff nurse in a cardiac intensive care unit, discusses how concentrated change within a short time span affects nurses. She notes that new leadership styles must emerge. Using the concept of *transformal leader* (60), she describes this as a commitment to a vision that empowers individuals with how things should be and, as such, involves staff in creating their future. The characteristics she describes in such leadership includes an organizational vision that can be turned into planned actions and, in the cases of nurses, it empowers them to grow and develop. The leader provides intellectual stimulation by encouraging nurses to use their imagination and develop new strategies to solve old problems. Change, then, is viewed as a system in which internal equilibration or adaptability is a necessary part of achieving goals. It is both planned and controlled, arises out of unfulfilled needs, and meets the vision and mission of the organization. Changed goals are developed through a collaborative process. The brief-change framework is used to describe the stages of denial of the change, through anger at change through the process of chaos and powerlessness and mourning for the past until, finally, the person can internalize the alteration as part of the role and reemerge into the system (63). Role conflict is a major cause of intradisciplinary unrest. Unless issues are brought out to the team and there is a high regard for relationship among staff, problems will remain unsolved. Transformal leadership includes high regard for both tasks and relationships.

Social workers who are trained in collaborative team skills may be frightened by other professionals who are trying to expand their roles to include conflict resolution. Additionally, the newer emphasis shared on team leadership still concerns social workers in health care centers in which role diffusion and identity has always been of concern.

This chapter depicts the sensitivity the social worker had about her role on the treatment team. The social work literature notes that social workers in hospitals historically have been sensitive about their professional domain and have been careful to avoid blurring their roles with those of other health professionals such as nurses. Additionally, their participation in planning for patients has always been at the discretion of physicians (Abramson and Mizrahi 1986; 1996; Dane and Simon 1991; Davidson 1990; Mizrahi and Abramson 1985). Mizrahi and Abramson (1985) note that the sources of strain that characterize the physician/social worker interaction began with the inception of social work in 1905 at the Massachusetts General Hospital. The authors believe such strain results from different socialization experiences in training. Social work training focuses on collaboration in the use of "self" in relationships and self-examination whereas the medical model emphasis is on the individual rather than the social environment; the disease orientation; and the importance of diagnosis, cure, and discharge. The physician role emphasizes decision making, moral authority, and expertise. Paternalism, even if it is benign, is meant to contain patient anxiety. Social workers today still encounter many instances of role blurring with nurses. The clinical nurse specialist with a master's degree in nursing, like the social worker, may define his/her role as helping with the emotional aspects of illness, patient advocacy, and quality of care. This causes duplication of services and competition. Davidson (1990) points out that the shortage of nurses "raised the starting salary for a nurse with an associate degree to $30,000 in some areas, [and] social workers who have a master's degree but are paid less must recognize their comparatively less essential role in health care" (230). Social workers need to stress their worth in the health care arena; it goes beyond medical services and includes expertise in family relations, cultural and organizational contexts, and group facilitation.

Differences in status and functions of social workers and other professionals have consequences for teamwork. As depicted in the narrative, the social worker emphasizes collaboration. This stems from the professional training of social workers. However, this concept of collaboration works well when other professionals recognize the unique expertise of the social worker. Role expansion requires that the social worker first establish his or her expertise in areas that are helpful to the team's planning for patient well-being. This includes the ability to arrange transportation, nursing home placement, finances, and support services. As the health care system is changing and all professionals are struggling with their own authority and roles, it is important for social workers to first claim authority for those tasks that they have been able to perform effectively. Davidson (1990) notes that the role of nurses has expanded in areas that have been traditionally based in social work, such as discharge planning, and that social workers believe nurses are better qualified to perform these functions. She suggests that, rather than claiming tasks and territory, social workers need to demonstrate areas in which they consistently do better than other professionals such as helping families plan for care at home and supporting distressed patients. Colleagues respect competence rather than tasks and territories. However, the fear of shrinking services and roles and the emphasis on collaboration for social workers have made the hospital environment one of fear, frustration, mistrust, and lack of appreciation.

As environments change, this is a natural phase of development. Redefining roles and establishing role authority is not static. It is an integral part of ongoing practice. Davidson (1990) notes that awareness of shifts in power is an important part of visibility for social workers especially as administrative control is shifting away from medical management. Ignoring the shift will not help social workers get support for their roles and presence in a hospital. Some of this will require a change in focus such as helping a hospital meet its needs to achieve credibility and accepting that conflict is not necessarily unproductive but rather part of the nature of changing conditions. However, professional anxiety about conflict cannot be left unattended.

Dane and Simon (1991) refer to social workers as guests in host settings, meaning their mission and decision making are defined and dominated by people who are not social workers. They must "justify their indispensability on a regular basis to either the mission or overall welfare of the host" (208). Additionally, the intensification of bureaucratic control over service delivery with the emphasis on efficiency and cost containment may interfere with patient problems and services and ultimately cause ethical problems. They further note that social workers who have relinquished responsibilities to other disciplines have suffered losses. Most notably is discharge planning because it has become a priority in current cost containment environments. This chapter illustrates how the social worker reacts to some of these changes. Think about her response to the needs of the patients in the support groups. She lamented the shift in support group focus from emotional needs of the patients to one of dealing with insurance issues. She did not view this as an opportunity to expand her role or as fulfilling an emotional need of the patients. This was clearly an opportunity that was missed. Discharge planning, which was now the responsibility of the nurse, was not seen as an area of collaboration. Think about how the information in her support group could have strengthened her collaboration with the nurse. Abramson and Mizrahi (1986, 1996) stress the importance of social workers understanding the nature of physician training and socialization in order to effectively function on a team. They note that physicians may use defense mechanisms such as denial and detachment to work through their stress and pressures. An empathetic social worker can enable a physician to work through a difficult team issue. Furthermore, they note that there is greater importance in teamwork and collaboration as part of health care reform because of increased emphasis in elimination of duplication and fragmentation through referrals, networking, and coordination. In the managed care environment and because of the deprofessionalism that is occurring, efficiency will depend on the ability of social workers, physicians, and other health care professionals to collaborate effectively in the provision of care to patients. Their research data furthe suggests that these changes are affecting all health care professionals, not just social workers, in that physicians are also valuing collaborative relationships and interactions and are investing in having positive relationships with others. These issues as depicted in the narrative require team-building skills and problem recognition. Part of this process will require that professionals become aware of the changes in their environment and begin to view these changes as a positive way to build their teams. The following exercises will enable you to envision a way to build effective teams.

Practice Skills

Client

1. Describe the role changes Jack and Violet are experiencing.
2. Describe the role changes the other group members are experiencing as a result of their changed medical status.

Social Worker

1. Using Lee's (1990) model of planning an effective team meeting (137), role play how the social worker in the narrative might conduct a productive interdisciplinary team meeting.
2. Discuss how issues of professional domain, role blurring, role conflict, and role change interfered with effective patient care planning. Identify the key reasons why the social worker was "scapegoated." What were her assumptions about her performance as a social worker?
3. NASW Code of Ethics (1996) describes conflicts of interest as an ethical standard that requires the social worker to maintain professional discretion and impartial judgment so that the client's interest is primary. Social workers should not take advantage of any professional relationship or exploit others for personal or business interests. Describe how Reenie responded to the ethical dilemma in Chapter 2.

Team

1. Using Billup's (1987) model for interprofessional teamwork as described on page 83 of our text, assess the key points in the narrative where interdisciplinary team communication broke down.
2. What were some of the key issues of tension that existed among team members? How were these resolved?

System

1. What is the response of the hospital system, as represented by the vice president, to a possible ethical dilemma?
2. What is the team's ethical responsibility to the system in this case?
3. How do paperwork requirements by the system impact assessment of the client's problem? What might the team do to change this?

3

Disability: The Patient and the Team Deny Change

Reenie was dashing up the stairs to meet with the team when her pager went off for the umpteenth time. Again. She shuffled her folders from one arm to the other, patted her lab coat searching for the location of the increasingly loud alarm. When she finally got it in the light, she was perplexed to see the unit's number. Again. Carolyn was beginning to make a habit of paging Reenie repeatedly. This was beginning to get on Reenie's nerves. She always returned her pages just as soon as she could get to the phone. They had worked together too long for Carolyn not to know that. Reenie shoved the pager back in her pocket, sucked in air, and took off up the next flight of stairs.

As Reenie opened the door into the hallway, she heard the hospital operator paging her overhead. This was definitely getting on her last nerve. She turned on the unit to find Carolyn pacing. Again.

"There you are. I've been trying to reach you." Carolyn almost shouted at Reenie.

"So I noticed!"

"Well, why didn't you return my page?"

"Carolyn, you didn't give me a chance. Have you ever known me not to answer my page?"

"Everything's faster now, Reenie. You've got to step it up!"

Reenie could feel her teeth clamp down on her response. "I cannot possibly move one bit faster. What is wrong with you?"

"Thank you. Glad to have gotten your careful attention," Carolyn responded with equal disdain. "He's been here already. He came through this morning. Went up one side of the hall and down the other, posting those blasted signs."

"Who? What are you talking about?"

"Pearman. He put up the signs!" Carolyn's face was getting redder as her speech got faster.

"Take a deep breath, Carolyn. It will do wonders for both of us. Now what signs?"

"Go look. Signs, notices, whatever you want to call them. I have a page in to Dr. O but he is in with a patient at his office. Look at them."

Reenie examined a couple of the doors closest to the nurse's station. Bright fluorescent pink and green signs were indeed posted at every room. And each one had the patient's name, diagnosis, date of admission, number of insured days available and, in very bold letters, date of discharge. Upon reading them, Reenie joined Carolyn in her outrage. First of all, none of the discharge dates seem to match what the team had decided in their weekly meeting. Where Mr. Pearman might have gotten them was a complete mystery. But of more concern to Reenie was the fact that personal information was posted in neon at every door.

"What does he think he is doing, Carolyn?"

"I don't know what he thinks he is doing, but he is not going to do it on this floor. I won't have it. And Dr. O won't have it either. You can be sure of that."

Josh approached the desk. "Top of the morning to you, ladies. What are we so sure of today?" Josh jumped unknowingly into the middle of the mess.

"Have you seen the signs on the patient doors?" Carolyn demanded.

Josh looked up curiously. "What? Oh, yeah. Nice job."

"Nice job?" Reenie and Carolyn responded in unison.

"Who's side are you on, Josh?" Carolyn knew she had better define the enemy quickly.

"Man, you guys are jumpy. What am I supposed to say? The group notices are . . . bright?" Josh was baffled by the big to-do over notices that Reenie posted routinely each week regarding her support group.

"They are not the group notices. Come look at them, Josh," The young therapist wandered over to where Reenie was shaking her head as she stared at door after door. Even he was offended when he finally realized what was posted.

"Carolyn, these discharge dates are all wrong. And they are supposed to be inside the room. You get new staff or something?"

"My staff and I had nothing to do with this. And we will continue to have nothing to do with this."

Josh glanced at Reenie for an answer. "Pearman's work, Josh," Reenie filled in the blanks for her colleague. "He apparently posted all of these this morning. None of the dates even match what we decided."

"Did you call him and tell him? We need to get these corrected," Josh commented naively as he began to remove the notices from the doors.

"I have a call in to Dr. Oliviero. I believe he'll set Mr. Pearman straight. He cannot change every discharge date on this unit, I don't care if he is Mr. Vice President of this and that muckety muck. Dr. O and I have been taking care of patients since before he learned how to wipe his own behind. We will not stand for this."

"You think Pearman did this on purpose? Changed all the discharge dates on purpose?" Josh was incredulous.

"I don't think. I know. He told me so. When I asked him what in the blazes he thought he was doing!"

"He should not come in here and change a team decision. That is not how things work." Reenie echoed Josh and Carolyn's concern. For the first time in a few days, the team was in sync.

• • • • •

"Violet, what are you doing on the floor?" Jack was exasperated to walk in from his morning's work in the study to find Violet sprawled across the bedroom floor with God-only-knew-what scattered all over the carpet around her. "The house is a disaster. Where is that woman? What's her name?"

"Who?" Violet asked innocently.

"The one from the agency that is supposed to watch you . . . uh, keep this place clean." Jack was not accustomed to clutter. Even though Violet never had been as tidy as he was, his housekeeper had always stayed with her to make certain that clothes were hung, papers put away as soon as Violet was finished with them. Of course, that was the housekeeper Jack had from years before his marriage to Violet until about four days after her return home from the hospital. Violet demanded so much help, and was so rude, that the housekeeper, after fourteen years of employment, just picked up her purse and walked out four days after Violet came home from the hospital. No resignation, no notice, nothing. In the days since, Jack had run through several potential housekeepers. Violet was running them off faster than he could interview them. That he understood, to a certain extent. Violet was not tidy, but she was particular about her routine, about her body. It was understandable that the inconvenience of her injury was making her a bit difficult. But this. This was nothing but a holy mess. And the plumber would be arriving any minute to install the hand rails and grab bars on the tub in the master bath. Jack took a deep breath. "Excuse me, ma'am. Where are you?" he bellowed, still unable to remember this latest helper's name.

"She left," Violet said from some faraway place.

"She left? Please tell me you are kidding?"

"No, I am not kidding. . . ."

"What happened this time?"

"She wouldn't draw my bath. I told her I was ready for my bath and she refused to draw it. I told her that would be just fine and that she could run along and sit on her posterior in her own house."

"Violet, how could you? Look at this place. What were you thinking?"

"This? This is nothing, Jack. Don't worry."

"Well, if it is nothing, then why is it strewed from here to tomorrow all over the floor when the plumber is on the way?" Jack bent and began to clumsily scoop up the array of newspaper clippings and old photographs. "You know you are not to get in that tub until we get the rails attached. The agency lady knew that also, which is why, thankfully, she did not draw your bath."

"Hey, leave that alone. I am putting it in order!"

"Order?" Jack surveyed the area with a smirk. "I do not see you putting anything in order. Come on. Let's get this mess, and you, up off the floor."

"No! This is homework. I have to have these things around me where I can work on them."

"Homework?"

"For my group."

"Your what?" Jack was absentmindedly glancing at the photographs he had picked up. He held one up to Violet, as if comparing old to new.

"The group meeting at the doctor's office."

"Oh, that. What does all of this have to do with your exercise regimen?"

"Nothing."

"Then why are you doing it?"

"We're going through our past. We're supposed to be going through our past."

"Looking for what?"

"A way to deal with the present and move to the future."

"Violet, are you sure you got this right? I did not hear the physical therapist mention anything like that, trust me."

"Not the physical therapist. The social worker."

"Oh, the social worker. That group. What is it she wants you to do?"

"Look at our past."

Jack glanced at his watch impatiently and gave up trying to understand the concept. "Okay, but do we have to trip over your past all week?"

"I'm working on it. Please, Jack, you are disturbing my concentration. I have to get the feel of this, get it arranged in the book just right. It's an artistic thing. You wouldn't understand. Now go. I need my creative space."

"Well, your creative space is going to get in the way of the plumber who is coming to work on your bathing space, if you don't mind," Jack was uncharacteristically terse.

"He'll have to work around me. I am choreographing my past, dancing lightly into the future." Violet danced a yellowed article over to a corresponding photograph.

"Geez, Violet. Give it a rest."

Jack jumped at the sound of the doorbell. He tried moving piles closer together.

"Stop it!" Violet protested with a quizzical look. It was not like Jack to ignore her request for creative space. He always said that he understood the artist temperament and he believed the end more than made up for the means. But today he was quite pushy. The doorbell rang again.

"The doorbell," he called out. "Could you get that? . . . Oh, yes, the help left. I forgot." Jack frowned at Violet as he headed toward the front door. "Just a minute. I'm coming!"

• • • • •

Dr. Oliviero and Mr. Pearman stood nose to nose at the nurse's station, each clutching a neon flyer that had been ripped from the front of a patient's door.

"You do not set the discharge dates for my patients." Dr. Oliviero was furious.

"Discharge date is dictated by managed care experts integrating empirical data with unique patient information, doctor. It is cost-effective and it is quality. And most important, sir, it is good financial sense. These are the discharge dates. I suggest you and your team do some serious planning to determine where these folks are going to fit into the continuum of care on those dates. And I do mean proactive planning, not your weekly social gathering," Mr. Pearman's voice was just as controlled and firm as Dr. Oliviero's.

"And I suggest you plan to spend some time in your boss's office, because I am getting on the horn to him right now."

"Dr. Oliviero, times have changed. Health care has changed. Your practice must change."

"The only thing that has changed is that greedy entrepreneurs like yourself are trying to make a factory out of medicine. Well, it won't happen, my friend. People are not just parts lined up on a conveyor belt."

"I agree with you. However, protocols have been studied, tested, validated."

"Medicine is an art as well as a science. Now get out of my face." Dr. Oliviero flung the notice in the hazardous waste bin as he stormed off the unit.

Frank Pearman glanced at the team members glaring at him. "Get to work on those discharges," he said as he followed the physician's exit. "It is the right thing to do for these patients."

The team was abuzz even before the elevator doors closed.

• • • • •

Jack flung the door open, waving the plumber through the door.

"Steve Woodson," the gentleman introduced himself simply as Jack was already headed back to the bathroom.

"Jack Mason. Bathroom is back here. Need to put those bar and rail attachments in. Wife needs a little help getting in and out right now. This is my wife, Violet. Please don't trip over her past."

Steve stopped at the sight of Violet, tipped his baseball cap. "Pleased to meet you, ma'am." Noting the items strewn about the floor he added, "Quite a job, putting all those pictures in order. Been meaning to do that myself, but . . ."

Jack interrupted impatiently, calling from the bathroom, "The tub is in here." Steve tipped his hat again and followed the sound of Jack's voice. He surveyed the marble bathtub carefully.

"Quite a beauty. What is it exactly that you want done here?"

"Bars, rails, whatever it needs to be, what did they say? Handicap-accessible?"

"Why would you need a handicap-accessible shower?"

"Something for the wife to hang on to while she gets in and out."

Steve was deep in thought. "She doesn't just want those pretty little butterfly stick-on grippers? You can get those pretty cheap down at . . ."

"My wife has had a stroke," Jack was curt. "She needs a handrail to hang on to as she gets in."

"Oh, a stroke. Well, then, you are going to need more than a handrail."

"What are you talking about?"

"She paralyzed?"

"No. Well, she has weakness on one side. Right now."

"Now my mother had a stroke. I know just what you need. But I'm going to have to tell you, sir, you need more than a handrail."

"Fine. Rails, bars, whatever."

"You need a different tub. In fact, she may need a free-standing shower instead."

"Nonsense. My wife loves this tub."

"Yes, sir. You going to lift her in and out?"

"That is what the rails are for. I thought you were knowledgeable about this sort of work. Obviously . . ."

"I don't know about knowledgeable, but I do know if your wife is just a little paralyzed, she can't get down in a tub and get back out without somebody lifting her, rail or no rail. You seen a doctor about this?"

"Of course we've seen a doctor. She just got out of the hospital. All the occupational therapist said was handicap-accessible. . . ."

"Now if you have a therapist, I'll be glad to put in a call about specifications."

"I just want handrails and bars, for God sake. What is not to understand about that?" Jack's voice was rising.

"Yes, sir, I understand you want handrails and bars. I can't do that, however. It just is not safe. Like I said, I can call the therapist and discuss it."

Jack raked his hand through his hair as his reddening jaw tensed. He glanced from his watch to Violet still absorbed in her growing stacks of newspapers and photos on the bedroom carpet. "Fine. Call the therapist. I'll get the number. Do whatever you have to. I have to be out for a while—work. You just do whatever you and the therapist agree to."

"Yes, sir." Steve surveyed the business card Jack jabbed at him. "I'll get on the phone right now."

"Fine. There is a phone right over there next to the wash basin. I will be back in . . . a while. Do what you need to do." Jack turned and strode over Violet's "past" into the hallway and out of the front door. Steve nodded at Violet, turned and went about his work in the bath.

• • • • •

"What does he mean by 'virtual team meeting'?" Carolyn was confused. "How is that different than what we have been doing?"

"We'll meet, but not all in the same place together." Josh tried to explain to the technologically disadvantaged. "We will hook up by computer."

"We only have one computer for the whole department. How am I going to find time to type a report for you guys? This makes no sense whatsoever." Reenie was put out with yet another bureaucratic brainstorm to save time that would just end up meaning more unpaid overtime for her.

"Not a report, Reenie. We would all meet in a virtual conference room, like a chat room on the net." Josh persevered.

"Pearman says we don't need to talk about all the patients anyway. You know, he's got them all on critical pathways. He says use the computer and only address those that have 'fallen off' the pathway."

"He really doesn't have a clue, does he? His concept of 'paint by number' health care just doesn't cut it. You have to go outside the lines to pull the whole picture together." Reenie was growing increasingly weary.

"All I know is Dr. O is going to hit the 'virtual' ceiling on this one. He is pretty tired of Frank's ideas for improved efficiency that don't take into account the needs of the patient."

"Carolyn, what happened when Dr. Oliviero went to administration about the notices on the patient doors. They didn't stop Pearman did they?"

"The CEO is out until next week. The rest of those 'yes' people don't make a move without his approval. Dr. O is waiting to talk to him."

"We had an inservice this morning on our new reporting requirements. We have to turn in a report every month that calculates how much money social workers have made or saved for the hospital. Supposedly Pearman's idea, but the directive came out of the CEO's office."

"Don't you charge per unit of service?" Josh relied on his department's procedures as a frame of reference.

"No, we have never charged. We have always been considered a basic component of hospital service, like the bed and nursing."

"So you don't make money. How are you going to show that you save money?" Carolyn was perplexed.

"Well, say Mr. X's discharge is being delayed because the equipment is not ready at his house. If we find an equipment company that can get the stuff out there stat so that he can go home, we have saved one day of hospital stay. One-day stay would cost the hospital at least $200, so the amount we saved is $200."

"Hmm, that seems like pretty soft calculation to me." Josh tried to follow.

"We do save the hospital tons of money," Reenie was indignant. She spent half her time trying to explain what social workers do, and here her own team members still didn't seem to have a clue. She was losing patience fast.

"Of course you do, Reenie. But it is like nursing, hard to translate into dollars and cents." Carolyn tried to arbitrate.

"I'm sure it won't be that hard, with all that we do." Reenie was more than just a little defensive. "They may end up adding staff when they see how much one social worker can save."

"That would be great. You guys are stretched pretty thin," Josh fortunately concurred. "But really, this way of doing team conference could save you valuable time, Reenie. And it could be fun, meeting in a chat room instead of that stuffy old doctor's conference room."

"Yeah, but can Dr. O deliver virtual donuts?" Carolyn broke the tension.

"Oh, man, no donuts! That would be the worst part!" Reenie was relieved to be on a safer topic. "It isn't going to fly with Dr. O anyway, so I'm not going to worry about it. As soon as Dr. O corners the big boss, we'll be back to business as usual, I'm sure. If it ain't broke, don't fix it—hasn't Pearman ever heard of that?"

• • • • •

"I have to go to the bathroom," Violet blurted to the empty room. Her statement was drowned out by the sound of clanging and chipping singing out from the bathroom. Violet repeated herself, a little more loudly. Still nothing. She screamed one last time. The clanging stopped.

"Beg your pardon, ma'am?"

"I have to go to the bathroom. Now."

"Yes, ma'am." A few more clangs then Steve appeared at the door of the bathroom. "I'm out of your way now. Sorry about all the tools and dust. Quite a job." Steve stepped through the bedroom and into the hallway. Violet did not move.

"I can't get up."

"Beg your pardon?"

"I said I can't get up, you moron. My foot must have gone to sleep. Help me up."

"Yes, ma'am. Sure thing." Steve leaned toward Violet offering his hand. She grabbed hold and pulled, but could not get up. Steve noticed the paralysis on her left side. He changed positions so that he was beside her, his arm around her waist. Gently, he lifted Violet until she was upright, leaning heavily against him.

"I'll need my stick." Violet could not bring herself to use the word *cane.* It just did not fit with her image of herself, even if it was just temporary.

"Yes, ma'am."

"And stop calling me ma'am. I'm young enough to be your daughter."

"Yes, m . . . Mrs. Mason. You sure you can manage with that cane? You're leaning pretty heavy."

"Just hand me the stick. I will be fine."

Steve retrieved the cane with one hand while holding Violet up with the other. He handed it over, made sure it was secure in her hand and on the floor before easing away. Violet stood awkwardly but independently. "Well?" Violet gave Steve a sharp look. He glanced questioningly at her in return. "I said I have to go to the bathroom."

"Oh, yes, yes. Please excuse me." Steve headed once more for the hallway. He stood there patiently waiting for several minutes, before hearing a terrible crash from the direction of the bathroom. He took off running, stopping just short of the open bathroom door. "Are you okay, Mrs. Mason? What happened?"

"I need a little help," came the muffled reply. "It's okay, I'm decent."

Steve stepped through the door to find Violet toppled onto the floor, her "stick" between her body and the cold marble floor. Violet was terse. "Help me up, idiot."

Steve had to work his way around, but was finally able to get behind Violet, his hands under her arms as he sat her up. From there he resumed his position by her side to help her back to standing. As he lifted her, Violet leaned into him wordlessly. "Mr. Mason should get some help for you," Steve commented as Violet got back on track.

"Nonsense," Violet was nonplused. "I don't need any help usually. I tripped over one of your tools. I'm fine. I won't be needing anymore help. Why don't you run along and finish up another day."

Steve glanced around at the mess on the floor of the bedroom, then back at his half-finished job in the bath. "No, ma'am, I believe I'll just keep working until Mr. Mason returns." He was certain that Violet should not be left alone.

"Suit yourself." Violet settled tentatively on the edge of the bed, then slid back down to her spot on the floor. I have work to do."

Steve bent down and shuffled through one of the piles of newspaper articles. He read several intently. Violet watched him out of the corner of her eye, trying to read his reaction while acting indifferent to his presence. "This is you, Mrs. Mason? You danced in the ballet?"

"I am a principal in the ballet, yes."

"A principal? And that means . . ."

"I dance the lead roles."

"Now that is amazing. I've got two good legs and can't dance a lick. How do you dance with your stick?"

"I do not dance with the stick. I am taking a short leave of absence from the company while I recover from this malady. I should be dancing again in six to eight weeks. These are all from my career to date."

Steve held up a full-page color ad featuring Violet in all her dance finery. "So beautiful." He put the paper down and studied the woman before him. "Yes, ma . . . Mrs. Mason, you are probably the most beautiful, graceful woman I have even seen in person."

Violet could feel an uncharacteristic blush. "Even with the stick?" she asked wistfully.

"Especially with the stick. Adds a certain character. When its not stuck between you and the bathroom floor," Steve added with a chuckle. Violet was quiet for a moment, then joined Steve in his laughter. The two of them laughed louder and louder, egging each other on, until they both were gasping for air.

"Well, the ballet could certainly use some character," Violet finally managed a reply. "Hey, would you mind handing me that stack of photos?" Violet enlisted the plumber's assistance in her project.

Steve eased onto the floor in the middle of Violet's piles of the past. "No, indeed I don't mind a bit." Steve lost all track of time as he watched this woman put together the sequences and meanings of her past. He saw something of himself as he watched her, remembering how, when he returned from 'Nam, he had sorted through all the pieces of what had been his life before the draft and tried to make them fit. He had been determined to put them all back together with invisible tape. Somewhere along the way he had realized that tape doesn't last, and that there was no reclaiming the past. His life had been changed unalterably. He had to learn to move forward to some new truth he could call his own. It had been a long and solitary path, but one which finally brought him peace. Steve watched Violet as she studied a picture from long ago. She smiled up at him distractedly.

"I can tell you're a dancer," Steve observed. "You can tell by the lightness in a person's eyes."

"I'll show you how I dance. Come here," Violet commanded.

"No, ma'am. I think you better just show me another picture."

"I can dance right now. I'll show you."

"You don't have to prove anything to me," Steve continued to protest.

"Fine. I'm going to dance now, with or without you." Violet began to pull herself up using the bed, inching around to her platform walker. Steve reluctantly held the walker out to Violet and offered his hand. He would keep her as safe as he could until Mr. Mason returned. It was the least he could do. Violet studied Steve's face for some time before deciding he was not mocking her. She took the walker and his hand. Once upright, she began tentative moves around the room. Her moves were clumsy but intentional. When she stumbled, Steve steadied her. When she finished a circle around the room, he applauded loudly and bowed to the dancer. "Thank you," he said simply as he helped ease Violet back down on the floor.

"I'll be much better when I'm stronger. Without the stick."

"Of course."

Violet returned to sorting her piles. Steve rocked back on his heels and got up, returning to survey the bathroom. Maybe there was a way to save Violet's bathtub and still make it safe. He got out from his pocket the therapist's specifications he had jotted on the back of an envelope and went to work with his measuring tape.

• • • • •

"Ladies and gentleman, I called this meeting today because, frankly, we need to talk." Frank Pearman kicked off the meeting in the administrative suite. Carolyn, Reenie, and Josh glanced quickly at each other, then turned to Dr. Oliviero in almost complete unison.

"More than that, my good man," Dr. Oliviero did not disappoint his team. "You need to listen."

"That may be. Wouldn't hurt any of us to listen to each other," Frank countered. "But you all are not in a place to hear. We have a number of issues on the table that must be addressed, like it or not. You as a team have to figure out how to respond to the concerns at hand."

"We, as a team, sir, have functioned quite well for several years. Hundreds of patients have benefitted from the expertise of this team. Without your help, certainly, and definitely without your condescension." Dr. Oliviero was not going to let this young whippersnapper put anything by him.

"You are absolutely right, good doctor. You have helped thousands of people, in fact. I agree with you one hundred percent." The team members sat silently, waiting for the catch. "What I must challenge you to do now, is figure out how you will continue to help people in this changing environment."

"We'll help them the way we have always helped them," Reenie ventured tentatively into the discussion, relying on one of her favorite sayings. "If it ain't broke, don't . . ."

"Yes, I know, 'don't fix it,'" Frank finished the sentence for her. "And I agree with that, Reenie. Sound management concept not to tinker with something that is working. However, what you all are missing is that something is broken. Health care has changed, and you all, individually and as a team, have not. It's broken, Reenie. You must figure out how to fix it."

"How can you say it is broken?" Carolyn was indignant. "What evidence do you have that we need to change anything? Our patients are going home functionally improved and happy with our care."

"Your patients are exhausting what little bit of coverage they have for rehabilitation in their stay on your program. And they are going home ignorant to the fact that they could have been discharged earlier with an outpatient program that would have conserved their benefits and gotten them to the same level physically. Some of them are getting billed for equipment that is no longer covered under their plans but none of you have bothered to check that. The hospital lost $30,000 last reporting period on your unit alone in spite of a full census. That is money that could have been used to hire additional staff had it not been squandered by your inattention to the changing environment. That additional staff just might be in the Social Work Department, Reenie. An extra staff person that could take some of the weight off your shoulders which perhaps could prevent errors in judgment like including irrelevant information on an incident report," Frank on a roll, waved the report on Violet Mason's fall in front of the group.

"Irrelevant information that could open the hospital up for an unnecessary lawsuit by a patient and her family who will waste valuable energy looking for someone to blame rather than concentrating on resolution of their loss and grief so that they can get on with their lives. And the hospital, of course, would settle out of court to avoid the kind of publicity that managed care companies are slobbering over to keep us out of their networks, which would in turn keep us from getting paid for any patients, which would in turn close the doors here. And I do believe, folks, that would have a definite impact on your ability to continue to care for patients. Yep, you have got some definite fixing to do."

"I cannot believe your attitude, young man. In my day, an administrator would treat patients and staff alike with respect. You don't know the meaning of the word," Dr. Oliviero sneered.

"I understand that what I am saying may not seem respectful, Dr. I absolutely understand that. But I happen to think lying to you and pretending that you could go on doing things the same old way would be the ultimate disrespect. And I agree with you, you deserve better. I'm going to leave you all to discuss your ideas for improving patient care within the current environment. Take this whole morning, I'll have lunch sent in to you. Just remember this. The only thing you get from digging in your heels is two broken ankles. Let me say it one more time: The way you are providing care is broken, my friends. See what you can do to fix it." Frank stood up abruptly and clicked out of the meeting. The team sat in silence for a minute before clamoring to respond to the administrator's comments.

• • • • •

Reenie prepared for her weekly group with the stroke patients. She was distracted still, chewing on her new reports and on Pearman's proposal that the team hold "virtual" conferences. Reenie wondered how long it would be before this group would be held by computer, everybody linking up from their homes, able to see words and maybe faces, but not able to reach over and touch the hand of those who might shed a tear or two in the telling of their story. Touch would be a terrible thing to take out of healing, but its loss was beginning to seem inevitable. Heck, someday the patients themselves would be virtual. Reenie chuckled to herself, choosing not to share her ruminations with those group members wandering in. They already knew enough about the changing nature of health care, no use burdening them further.

"Great. I see you all brought items for the life review today," Reenie was pleased as she surveyed the bundles brought in by the group members. "Who wants to start?"

"I will," Violet volunteered readily. She passed around her scrapbook as she described her life as a dancer, starting with her first class when she was three, through the years and years of training and practice, right up to her most recent triumph as principal in the last production.

"And how does it feel," Reenie probed gently, "to know you will not dance again."

"What are you talking about?" Violet almost bolted out of her chair toward the social worker. "I will dance again."

"Well, of course you will find ways to express yourself in dance again, but how does it feel to know you will not be the principal, you will not take the stage again."

"You are lying. Stop it! You know I will dance again. You know I will! Just as soon as I get rid of this stick." Violet shoved her platform away from her, sending it clattering to the tile. Reenie was surprised by the depth of Violet's reaction, but quickly recovered.

"I'm sorry. Yes, you will dance again. How does it feel right now, just right now, while you cannot." She would have to move slowly with this one. She clearly had a lot to lose, and she was well defended against the possibility. Reenie was amazed once more at the power of denial.

Analysis

The chapter narrative begins with the social worker, Reenie feeling hurt and perplexed by Carolyn's increasing anger toward her. Reenie is relying on previous boundaries and relationships which protect her from examining the profound changes that are taking place in the organizational environment of the hospital. Carolyn is angry about the changes that are impending and wonders how it will affect her professional tasks. She notes that "everything's faster now, Reenie. You've got to step it up." Like Reenie, she is intuitively responding to a variety of issues but seems incapable of an analytic problem-solving approach. They both are unproductive in their responses and displace their anger on each other and Josh, the young rehabilitation specialist who appears, in their eyes, to be unresponsive to the calamities of change. The narrative focuses on two ethical issues. One is the ethical dilemma of patient confidentiality as personal information is posted on patient doors. The other is the intrusion of the managed care system that is affecting the clinical decisions about patient care felt by the team.

This is illustrated in the narrative by the social worker who cannot adequately express to the team major dilemmas that have been presented in the first three chapters. She has abdicated her authority in decision making to those she perceives as having more important skills and, as such, she has lost her ability to be effective in interprofessional relationships and team functioning. This has lessened her influence with the team. This could have been a good opportunity to use social work skills to identify ethical conflicts and analyze team functioning in a more systematic manner. A collaboratory model is the only way difficult and pertinent ethical problems can be examined. The main benefit of this is that communication among team members will begin to take place. When the team in the narrative finally does come together, it is in anticipation that the doctor will "fix things up" because this is how things happened in the past. Guidelines for resolving ethical dilemmas are now part of the NASW (1996) revised Code of Ethics. Reamer (1998) points out that the revisions of the NASW (1996) Code of Ethics include resources social workers should consider when they face ethical conflicts. This includes ethical theory, literature on ethical decision-making strategies, social work practice theory, and research as well as relevant laws and regulations and other relevant codes of ethics. The code could have offered Reenie an opportunity to examine issues relating to privacy and interdisciplinary collaboration as well as a supportive basis to challenge funding limits of managed care contracts. Reamer suggests that the profession must then intensify its efforts about the new revisions to the NASW Code of Ethics in order for social workers to be able to adequately use the code for new ethical conflicts that are arising due to technical developments and financial arrangements that are greatly affecting practice delivery.

In examining some of the patient issues, Violet begins the process of poststroke adjustment. The first thing that is noticeable is that Violet's behavior appears to have changed. Violet has become demanding and rude as she is concentrating on a task of reviewing her past as a "way to deal with the present and move to the future." The strain of family caregiving is evident in this segment with her husband's difficulty in dealing with a person who has experienced both physical and emotional changes.

Burack-Weiss (1995) points out that individuals are living with chronic illnesses that would have been considered fatal as little as a decade ago. While they may function, they also rely on those close to them to meet some of their daily needs. This type of caregiving has been primarily the responsibility of women. Men take this responsibility when illness affects a spouse or there is no woman available to help. The stress of caregivers is much documented in the literature. Little is known about the stresses and strains of caregiving among young married couples, especially husbands. It is not surprising that Jack's need for support was not a key issue with the treatment team. You might assume that the team was too concerned about holding on to known patient support services and that creativity and new programs can only be developed when the environment is stable. Poststroke patients have been shown to experience a variety of mood and behavioral changes as a result of brain injury. These changes include inappropriate responses such as laughing and crying disproportionate to internal and external stimuli (Mukand, Kaplan, Senno, and Bishop 1996) to depression and anxiety (Castillo, Schultz, and Robinson 1995). In addition to feeling the burden of caregiving, Jack must now contend with personality changes in his wife. Tension arises between the two as Violet is involved in a project for her support group for poststroke patients. Jack has no support group to help him deal with the changes he is experiencing. There was no discussion during the family conference about the behavioral and psychological changes that may occur poststroke. Nor was there any discussion about the effect of the stroke on the marriage of Violet and Jack. Why do you think that was? Similar to Violet's change in behavior, the changing nature of authority from medical to administrative affects the behavior of Dr. Oliviero. Dr. Oliverio confronts Frank Pearman in a hostile manner as he stands firm in his territory trying to affirm his role in determiing discharge dates for his patients. Dr. Oliviero has no support group to help him "review the past as a way to deal with the present and move to the future." Frank Pearman responds that discharge dates are "dictated by managed care experts integrating empirical data with unique patient information." This statement emphasizes the shifting authority in the hospital. Frank Pearman does not consider the doctor as head of the team. The doctor's judgment about patient care based on clinical needs must now bow down to administrative expertise. To make matters worse, Mr. Pearman views the support groups in Dr. Oliviero's office as social gatherings and thus further emphasizes the changes that administrative control might have on physician practice. Interestingly, they both leave the confrontation believing that their approach is the right thing to do for patients. Readers are left to wonder whether either approach is the right thing to do.

The use of computers to provide and store patient information presents another type of ethical dilemma. There appears to be a proposal for a "virtual team meeting." While Reenie and Carolyn are trying to understand how a computer can replace a team meeting, Josh is more accepting of the use of computers and is fascinated about staff working "like a chat room on the net." New uses of technology can replace human contact. Younger professionals are much more attuned to technology and accepting of its possibilities. On the other hand, protocols called "critical pathways" to define treatment appropriateness are also replacing human decision making by using standardized models of practice as guidelines. The team regards all new ideas as Frank's ideas for excluding the needs of the patient, although clearly that is not the case. Another change the team members must adapt to is a cost justification of their unit. Josh, the rehabilitation specialist, is surprised to learn that social work never charges for service. Carolyn challenges Reenie to explain how she is going to show that she saves money since she doesn't make any. Reenie gives an excellent justification of the role of social work but is disheartened that her own team members do not appreciate or understand her contribution. The scene ends with the team members reinforcing their own value and importance to the hospital. They feel justified that they cannot accept the benefits of any kind of change. They seem unaware that their skills may not be as valued as they believe they are, and thus continue to support each other's denial about the changes that are taking place in the hospital.

Violet begins to test out her mobility with Steve, the plumber. She is demanding of him and even rude. Steve appears perplexed by seeing two images of her—one is of a young woman who is disabled and brash and the other is of a woman who had an important role in life and is still involved in that role. He can integrate these images well and relates to both the past and present situation of Violet. It is possible that his experiences in Vietnam made him acutely sensitive to tragedy and destruction of young people. He intuitively senses a person's need for both physical as well as emotional safety. To this extent, he provides a model of supportive attention. He demonstrates his ability to compromise as he uses the therapist's specifications to save Violet's bathroom and make it safe.

The final scene focuses on the group. Violet volunteers to go over her scrapbook. Reenie misunderstands the importance of the scrapbook and gently asks, "How does it feel to know you will not dance again?" While this statement is an accurate interpretation of what a social worker would expect a poststroke patient to grapple with, it also reflects Reenie's inability to understand the effects of denial. This is an interesting reflection because Reenie has not been able to recognize or deal with the power of her own denial in her ability to accept change. This denial stirs her feelings of loss and grief as she ruminates about computers replacing the art of communication on a face-to-face basis. She is blind, however, to the idea that other people using different methods of communication or accomplishments feel the same loss and grief when their primary mode of expression is altered. Perhaps Violet's reliance on a cane or walker is as much an intrusion into her area of expertise as the use of computer models and electronic communication interferes with Reenie's expertise in human interactions.

What are some of the issues Reenie is struggling with? She has voiced her concerns (at least to herself) about patient confidentiality and information sharing. Why has it been so difficult for her to articulate these issues to the team? Solomon and Mellor (1992) note that barriers within the interdisciplinary team are usually related to the acceptance of a functional team. This includes a respect for others and the ability to share power. There are times when medical knowledge and expertise is the critical component, but at others times, another discipline's expertise becomes crucial. Recognizing which discipline should take a leadership position at any given time is a skill that is needed by each team member. Solomon and Mellor suggest that the following factors are needed to make the interdisciplinary team work: (1) Members need to believe in the interdisciplinary model (many times they are only interdisciplinary in name and workup); (2) every discipline tends to believe that it is not only the hardest working, most stressed discipline, but also the most capable and caring. Professional respect includes the recognition that this belief is invalid—all disciplines have their own types of obstacles and struggles; (3) team members must be able to disagree and to accept that under some circumstances, solutions may not exist; and (4) the team cannot be too large or a loss of group dynamics will take place and each discipline will return to a self-serving stance (183–184).

Saltz (1992) believes one of the first tasks of an interdisciplinary team is to gain a comprehensive assessment of the patient in order to provide data and impressions for discussion in the initial team meeting. Each team member has a unique and overlapping role in evaluation. This multidimensional assessment forms the basis of an optimal rehabilitation plan. Interdisciplinary health teams operate in an organizational context which may dictate their structure and mission and the defined roles of each member. Norms for individual behavior and the group as a whole must be balanced with attachment to professional reference groups. The patient and his or her family are also part of the team. Team efforts must be coordinated with the family to avoid giving conflicting messages. Sands (1989) views the interdisciplinary team as a culture. Interdisciplinary teams are part of cultures in which interactions are patterned, rules are employed, specialized vocabulary is used, and meaning is contextualized. Unique professional cultures require adaptation of team and understanding of their language. Mellor and Solomon (1992) note that differences in individual members, as in the development of any group, have to be resolved as the group moves toward cohesion. This is especially difficult when there are different disciplines: "Each discipline or profession has a different status in the eyes of the world—medicine is accorded more deference than the others, nursing vies with social work" (207). Additionally, stage of career, level and type of credentials, organization and administration of each discipline, clinical experience, and licensing all affect the development of a team. Terminology and use of jargon can also be problematic. Social workers may use the words *social support networks* differently from nurses, notations on charts can have different meanings, dehumanizing jargon can create misunderstandings. The interdisciplinary team can be a battleground for different disciplines or a battle of turf. Role blurring is a real threat. Teams respond by underscoring their specialized expertise, using more jargon or retreating from sharing. Membership in an interdisciplinary team is not always comfortable, not always easy and demands much from its members. Teams also must not get so comfortable with themselves that they lose the flexibility that results from each discipline being able to question the others.

Abramson (1984) points out that members of interdisciplinary teams also have a moral responsibility to their own professional values. Sometimes this may interfere with the group's decisions. On one hand, effective team action will mean some compromises must be made. On the other hand, each team member "must carry out his/her assignment in accordance with his/her own standard of excellence and code of ethics" (39). Conflicts of obligations can also take place when the social worker has obligations to the patient, the team, personal moral principles and beliefs, and to outside forces that affect patient functioning. The social worker's primary responsibility is to the client; but to enable what is best for the client, collaboration with other parties is necessary. Much of the conflict that was depicted in the narrative focused around the changing nature of the interdisciplinary team as a result of the influence of managed care protocols. In order for this team to begin the process of rebuilding itself and dealing with major changes, team members must first agree to formulate the problem. The next series of exercises will help you learn these skills.

Practice Skills

Client

1. What interventions were needed to assist the client and her husband in making effective role changes?
2. What services could have been offered to address the needs of the caregiver?

Social Worker

1. How might the social worker have asserted her authority in decision making?

2. What social work interventions with the team and with the system might have enhanced the social worker's ability to continue to provide needed services? What role does denial play in her ability to implement these interventions?

Team

1. Use Solomon and Mellor's (1992) model of team formation described on page 106 of this text to analyze the members' belief in interdisciplinary teams, their professional respect for each other, their ability to express their conflicts, and the composition of the group as it affects their dynamics.
2. All the players in this chapter find themselves embroiled in conflict. Burns (1989) identifies the integral role of effective communication in avoiding and effectively managing conflict. He identifies fifteen tactics virtually guaranteed to ensure bad communication and conflict:
   a. Truth (you are right and the other person is wrong)
   b. Blame
   c. Martyrdom
   d. Put-down
   e. Hopelessness
   f. Demandingness (without directly identifying what is desired)
   g. Denial
   h. Passive-Aggression
   i. Self-blame
   j. Helping (try to solve the problem rather than listening)
   k. Sarcasm
   l. Scapegoating
   m. Defensiveness
   n. Counterattack
   o. Diversion

   Which of these tactics is used by the characters in Chapter 3? What are the results when these communication tactics are used?
3. Conversely, learning to actively listen is a key to Burns' (1989) five secrets of effective communication.

   The Disarming Technique: Find some truth in what the other person is saying, even if you feel convinced that what they are saying is totally wrong, unreasonable, irrational, or unfair.

   Empathy: Thought empathy—paraphrase the other person's words; and Feeling empathy—acknowledge how the other person is probably feeling.

Inquiry: Ask gentle, probing questions to learn more about what the other person is thinking and feeling.
I "feel" statements: Express your feelings with *I feel* statements rather than *you* statements.
Stroking: Find something genuinely positive to say to the other person.

Did any of the characters use any of the five effective communication skills? If so, who and with what result? How might these skills have been used to diffuse conflict and support effective communication among team members?

4

Change: Crisis, Conflict, Opportunities, and Rehabilitation

"Well, we might as well just sell stock in our services and provide care to the highest bidder." Dr. Oliviero was red-faced again.

"Do you think it is true? You really think they would go through with this?" Carolyn was hoping against hope.

"Nothing drives anything anymore except the almighty dollar." Reenie joined in the fray.

"You are absolutely right, Reenie," Dr. Oliviero continued, "Unfortunately, I think there is an excellent possibility that it might be true. It would be a sad day. A sad day, indeed. But in this day and age in health care? A definite possibility. The for-profit jackals are circling anything with the faintest scent of money. It is nauseating." Dr. Oliviero began to get distressed.

"I don't even know if I would want to continue working here if it happens," Reenie was distraught.

"You're leaving?" Josh, as usual, joined the conversation a little behind.

"Not unless we merge with HealthOne," Reenie tried to catch him up.

"Merge with HealthOne? This hospital? Not a chance." Josh was certain that a merger was far too sophisticated a business maneuver for this not-for-profit hospital.

"Don't be too sure," Carolyn plopped the newspaper article on the counter in front of Josh. The physical therapist grabbed the paper and began poring over the article.

"Does it say what they are going to call it? Metro HealthOne, or maybe HealthOne, Metropolitan, or . . ." Josh seemed excited.

"My goodness, Josh, don't dig our grave yet?"

"You're overreacting, Carolyn. This could be big."

"It's going to be big all right. One big headache," Dr. Oliviero began. "I've heard it from my colleagues. We won't know whether patients are coming or going, and no one will care that we don't. We'll have to know what plan the patient is on, and get precertification from somebody who has absolutely no medical training but can type 120 words a minute every time we want to take the patient's blood pressure. I'll probably have to fill out some form if we want to take their temperature as well. It will be big, all right. The biggest pain in the . . ."

"Hey, it says they would probably combine the rehabilitation program in one facility or the other. Think it would be here or at HealthOne?"

"Josh, we don't care where it might be. We care that this hospital maintains its commitment to service and quality. I don't think HealthOne shares that same mission."

"Yeah, but they have state-of-the-art equipment at all their facilities. We can't even get a decent equipment closet going. They have aquatics at all their locations."

"The patients don't stay long enough to dip their big toe in that almighty pool. They are out the door about five minutes after the ink is dry on their admissions papers."

The fax machine on the unit started to whir as the group stood discussing the relative merits of a possible merger of the hospital with such a large for-profit corporation. Carolyn began to sort through the pile of papers spewing out, becoming more agitated with each page. "At the rate we're going, it may not matter whether we merge with HealthOne or not," Carolyn announced. "Look at this, Dr. Oliviero. We have to document medical necessity for all the procedures performed this week—outliers!"

Dr. Oliviero shuffled through the papers, then cocked his wrist and let the whole pile fly for the nearest trashcan. "Someone else can play with those. And some guy in his plush leather chair can worry about mergers. In fact, I don't want to discuss it anymore. Carolyn, let's take care of our patients."

Dr. Oliviero marched off to the first patient's room, his faithful nurse right behind him.

• • • • •

Jack unlocked the door slowly, his movements slowed as much by dread as weariness. He was not getting much sleep these days. Violet was not sleeping well, and when Violet didn't sleep well, no one within earshot slept well. So, he was tired. More tired than he could remember being. More tired than those early days when he was trying to get the company up and going. There were many long hours and tremendous work then, but there was something to show for it at the end of each day. These days he felt more like he was marching in place. A very muddy place, at that. Violet still needed so much, and Jack just could not keep neglecting the company to cater to her every whim. Violet wanted attention when she wanted it and not one second later. Jack supposed she had always been that way, but now . . . well, now it made him tired. Jack leaned heavily into the door, preparing himself for the evening. He was greeted by the sound of a hammer clanging against porcelain. The noise reverberated in his head as Violet greeted him at the door. "Jack, you're late."

"Work. Way behind at work, honey. How was your day?" Jack tried to focus his attention on Violet as the banging continued from the bathroom. He glanced at his watch. It was well past 8 P.M.

"Great. The ballet delivered this," Violet waved folded stationery in front of his face as a loud crash jolted the floor.

"What in the world was that?" Jack asked, moving past Violet.

"It was an invitation to the annual charity event. They sent it over by courier."

"Not that. That noise. What is the noise?"

"What should I wear? Something that doesn't show this brace." Violet lifted her skirt to examine the custom-made orthosis bracing her ankle. She seemed oblivious to the noise.

"Is something wrong with the plumbing?" Jack made his way into the master bedroom and headed for the bathroom. He was almost to the door when Steve stuck his head around the door.

"Evening, Mr. Mason."

"Steve? What are you doing here at this hour?"

"Trying to get out of your hair as soon as possible. Your misses wants her bathroom pronto, you know."

"Yes, I'm sure she does. I thought you would be finished by now. Just putting up some rails. How long does that take?"

"Rails? Oh, no, sir. We're remodeling."

"Remodeling? What do you mean, remodeling?"

"I spoke with the therapist, like you suggested, Mr. Mason, and this is what we came up with," Steve answered, unrolling a crumpled, roughly drawn blueprint. "If we move the commode here to this spot, we have room to widen the shower enough that I can build in seating. Now, I couldn't do much with the tub, but we are looking at a device that will lower and lift that I think I can install here if we move that linen closet to this space out here in the bedroom."

"What do you mean that spot? That spot is my dressing area. All I want is some rails, man. What in the world are you doing?" Jack was incredulous.

"You said to talk to the therapist and do what needed to be done."

"Rails. That's all. Where to put the rails. Now is no time to remodel. I don't understand why you are doing all this."

"Your misses likes a shower and a bath, she said. Just trying to make it safe for her, Mr. Mason."

"We just need some rails. Put them in now, take them down when she no longer needs them. Is that so hard to understand?"

"She's going to need this for a long time. I'd say that arm is not going to come back, Mr. Mason. These changes are for good."

"You don't know what you are talking about. This is temporary. It has to be temporary. I can't take it much longer." Jack's voice rose more than he intended.

"What are you saying, Jack?" Violet's voice was small and frightened behind Jack. He had not meant for her to hear him, had not meant to lose his temper. He whirled around and brushed past her.

"Look, Steve. It's late. Pack your stuff up and go home. I'll talk with the folks at the hospital when I get the chance. I'm going to bed."

"Whatever you say, sir." Violet watched quietly as Steve packed his tools. Jack sat on the end of the bed, rubbing his temples. Steve tipped his hat to her as he walked past them on his way out the door. "Good night, folks. I'll see ya when I see ya." Jack brushed by Violet into the bathroom, tripping over a plumbing part leaning against the counter. Jack slammed the door shut.

• • • • •

Reenie trudged toward the nursing station. She was not looking forward to helping Carolyn with the paperwork that had been fished out of the trashcan. Carolyn had paged her to say that it simply had to be done, and that some of it had to do with the ordering of equipment, which, of course, was Reenie's responsibility. That and a million other tasks that kept her from actually talking to her patients these days. She spent more time with a number two pencil in her hand than the frail hand of a frightened family member. She thought some days about hanging it up, opening that bait shop in the Ozarks that sounded so tranquil. But she knew that, no matter what the system, the patients were better off for her being there. She had to believe that. It was what kept one foot moving in front of the other on days like this. As she approached the unit, she heard the familiar cadence of one of Dr. Oliviero's sermons.

"And I will not be insulted by having to explain why I need a CBC count on this patient. Any imbecile can look at my note in the chart and understand clearly what is necessary. It is an insult to my intelligence and to my professionalism. I will not have it."

"Dr. O, please. I know this is a pain. I know we shouldn't have to do it. But Pearman is breathing down my neck. I have a splitting headache. The patient in 34 is in the bathroom and I have no one to get her back to bed so I have got to do it myself. Could you please just sign these forms? I will fill them in later." Carolyn rarely spoke to Dr. Oliviero in this fashion, but today she was practically begging for mercy. She was so tired. Dr. Oliviero was in no mood for compromise, however.

"I will not sign these forms. It is demeaning to be asked."

"I know it is, but these days you sign them or the patient does not get what is needed."

"I will not practice like this. I refuse. I will close my practice down before I will sign these."

"Please, Dr. O. For me. Just sign them for me," Carolyn was embarrassing herself but she was desperate for cooperation.

"I will not. I will stop practicing medicine before I will sign these insulting forms."

Carolyn glared at Dr. Oliviero, then brushed past him into the nurse's lounge, slamming the door behind her.

Dr. Oliviero threw his hands up in the air. "That's it," he declared. "That is it. I will begin now to close my practice. I will not go on like this."

"Dr. Oliviero, you don't mean that!" Reenie had never heard the physician make such a threat.

"I most certainly do mean it. What is the point, Reenie?"

"The patients, doctor. The patients need you no matter what system they are stuck with."

"I am no longer allowed to do anything for my patients. Medicine is no longer practiced by doctors. It is directed by bureaucrats and inept medical profession dropouts. I will not be a patsy for some corporate board sitting at the table dictating when a patient needs to have their blood drawn. They want to practice medicine in that fashion, they come right down here and do it themselves. It is insulting to me, to Carolyn, to you . . . this is a sad day."

"Physicians like you are our only hope, Dr. Oliviero. Who is going to change the system if you stop practicing?"

"This is one heck of a system, Reenie. I don't know if changing it is even possible. Such complex reasons for the mess we're in. And money-hungry suits fueling the hysteria for their own financial gain. I don't know who is big enough to fight it."

"You are, Dr. Oliviero. I know you are. You and your colleagues have to speak out about what is happening."

"I'm tired. And I don't even know if I know what is going on."

"Get informed. Get active in the local Physicians in Managed Care Group. If you don't, that grandson of yours that is in medical school will never know what it is to practice the art of medicine. He will be another mechanistic businessman in the business of health care."

"You are not playing fair now, Reenie. Let's leave my grandson out of this. And what about you? What are you doing to make a difference in this whole mess? What do you recommend we do next?"

"Well, I think we need to demand some changes."

"Yes, well, what shall we ask for?"

"Well, I support the social workers' organizations, their stand in this."

"What do they say, Reenie? What do they suggest we do to change the situation?"

"I don't know the details, Dr. Oliviero. I'm not as informed as I need to be. I just know we need you to have a fighting chance. Your patients need you and I need you."

"Alright, alright. I'm just tired today. I'll make a deal with you. You get some information from your colleagues and share it with me. I will attend the next meeting of the Physicians in Managed Care before I throw in the towel."

"Deal. Thank you."

"No long-term promises."

"I understand," Reenie glanced at her watch as Carolyn finally emerged from the lounge. "Oh, I've got to run. I'm meeting Jack Mason in my office in five minutes."

Reenie saw Mr. Mason standing outside her office door as she rounded the corner. She had hoped for some time to collect her thoughts before he arrived but that kind of time was a luxury she could not afford these days. She would have to call on whatever reserves she could muster to get her through this last stretch of the day. She was concerned about the Masons. Mr. Mason had been vague when he called requesting a meeting. Something to do with the safety specifications for the bathroom. She had tried to steer him to the occupational therapy department, but he was insistent on a meeting with Reenie.

"Hi, Mr. Mason. Sorry I am running a little behind today," Reenie shifted her armful of papers to open her office door. "Come on in and have a seat." Jack followed Reenie in through the door as she hurriedly scraped more mounds of paper off of the available seating in the small office. "What can I do for you today?"

"You can call off your plumbing hounds!" Jack laughed, not as easily as he had in the days before Violet's discharge from the hospital.

"Plumbing hounds?" Reenie was mystified.

"This fellow who you asked to install rails in the bathroom has become a one-man demolition derby."

"The occupational therapist gave you a list of numbers . . ." Reenie was still trying to sort things out.

"I don't mind him putting up rails. Heck, I don't even mind a bench or something in the tub for Violet, but what I don't like is his insinuation that these changes need to be permanent."

"What changes are you referring to, Mr. Mason?"

"The changes you all apparently told him to make in my bathroom."

Reenie shuffled through the scraps of paper on her desk, looking for her notes related to Violet Mason. "Oh, okay," she responded, zeroing in on a scribbled message from the occupational therapist. "It looks like the OT talked with a plumber you hired to make the bathroom accessible. Let's see, he was asking about the possibility of a lift for the bathtub so that Mrs. Mason could take a bath rather than a shower?"

"See, that is exactly what I am talking about. Why in heaven's name would we need a thing like that for the short while that Violet will not be able to take a bath? She can surely take a shower until she gets her strength back in her leg and in that arm."

"Mr. Mason, tell me what you understand about your wife's leg and arm." Reenie began to probe gently.

"I know what you all told us. That she needed therapy, still needs therapy, to recover the use of her arm. The leg has already come way back."

"Yes, you are right. Mrs. Mason needs continued rehabilitation. She will continue to learn compensatory strategies to deal with what has been lost in motor functioning. But she will probably never be 100 percent again."

"Violet will be 100 percent again. She wouldn't settle for less than 100 percent. You have never seen her dance, Reenie. If you had seen her dance, you would know. She will not go out on that stage again until she is fully, 100 percent recovered."

"She will probably never dance again, Mr. Mason. Not as the primary dancer with the Metropolitan Ballet. Her leg and her arm will not come back 100 percent."

"You don't know what you are saying. Dancing is Violet's life. She will shrivel up and die if she cannot dance. She will dance again."

"I know these are hard facts to hear, Mr. Mason. But you must hear them, for Mrs. Mason's sake. She is not going to recover the full use of her arm and leg. She is not going to dance with the ballet company again. She needs your support in coming to terms with that."

"I cannot accept what you are saying, ma'am. I'm sorry, but you are wrong."

"You may not be able to hear me right now, but know that you and Mrs. Mason both have a world of adjustments to make. Life will go on, it will even be good again. But it will be different."

"Good for Violet means dancing, being whole physically. How can I, uh, she, take it if she is not physically whole. She won't need that hideous brace forever."

"She may. Change is hard, Mr. Mason. You are absolutely right that this will be hard for Mrs. Mason and for you. But denial that changes are needed just makes it harder. Mrs. Mason feels guilty, you feel frustrated . . ."

"This nutty plumber. He's talking about taking out my dressing area so that he can install this lift gizmo."

"It could be a great idea. It could certainly allow Mrs. Mason more freedom in the bathroom. Let me call the occupational therapist . . ."

"So you are telling me that this bozo is right, that the whole bathroom has to be redesigned? Violet is not going to get better."

"She may get better, Mr. Mason, but she is not going to get 'well.' I'm sure there are things that could be done to make the bathroom space usable for both you and your wife. I'll just get the OT over here."

"The changes are permanent."

"Your wife will have permanent deficits, yes."

"Never mind, Reenie. Don't call the OT. Let the madman plumber do what has to be done. So be it. Just don't expect me to stay around and watch it. I'm not the man for the job."

Reenie watched Mr. Mason's back disappear beyond the office door. She had seen it so many times before, so many family members at the moment of realization that change was inevitable. She felt for each of them in this situation, and knew they each had to find their own strength. She hoped Jack Mason knew where to look for his.

She glanced around at the chaos that had become her office. In one corner, neglected and ignored, sat the computer that Pearman insisted everyone must have. She recalled her conversation with Dr. Oliviero, and her promise to research the managed care positions of professional social work organizations. She pulled out a file of newsletters, each bearing the Web addresses she had filed away carefully, thinking they might come in handy someday if she ever learned to surf the net. Another glance at her to-do list and the pile of papers to finish for Mr. Pearman told her clearly, today is the day. She rolled reluctantly over to the computer and tried her hand at the sign-on instructions taped to the front of the monitor. This would link her up to the hospital's network which would then give her access to the Internet and to all the social work references out there in cyberspace. At least, that's what she hoped would happen.

Reenie typed in the password carefully recorded in her notes from the computer training center. A message blinked back at her. Log-in incorrect. How could that be? She typed the password again at the prompt. Again the same message. Irritated, she called the computer training center help line. The voice on the other phone explained matter of factly that she was first to enter her name code, then the password. Reenie was certain if this had been part of the training she would have written it down, but she was as polite as possible to the computer nerd on the other end. She dutifully typed in her name code, hit enter, then entered her password. A whirring noise told her she must have done something right. For the next few minutes she struggled through her notes, moving clumsily from one screen to the next, searching her way toward cosmic wisdom on managed care and social work. She entered the words at the search prompt and waited for the magic answers to appear. A note flashed across her screen announcing the finding of 10,306 items. She spent the next 15 minutes staring at a small blinking hourglass sitting in the middle of her screen. Her pager went off 6 times. She waited another five minutes, and still no further response from the machine. The blinking hourglass continued to mock her. In disgust she gave up, flipping the power switch and vowing to trek to the library at the very first opportunity. She would just have to do things the old-fashioned way.

• • • • •

Jack rubbed his temples as he tried to concentrate on the work in front of him. Jack needed to be at the office but someone had to babysit. Not Violet so much as the blasted plumber. He was like a terrorist sitcom character who moved in and would not go away. He had been working on the bathroom for days now, and apparently he could do nothing quietly. The bathroom was unusable at this point. Violet and Jack had been relegated to the guest bath while Steve finished his masterpiece. Worse yet, Violet seemed to like the bozo. Actually, it was some relief to Jack. Steve seemed content to field Violet's onslaught of questions, didn't seem to mind her intrusions. Violet needed constant attention. That had always been true. Jack had been more than happy to lavish her with attention in the past, but now he was distracted, worried. The hospital bills were extensive, even with insurance. There were so many "disallowed" items. And Jack had taken so much time away from the business that profits had begun to slip. The company was still young enough to require the founder's touch to keep investors and employees interested and inspired. Jack simply had to take a break from Violet and turn his attention to business matters at hand.

Jack began entering the numbers into the computer one more time, having already lost his place when interrupted by Violet. He hit the final enter button just as a loud crash, followed by a scream from Violet and muffled yells from Steve broke his fragile concentration. His finger slipped off enter and landed on delete. Jack jerked it off the button but not before he saw 30 minutes of data disappear from his screen. He picked up the keyboard and smashed it to the floor, tripping over it as he headed out the study door to find out what newest commotion had caused this latest glitch. He rounded the corner into the bedroom to find Violet sprawled on the end of the bed, hysterical.

"Violet, what is the matter? What has happened here?"

Violet tried to answer, but could not get any actual words out. Jack ran to the edge of the bed before he realized she was laughing and not crying. "Violet, for goodness sake. What are you laughing at?" Violet could only gesture somewhat helplessly toward the bathroom. Jack whirled around to the doorway. It was then that he heard the sound of rushing water. Steve was hunched under the sink, soaking wet, working frantically. Above him, a stream of water shot straight in to the air from the spot where the hot water handle should have been.

"What in the . . ." Jack sputtered.

"Oh, hey, Mr. Mason," Steve bumped his head as he raised up to greet Jack. He was surrounded by expensive towels stitched with the Mason monogram now soaking up the rising water on the expensive tile. "Slight problem here."

"Why does the bathroom look like the Poseidon Adventure?"

"Problem with the handle there. Almost have this taken care of." Steve made the last turn of the wrench which stopped the flow of water into the bathroom. He sat up, laughing. "Had a little trouble getting the old handle off of there."

Jack was livid. This was absurd. He was working his tail off to keep things going while a madman destroyed his house and all his wife could do was laugh hysterically. "You are supposed to be fixing the bathroom, not destroying the house. What in the world was wrong with the handle that was on there? It was practically brand new. Imported from Italy. You remember, Violet—you found them in that little shop last time we were in Europe. A perfectly good handle."

"Beautiful handle. I wrapped it and stored it under here, Mr. Mason. But Mrs. Mason can't turn it off with that one hand right now. Can't get a good grip on it. She needs one like this." Steve held up an adapted handle for Jack's inspection.

"I don't want that one. I want the one that was on there."

Violet found her voice. "Jack, don't be so petty. I can't use the old one right now. Steve says I need the adapted one."

"I don't believe you, Violet. Are you just going to give up just like that? You drove me nuts looking for just the right hardware for the bathroom. I think that is why we went to Italy in the first place. And now it's no big deal?"

"Jack, it is just a handle on a sink. It's not like you to overreact like this."

"They say you are never going to dance again, Violet. You just going to give up on that, too? Does that make you laugh like a hyena, too?" The pain on Violet's face shot through Jack's heart like a poison arrow. In that moment, he knew for certain what he had thought in the social worker's office. He simply could not do this. He strode to the closet, pulled out his overnight bag and began to stuff clothing into it.

"Jack, what are you doing?" Violet watched in disbelief, still perched on the end of the bed.

"I've got to get some work done, Violet. I can't work with that going on," Jack jerked his head toward the bathroom, where Steve stood awkwardly studying the sink handle. "I've got to get some sleep. I'll be in touch." Jack zipped the bag, and headed for the door, never looking back.

"So, Mr. Mason, you want the new handle or the old handle? Your call," Steve hollered after him.

"By all means, put a new handle on the sink. Put one in the kitchen while you're at it. Change every handle in the whole place while you're at it, why don't you?" Jack never looked back.

Steve flipped the handle in his hand. "The mister just needs a little rest, Mrs. Mason. He'll be all right."

"He's gone, Steve."

"Gone for now."

"Gone for good. I know him. He's not cut out for this."

"You going to be okay?"

"What choice do I have?"

"Yes, ma'am. I'll pack up my tools and finish this up tomorrow, what do you say?"

"Yes, that will be fine. And, Steve . . ."

"Yes, ma'am?"

"Put in the new handles, please. As soon as possible."

"Yes ma'am, will do." Steve picked up slowly, listening to make sure Mrs. Mason was okay. When he could stall no longer, he exited the bathroom and headed for the entrance. "Good night, ma'am. I'll see ya when I see ya."

• • • • •

"So what are you saying, Josh?" Carolyn was not sure she had heard the physical therapist correctly.

"I'm leaving." Josh was nonchalant.

"Leaving for the day, leaving this unit, leaving the hospital?" Reenie tried to clarify.

"Leaving the hospital. Turned in my resignation today, gave my two weeks notice."

"Why? It was Pearman, wasn't it? He has been on everybody's back for weeks now. I don't know why any of us take it. We should all leave. Except the patients need us." Reenie sounded the familiar refrain as if she was trying to convince herself. "The patients need us, Josh."

"Well, I'm going where there are other patients who also need physical therapy."

"Where are you going?" Carolyn asked, an edge to her voice.

"I signed on with PrimaStaff to work contract wherever they want to send me. And for the bucks they are paying, trust me, I will go anywhere."

"PrimaStaff? You're going to leave here to work for a 'temp' agency? What is the attraction?"

"The money is incredible, Carolyn. And the flexibility. And they want me so bad—that counts for something. They're not like this place—you now have umpteen lunch meetings and you better stay until you get that paperwork done. I'll get paid for every minute I work."

Carolyn raised her eyebrows to Reenie. "Say, that would be a change of pace, wouldn't it?" Reenie concurred with a shake of her head.

"And I should have time for my other endeavors. Friend of mine is the clinical director at this really cool outpatient sports clinic. All the professional players go there. She's lining me up with some one-on-one training with these guys in the evenings."

"So, you're taking a job so you can increase your autograph collection?" Carolyn was getting close to surly.

"No, I'm taking a job where my salary is double and I'll be able to have a life. Might even be able to pay my student loans off."

"Money isn't everything. I could probably go somewhere else for more money, but the patients here need me . . ." Reenie trailed off, sounding a bit uncertain.

"Those guys need therapy just like these guys do. You ladies sound like sour grapes to me."

Carolyn and Reenie made guilty eye contact. "Well, it's just that we're going to miss you, Josh," Carolyn recovered first.

"Yeah, Josh, we've gotten used to having you around. We're crushed that you could even think about leaving the company of such an accomplished team." Reenie followed Carolyn's lead, even though she was quite upset.

Like she needed one more thing to deal with. She knew from experience that the team would have a contract physical therapist assigned—probably a different one each day. This person would do a competent job of providing physical therapy, but would not see him- or herself as a part of the team in any way. And the team certainly did not need that right now. Reenie felt like they were fighting for their collective lives with Pearman already. He probably would try to use this as an excuse to break up the team for good since he had no clue about the team's impact on quality of care. Reenie almost laughed out loud. Like Pearman cared about quality of care. Yeah, right. He was just another suit trying to make the biggest buck possible. And right now, Josh didn't seem that far away from him. Josh should understand that this was the worst possible time to leave the team, yet he didn't seem to care. He didn't even have the decency to apologize for his decision. Reenie was working herself into a pretty good frenzy inside her own head, only vaguely aware of the voices swirling around her. She snapped out of her reverie only when Dr. Oliviero waved his hand in front of her face.

"So, Reenie, what do you think about it?" the doctor was repeating his question.

"Oh, I just hate it. The only thing I want to hear is that it is not going to happen."

"Any chance you're going to change your mind, Joshua?"

"No, sir. I've made my decision."

"Well, Reenie, looks like we're going to have to regroup. We've lost him. This doggone managed care is changing everything."

"It's not really managed care, Dr. Oliviero. It's the opportunity . . ."

"Trust me, it is managed care." Dr. Oliviero did not want to hear any other explanation for the loss of one of the most promising young therapists he had come across in a while.

"I'm sorry, guys. It is just the chance I've been looking for to do something new. You will be all right."

"Yeah, we'll be okay, Josh. But we won't be the same." Carolyn spoke from years of surviving team changes. She did not look forward to breaking in a new member. That is, if Pearman let them hire a new member. The problems of teamwork were definitely shifting.

• • • • •

Violet checked herself in the mirror one more time. It had taken her most of the day, but she was finally ready. Discarded gowns lay crumpled on the floor in the walk-in closet, all rejected in the search for just the right dress for tonight's annual ballet charity ball. Violet had not seen her fellow company members since her accident and she was determined to look her best. She knew that all the lights would be flashing in her direction and she must reassure her company and her public. She added the long gloves, thinking them a nice touch that took attention away from her arm, still dangling uselessly. Fortunately, the formal attire hid the brace. Violet was determined to make the gala without her cane. She still tired with long distances, so she would use the wheelchair to get downstairs, then get into the van on the lift. She would have the driver deliver her to an address a couple of blocks from the gala, then wheel herself as close as she could without being seen, find a place to stash the wheelchair and wing it unassisted for the rest of the time. At the appointed hour, she would recover her wheelchair and meet the van to return home. She had been practicing walking around the house without her cane and was certain she was ready. It would have been a good sight easier to accomplish, of course, if Jack were going with her.

Jack. Violet took a deep breath. Jack. This was also the first time her friends would see her without Jack at her side. She would explain that work demanded his attention but they would know. Jack Mason had not left her side at a soiree since the night they met. Well, they could talk all they liked. Violet was not yet ready to discuss her situation. She needed to make her first public appearance as unencumbered by distractions as possible. And, who knew, with all the handsome gentlemen that made these events, she might meet someone tonight ten times the man Jack Mason turned out to be. Violet missed him terribly, having become accustomed to having a constant suitor by her side, especially one who adored her as much as Jack. As much as Jack used to, that is. He was a great disappointment to Violet. She had thought him to be strong enough to handle anything. She thought she had married a man, not a boy who would run at the first rough spot in the road. The tear rolling down her cheek brought Violet out of her reverie. She wiped her face, determined to focus on the future tonight, not on what was or might have been with the prince charming who had now ridden off into the sunset without her. Life would simply have to go on.

Violet made her way to the phone, using familiar furniture and walls for balance in a manner that had simply become habit for her. She dialed the MetroVanAssist service that Reenie had referred her to. She would allow the accessible van and assistant/driver to deliver her to the address she had selected near the gala, then carry out her plan for a "normal" entrance.

"Good evening. MetroVanAssist. How may I help you?"

"This is Violet Mason. I need a van pickup in half an hour."

"Just a moment." There was an interlude of muzak before the voice crackled back on the line. "Name again?"

"Mason. Violet Mason."

"I don't see your name on the schedule, ma'am."

"No, no. Look again. You processed my application. I have my card right here."

"Yes, ma'am, you are in the system. I pulled up your information. But we don't have you on the schedule to be picked up this evening."

"Of course you don't have me on the schedule. I'm telling you now. I need to be picked up in half an hour. Now put me on the schedule."

"Can't do that."

"What do you mean, you can't do that?"

"You have to call a day in advance for the van service, ma'am. We schedule twenty-four hours in advance."

"I don't have twenty-four hours. I have to be picked up tonight. I have to appear at the gala tonight."

"I'm sorry, but the schedule is full. We don't have a driver who can pick you up."

"What am I supposed to do? I have to be at the gala in one hour. I must be there. Do you understand that?"

"I understand, ma'am, and I'm sorry. We cannot pick you up. Do you have a friend you could call?"

"My friends are not accustomed to hauling around a wheelchair, thank you very much."

"There are some buses on each route that are wheelchair-accessible. Perhaps you could take one of those."

"How can you get a wheelchair up those steps?" Violet was amazed at the idiocy of this person.

"They lower to street level, ma'am, with a lift. Quite user-friendly. Let me connect you with the information line for MetroSystem."

Violet hung up abruptly. She did not have time to sort through the bus schedule to find some kneeling bus. She would end up looking like a fool for certain in such a contraption. She was angry and confused. What kind of van service was this? Who ever heard of having to call for a ride twenty-four hours in advance? She would have to speak with the supervisor tomorrow. Tonight she had no time. She had to figure out how she was going to get to the gala.

Violet gave it careful consideration. Her entrance was crucial. There had been media reports about her accident, but no pictures since she first went to the hospital. She must appear normal tonight. Her career depended on it, she was certain. There was only one possibility. She would have to take a cab. She could hail a cab downstairs to take her directly to the gala. That was a better idea than the van service, anyway. Make the entire ride in the cab. It wasn't really that far to go without her wheelchair. Violet was amused that she had not figured this plan out sooner. She grabbed her black evening bag and headed downstairs.

Violet wavered a bit as she locked the door, but the wall provided the balance she needed to make it to the elevator. She held on to the doors just a bit as she made her way into the elevator car. Still determined, she pushed the ground floor button. The motion of the car as it resumed its ride downward threw her off balance. She banged against the wall just a bit. She cursed the building owner for not having installed handrails in the elevator. As jerky as it was, any normal person would need to hang on. Violet had almost gotten her balance when the elevator screeched to a stop on the first floor, sending her reeling the other way. She reached toward the opposite wall, but it was too far away. She landed square on her backside in the middle of the elevator. The doors opened, and Violet startled a young couple who almost stepped into the elevator before they noticed her occupying the floor. The young man reached a hand to help her up as they both inquired as to her well-being. Violet tried to pull herself up with his help, but the weakness in her leg kept her from getting the push she needed.

"Be careful now, you must have hurt your leg in the fall," the young woman blurted before spying the brace on Violet's leg. "Oh, no, you've already hurt your leg. Is that a cast?"

"No, it's a brace. Weak leg from . . . an accident. That's all. Just a little weak."

"Here, let me help from the back. I think we can get you up." Violet was finally righted with maximum effort from the couple. "Do you need to sit down? Can we help you back to your apartment?" Violet wanted nothing but to be away from these strangers who had to lift her from the ground. She could not bear to be in their presence one second longer.

"No, thank you. I'm fine," she lied. "I am meeting a friend here. I'll be fine. You run along. And thanks for your help." Violet hugged the wall as the elevator doors closed on the worried faces. The elevator took them up and away. Violet breathed a sigh of relief. She noticed how exhausted she was. She eyed the distance to the front door, and the expanse of sidewalk to the street where a cab could be hailed. She knew she could not make it without falling again. That blasted van service. How dare they stand her up like this on the night of the gala? They clearly had no idea who she was or they would have rearranged their precious little schedule to make sure they were at her front door right now. But they were not here and Violet was. She racked her brain for a transportation solution. She knew what she would have to do, but she avoided the thought as long as possible. When she was certain that she had been hanging on to the wall around the elevator for hours and could not possibly hang on one second longer, she let it come. The only solution. She would have to attend the gala in her wheelchair. If she could get back up to her apartment, she could get in the chair, wheel back down, hail a cab, and let the driver get the chair in and out for her. So much for her "normal" entrance.

But an image flashed in her head of Liz Taylor once more in a wheelchair. The public had seen her enter and leave hospitals and public events in a wheelchair and it did not seem to affect her career. The fact that she wasn't a dancer Violet ignored for the moment because she had to. She would arrive, *á la Liz Taylor*, the delicate, beloved star, in a wheelchair. She punched the up button with the last ounce of determination she could manage.

Violet boarded the elevator, more prepared this time for its bounces and sways. She made the trip back to her floor successfully, and the wall carried her to her front door. She managed to get in the door upright and made her way to the wheelchair sitting forgotten in the library. Violet placed her bag in her lap and rolled to the full-length mirror by the door. She studied the image reflected at her. Not bad. There was an air of Liz Taylor to her appearance indeed. Her AFO was visible as the dress rode up a bit in the chair. Violet tugged and shifted until the brace was covered, making a note to adjust her dress regularly to keep the brace covered. One last look in the mirror was enough. It wasn't perfect, but it would have to do. She could not miss tonight's event.

The trip downstairs this time was uneventful except for the elevator doors banging against the wheels of Violet's chair before she could clear them. She managed to turn, push the button, and get out of the elevator on the first floor. The wide entrance door pushed open as she banged against it, and Violet was outside the building. She felt a tremendous relief and sense of freedom. She had escaped the building on her own. She knew now that she would make it to the gala. Violet Mason was back.

Violet hailed a cab after only a few tries, and the cabby was helpful in getting Violet in the taxi and the chair in the trunk. He admonished her several times, loudly, to be careful. Violet cringed, but kept moving. On the ride over, she handed him a large advance tip and explained the kind of quiet assistance she would like once they arrived at the hotel. The cabby pulled up in front of the ballroom entrance, quickly retrieved the wheelchair, helped Violet out of the taxi on the side opposite the door, and sped away, promising to return at an appointed hour to retrieve her. Violet looked up at the massive building as the cab pulled away, and for a moment she seriously considered chasing it down in her wheelchair. Panic almost overtook her before she recovered, calling on the genteel image of Ms. Taylor offering her delicate hand to her admirers as she was wheeled out to meet her fans. Of course, Liz always had someone wheeling her. Blasted Jack. That's all right, though, Violet consoled herself. It would be better, she decided, for her to wheel herself. More convincing that she was going to recover, that this wheelchair was a temporary ornament, necessary only while she regained her strength. It wasn't perfect, but she would make it work, she vowed to herself as she began to make her way through the big glass door. Her heart began to beat in rapid anticipation. She felt like a warrior coming home after battle. She was ready to receive the spoils of her toil. She was ready to be admired and envied, the principal ballerina once more. Tonight had been a long time coming and, exhausted as she was by the trip to get there, her spirit lifted as she saw familiar faces in the ballroom ahead.

Violet wheeled herself into the ballroom, preparing herself for her usual cool presentation in the face of fawning admirers. She moved just inside the door and waited for the crowd to gather. And waited. No one made a move toward her. In fact, no one even looked her way. They did not recognize her, she realized. Of course, they did not expect to see her in the wheelchair. She would need to wheel herself to a familiar group to break the ice. She spotted some of the chorus dancers in the crowd. Normally they bored her with their dreams and gushing awe. Tonight they would serve her purpose, however. A group to identify her, giving her peers time to recover and make their way to her side. Fitting, she thought. That is exactly what the chorus was supposed to do for the principals. She wheeled her way over to the dancers.

"Hello, children. How are you tonight?" She approached them as if deigning to talk to them was the most natural thing in the world.

"Beg your pardon?" The girl with the long red hair responded, her voice bordering on rude.

"I haven't seen you all in a while. I was inquiring as to your well-being. A proper formality, I believe." Violet dared not cross the line. She must speak with them yet remain reserved.

"Who . . . Violet? Violet, is that you?" The anorexic brunette was the first to recognize her, her voice registering disbelief. They all turned to stare, none of them quite making eye contact. "You . . . you're in a wheelchair." Violet detected something unexpected in the young girl's voice. It was not the admiration she had anticipated, not even the disbelief which she could understand. It was something she was not familiar with, yet had a vague sense of having felt for someone else. Her eyes stung when it hit her gut what she had heard in the girl's voice. Pity. Pity! The thought knocked Violet against the back of her wheelchair. She was off balance, unable to reply in an appropriate manner. The other dancers just stared in her direction, staring for what seemed like hours yet never making eye contact. They began to shift awkwardly.

"How astute of you to notice." Violet finally managed. With all the strength she could muster, she did a twirl-about in her chair and rolled away as quickly as possible. She would not waste her time on these ignorant girls who were too young to have known how brave and beloved Elizabeth Taylor was, being wheeled about in her wheelchair. Violet was beating such a hasty retreat that she almost ran right over the ballet director who was chatting with the organizers of the fund-raising event. He had to step forward quickly to avoid being sideswiped. Still, he did not notice who was driving the speeding wheelchair. He never even looked at her, just kept up his conversation as if he had stepped lightly to avoid a moving piece of furniture. Violet was not prepared for this. This was not the homecoming she had planned. She searched wildly, looking for someone that seemed approachable, someone who would give her the star's welcome that she deserved. Someone who would look at her.

Violet wheeled to the side of the room to regroup. She watched the other attendees and felt strangely removed from this familiar scene. She had always stood in the middle of the room as people came to her. The event organizers, the director of the ballet, the other dancers, the press . . . all waiting their turn for a precious moment with her. She had stood, her arm draped comfortably through Jack's, as the young dancers had scooted by, trying to catch the eye of the beautiful ballerina and her handsome husband, hoping for some acknowledgment that they could write home about. She watched it happening still, but someone else was standing in her spot while she sat ignored in the corner. There was only one thing to do. Drink heavily. She had to practically run over a waiter to get her champagne, so she picked up two glasses at a time.

For a while, Violet sat and watched, thinking that no one noticed her. She began to notice, however, that there was a buzz in a group from time to time, a low murmur as they turned and stared in her direction. After some time, she saw someone whisper in the director's ear. He wheeled around in Violet's direction, disbelief on his face. "Violet, dear," he called out as he started toward her. She heard it in his voice. That same tone. Pity. She could bear it no longer. She turned and wheeled herself out the door, moving as fast as her good arm and leg would let her. The director gave up on her sometime before she reached the exit. She sensed him, and all the guests, frozen in the ballroom, watching her pitiable little exit. They would cluck to themselves quietly, then turn back to their inane conversations, life going on as it will.

Violet felt the fresh air hit her face, cooling the hot tears that rolled down her cheeks. She looked at her watch. Another hour and a half before the cabby returned. Gala guests were arriving still in their shiny cars with their perfect bodies. Violet had to find some place to wait. The neon light of a bar across the street caught her eye. She wheeled herself across the way, and through the darkened doorway. Once inside, she was confused about what to do. She clearly could not maneuver herself to a bar stool. The tables were all surrounded by chairs and she did not think she had the strength it would take to stand up and transfer to a chair. She looked around for other options but saw none. Fortunately, nobody was paying any attention to her here either. She had time to make her decision. She finally gathered every ounce of energy she had and stood, collapsing more than moving, to a chair at a table not far from the bar. Once she was safely seated, a cocktail waitress came by and Violet ordered another drink. She giggled to herself as she remembered there was no reason to worry—her designated driver would arrive in just over an hour. The giggles almost turned to tears again, but she caught herself just as her drink was delivered. Violet took a long sip. She was petrified. For the first time in her life, she was afraid of the future. Oh, come on, she thought to herself. Forget the future for tonight; I'll worry about it tomorrow. What? She was giggling again, unable to keep up with her own conversation. The alcohol was definitely taking its toll. Violet looked up, laughing, and her eyes met those of a man at the bar. He smiled at her, lifted his glass to her and took a drink, staring at her all the while. She lifted her glass with her good hand and knocked back her drink, meeting the stranger's eyes. Now this felt nice. Normal. Flirting across a crowded bar. How nice that she could still attract the attention of men in bars—she had not lost her touch completely. The gentleman made his way over to her.

"What a great smile you have," he greeted her.

"Thank you, kind sir," she answered, ignoring his lack of creativity.

"Would you like to dance?" he asked, motioning to the small dance floor. Violet wanted to disappear. He apparently did not see her entrance.

"No, I . . . I don't think that would be a good idea. I . . ."

"Oh, come on. Just one dance, that's all."

Violet shifted awkwardly, banging into the wheelchair behind her. It caught the man's eyes for the first time.

"Oh, jeez, I'm sorry. I didn't even see that. I'm really sorry." The man could not back away fast enough as he apologized.

"It's okay, really. No problem." Violet wished the floor would open up and swallow her whole. The man returned to the bar, his back turned squarely away. Violet drained her drink. She looked at her watch. Time to go to the bathroom before meeting her cab outside. She transferred back to the chair with some effort and rolled herself to the ladies room. This time she was grateful that no one seemed to notice her. She wanted to be invisible. She maneuvered into the small lounge, and stopped to look at herself in the mirror. She looked like she had been the loser in a dogfight. She was pale, with big circles under her eyes. Her hair looked as tired as she felt. She would be glad to reach the sanctuary of her home again. The conversation of two women in the lounge drifted into her consciousness.

"Dating is impossible these days. Where are all the good men?"

"Dating is a definite drag. Try being single in a bar and being ignored."

"Yeah, well, you think its hard for you. Try being single in a wheelchair, and in a singles bar. Then you'll know what being ignored feels like," Violet joined the fray. The women looked at her wordlessly, but acknowledged her reality with their nods of understanding. Violet turned wearily and wheeled herself out to wait for her cabby to rescue her from this hell.

• • • • •

"Let's get this show on the road, folks," Dr. Oliviero was in command again as he kicked off the team's regular patient conference. They were continuing to hold them in defiance of Mr. Pearman's push for computer communication. And they were setting their own discharge dates for the patients, in spite of Pearman's continued efforts to post some other discharge date daily in the patients' rooms. Another regular feature had been added to their conferences these days—managed care bashing. As pressure mounted on the team members to change their practice, their resistance grew stronger. Reenie had not made it to the library yet and Dr. Oliviero had not quite made it to the Physicians in Managed Care organization meeting. All the team members, with the exception of the contract physical therapist filling in for Josh, joined in the moaning. Too many demands, too few resources. It was in the middle of just such a discussion that Mr. Pearman joined this particular team meeting.

"Still meeting the old-fashioned way, I see," he observed as he invited himself into the conference room.

"Still meeting about taking care of the patients, yes," Dr. Oliviero responded coldly.

"Is that what you're doing?" Mr. Pearman asked.

"That's exactly what we are doing," Carolyn echoed the doctor's response.

"How can you be so sure?" Pearman challenged.

"What do you mean, how can we be so sure? We are talking about the needs of the patients." Reenie joined in the fray.

"How do you know what the patients' needs are?" Pearman asked.

"Almost fifty years of medical practice, that is how I know." Dr. Oliviero answered the challenge.

"You know what you think the patients' needs are, but do you really know?"

"What are you getting at, son?" Dr. Oliviero asserted his age and experience.

"I know what patients say they need."

"Yeah, right," Reenie couldn't stop her guffaw. "When was the last time you talked to a patient?"

"The last time I read a report from people who talked to patients to find out what they need was last night. Empirical data, systematically gathered and analyzed. When was the last time you did that?"

"I deal with people's hearts, Mr. Pearman, not with statistical research. You should try it."

"Oh, I have tried it, Reenie. Ever since getting my joint Masters degree in Social Work and Business. From that first job as the only social worker at the inner-city clinic until today. I deal with people's hearts."

Reenie was in shock. Her mouth literally gaped as she tried to absorb the fact that this managed care military maniac was a social worker. Carolyn filled in the silence.

"You are a social worker, Mr. Pearman?"

"Yes, I am a social worker."

"When did you stop caring about the patient?" Reenie recovered.

"I have never stopped caring about the patient. I realized from the surveys of patients that were published—empirical data that you hate so much—that how I thought one helped the patient was not at all how the patient wanted to be helped."

"I cannot believe you are a social worker," Reenie was still in shock.

"I cannot believe you are a social worker, either," Mr. Pearman shot back.

"What are you talking about? I work my tail off for these patients." Reenie was indignant.

"Yes, but you have not even bothered to find out if what you are so busy working on has any meaning in the quality of their lives. Do some research, Reenie. Use the information you have available to you. Catch up with the times. Join this century. Find out what patients need now. Not what you think they want, or what makes you feel comfortable giving them. Find out what they really need. Find that out and provide it. All of you. Do that and I will be off your back. Until then, you'll be seeing me every time you turn around. You make the choice. But make the right one, the one that is right for your patients, not you."

Pearman left as quickly as he had appeared, leaving the team in stunned silence. "I cannot believe he is a social worker," Reenie muttered several times as the team members fidgeted in their chairs.

"Let's take a break and regroup in an hour or so," Dr. Oliviero broke the spell. The team members shuffled their papers and filed out of the room, still trying to absorb their strange encounter with the now mysterious Mr. Pearman.

Analysis

Chapter 4 introduces a series of events that begins the process of change in the characters. As the title implies, the changes that take place are seen in stages of crisis, conflict, and opportunity. In each series of events shown, the characters can no longer deny the environmental forces that are shaping their professional careers. A resolution of these issues cannot take place at this time because change and recognition of opportunity is a process that first begins with individuals' capacity to acknowledge they are dissatisfied with the current state of events and have hope that change has some rewards for them.

The theme of the chapter centers on inevitable loss and abandonment as individuals prepare themselves for adaptation on both a professional and personal level. This feeling of loss is a normal stage of reaction to change because it reflects disruptions in the homeostasis of the individual. However, when issues of loss and abandonment are coupled with insight and mobilization, adaptation takes place. This is depicted in the behavior of Violet who faces the abandonment of her husband at the same time she is facing role changes. Nevertheless, she mobilizes herself to go to a gala event in an attempt to test her skills in reentering the world. The reader knows she will fail, but she will not experience failure. Rather this event will begin the process of a realistic assessment of the future and, with appropriate rehabilitation, a good transition into another role. The amount of energy depicted in this scene demonstrates the enormous burden individuals with disabilities must face just in order to get their basic needs met. Through Violet, the reader struggles with her feelings of anger, shame, and embarrassment and identifies with her hardship. This energy and struggle are a necessary step in the direction of independence and autonomy because they depict the individual's capacity to challenge and push him- or herself even though the outcome is unclear. This parallel surfaces in Reenie's quest for identity as well. Through a series of events, Reenie recognizes that her skills and place in her professional career are not where they should be. Her struggle with using new technology and databases, the computer system, and patient-driven statistics at first seem to overwhelm her. Rather than ponder it, she denies their value until it becomes obvious to her that her own disabilities in her role as a professional social worker are not only affecting her but the patients as well. Reenie's search for role identity is depicted as her acceptance that she needs to update her skills if she wants to find a relevant place for her soial work skills in the new systems of managed care. Although her first attempts to log-on to the net are unsuccessful, it is her first step toward adaptation. Like Violet's initial attempt to meet the challenges of her role, this highlights the enormous amount of energy change requires.

This chapter shows how easy it is for Josh to make changes in his career and accept a more fluid sense of belonging to his job. Could this be a function of his training and lack of experience in different settings? But for many social workers and other health professionals like Dr. Oliviero and Carolyn, new information systems and managed care requirements are out of keeping with their professional training and the past ways they've perceived their professional roles. As noted in previous chapters, the changes that are taking place in health care systems have been profound. Professional schools are first beginning to integrate these changes in course and field training. Some practitioners, like Dr. Oliviero in the narrative, have ethical dilemmas about the shift in emphasis from a nonprofit orientation to a corporate one which is characteristic of managed care organizations. Dr. Oliviero views the emphasis on vertical integration, consolidation of services, cost-effective treatment, and management through critical pathways as a model of care that is incompatible with quality patient care. No amount of flexibility and professional innovation could change the basic premise of managed care systems. Dr. Oliviero believes that the commitment of service and quality is no longer an integral goal of managed care systems. He views the documentation and certification that is required by health care providers as having no relevance to the delivery of patient care and as taking time away from what is deemed important by providers. Whether this type of documentation and subsequent data or empirically based system can actually benefit the patient is not viewed as a viable option. In short, it is not even given a chance. If there is to be a middle ground, there must be some acceptance that there can be better ways to deliver health care than what is currently taking place. It is interesting to consider whether both points of view are of value, whether quality patient care may actually increase by having good evaluative standard and protocols, and whether clinical paths might benefit patients as well as control costs. Is there some kind of synthesis that can incorporate both the older and newer models of health care delivery? To get to this point of synthesis, however, professionals must go through a lot of soul searching and be willing to make changes that they do not like at first and from which they do not see the immediate benefits. It is therefore not unrealistic in the early phases of changes to expect resistance and frustration and even hopelessness to the point of wanting to leave the profession, as Dr. Oliviero expresses in this chapter. Nevertheless, the seeds of compromise are beginning to take root in Chapter 4.

On a personal level, Violet is also exploring ways she must learn to be more adaptive. Both she and her husband are struggling to give up their illusions of their previous systems of living. Their career and personal roles are permanently altered. If we look at their situation as a parallel of the health care system, we might argue that at least the health care team has options—professionals in health care can learn new skills, find other positions in organizations that are in less upheaval—but Violet does not view her options in this same way. Her change is physical and structural and permanent, yet, does this change preclude other career paths or has she not yet reached into her imagination and creativity for ways that have not yet occurred to her? She can perhaps still pursue her career but in a different form with new skills and tools that use the best of her professional assets. To do this, she, as well as the health care team, needs to conceptualize a new vision of herself (themselves) that would use her (their) assets and acknowledge her (their) liabilities. Whether change is dramatic or subtle, professional or personnel, it requires enormous energy. There is no such thing as a small amount of adjustment when the requirement entails learning new skills that alter the way people perceive their major missions in life.

Josh and Frank Pearman are the catalysts that jolt Reenie to open her eyes and accept that change is inevitable and perhaps even beneficial. For Jack, this jolt of reality comes from Steve, the plumber who senses immediately that Violet's changes are for good, not just temporary adjustments to weather through. Later in the chapter, Reenie is confronted by Frank Pearman who reveals he is a social worker and challenges her with the accusation that she is not doing the best for her patients because she is out of touch with her skills. Although Reenie is shocked to learn of a social worker working for a managed care organization, she appears more shocked that he actually believes empirical databases can benefit patients. Reenie will begin the process of reformulation of her goals although it will be a slow and difficult task. It would be nice to think that change is due to insight and recognition of the value of other ways of examining professional skills, but Reenie will change simply because she has no choice. If her experiences are positive and make her feel useful, she may be more willing to open up even further. On the other hand, compromising for the sake of peace and acquiescing to requests that are demeaning in order to gain cooperation is not the kind of skill that is needed to create and maintain an innovative system. Dr. Oliviero is correct in not agreeing to sign forms that he believes undermines his professional authority and further erodes the leverage he has as a clinician with managed care requirements. This poses another dilemma. On one hand, Dr. Oliviero may be applauded for refusing to follow orders in a blind fashion just because someone demanded it. He views the request as both an ethical constraint on his practice and an imposition on his professional autonomy. His independence, his belief in the ethics of practice as superseding other requests are admirable. On the other hand, does Dr. Oliviero ever give up the authority of his clinical position and having the final word on decision making? Are his decisions harmful to others? Carolyn argues that she has the burden put upon her to get the papers signed and she is already overburdened with work. She also tells him that the patients will not get what they need unless the forms are signed. Carolyn ends up compromising *her* sense of professional integrity and authority for the sake of the patients.

Reenie confronts Dr. Oliviero and states that he can't close his practice because the patients need him no matter what system they are stuck with. Dr.

Oliviero countermands with the statement that medicine is no longer practiced by doctors, it is directed by bureaucrats and inept medical professional dropouts. Reenie encourages Dr. Oliviero to do something active about his complaints because people like him are the only hope to change the system. As she encourages him to organize and speak out with his colleagues, she slowly becomes aware that she is just as uninformed and out of touch with her professional organizations as he is. They both make a promise to get involved in their respective professional organizations. As Reenie begins a case conference with Jack, who is struggling with his own environmental changes, she begins to use her newfound advocacy skills to force Jack to understand the inevitable changes in his life. Her statement to him that life will go on for Violet and will even be good again but different is a reflection of the health care system changes that the interdisciplinary team is struggling with. Just as Jack must make adjustments and provide support for his wife as she comes to terms with the changes in her life, the interdisciplinary team members must help each other build an effective team-oriented system that is sensitive to the current changes set forth by managed care systems. This includes advocacy for change when the system is not responding to needs of patients and an open-minded approach to new ways of defining quality of care. The center of the conference focuses on the word "good" in that change may require an understanding on the patient and system level that getting better is not the same thing as getting *well,* and that getting *well* is a relative and subjective experience. In the following scene, Reenie forces herself to log-on to the computer and, although frustrated at her inability to succeed, unconsciously she has incorporated the lesson that life will be different and even good. Thus, this begins the process of adaptation to change. When Jack returns to his house and tries to return to his old ways of doing things, he finds that his home atmosphere is chaotic, his wife is laughing with the plumber. The plumber, Steve, seems to be able to focus on a task that enables Violet to feel valued and important. Replacing a handle on a sink represents to Violet her willingness to give up what she once treasured and to compromise beauty for utility. Rather than recognize the significance of this event for Violet, Jack misinterprets her response and cruelly tells her she will never dance again. In a strange and calm way, Violet seems to accept this. At the hospital, Reenie and Carolyn are informed that Josh is leaving. He is fed up with the paperwork and signs on with a contract agency that will give him more money and time to pursue other interests. Carolyn and Reenie react to his job change with feelings of loss and abandonment. They both view their team through a collective lens and believe his abandonment of the team reflects the triumph of managed care systems driving personnel decisions by the lure of money. They do not appear to understand his fluid sense of team and organizational allegiance and his interest in working with a wide variety of different kinds of patients.

Another focus of the chapter is on Violet. This chapter has tried to portray the everyday bravery that is necessary for the disabled to make even the simplest excursion into the outside world. Violet's first venture into the outside world begins with a call to a Metro Van Assist service to transport her to the gala. Violet's first reaction to calling the service for the disabled is normal; she assumes it works like a taxicab. She had no inkling that a reservation is required. This scene is presented to give some insight into the everyday concerns of the disabled. Her life requires endless planning to make even the simplest moves. Violet finds the image of her riding a bus that kneels down for her a further confirmation of how foolish she must look. Even a simple ride down the elevator becomes an arduous chore. She never even thought about whether elevators had handrails to help disabled persons. Now all of these little details in life have to be thought over and planned for, even as simple a thing as leaving the building. Despite her bravery and her belief in her recovery, the pity of individuals who were once colleagues overwhelms her. Her role as dancer is no longer viable, and with this loss come feelings of being ignored, discarded, and put to one side. She leaves the gala with a sense of being lost and ends up at a bar while she waits for her cab. As she begins to drink, she comes to the realization that she is afraid of the future. As she experiences the awkward rejection of a man who did not see her as disabled at first, she blurts out her despair of both being single and handicapped at the same time. She poignantly cries to two strangers in the ladies lounge, "Try being single in a wheelchair, and in a singles bar. Then you'll know what being ignored feels like." Her fantasies of rescue are gone, and Violet is left to tend to her despair.

The final scene depicts the team's rising battle with managed care. The team's open defiance of Frank Pearman's directives about computer meetings, discharge dates, and empirical databases pulls the members together in blaming the managed care system for all the problems in health care. Despite their bashing the system, little has been accomplished. Neither Reenie nor Dr. Oliviero have made it to their respective professional meetings or to the library. Frank Pearman enters their conversation and questions whether they really can assess their patients' needs. He confronts them with the fact that the use of systematically gathered empirical data helped him assess quality of care for patients from the patients' viewpoints, not from his own viewpoint. He challenges Reenie to consider newer ways of using information that is actually oriented toward helping patients. This interaction becomes a focal point of opportunity as Reenie begins to ponder some of the advantages that newer systems of quality management might be able to offer.

This chapter alludes to many issues of social work practice in a changing health care environment. One of the key issues raised was whether the team was prepared to enable the process of rehabilitation for the patient and her family. Four areas of rehabilitation needs were depicted in the chapter. They were (1) the physical-environmental changes in the household; (2) the relationship between the husband and wife; (3) the adaptation to mobility; and (4) the self in relation to the adjustment process. These four events demonstrate the contextual nature of adaptation. All of these adjustments occur as responses, and, therefore, treatment planning by the social worker should focus on the interrelatedness of events rather than their sequential nature. Mackelprang and Salsgiver (1996) argue that people with disabilities need to be viewed not just simply as patients and clients but as active and responsible consumers. This is consistent with social work philosophy that empowers clients to become active participants and decisionmakers in their rehabilitation process. This reinforces the strengths-based practice model. The independent-living perspective views social workers as adjuncts to the therapeutic process while the patient becomes the advocate and decisionmaker for the services needed. While the strengths perspective is an important component of patient advocacy and empowerment, patients need guidance from the interdisciplinary team on how to actualize their goals. Borrowing from the geriatric social work literature, Saltz (1992) and Saltz and Schaefer (1996) discuss rehabilitation as involving the integration of psychosocial information with knowledge of organic impairments coordinated through the interdisciplinary team and usually led by a social worker. According to Saltz (1992), the team should operate as a unit to optimally meet the needs of the patient by providing communication among specialists within the organization and insuring both quality of care as well as fiscal accountability. The term *multidimensional assessment* forms the basis of an optimal rehabilitation plan and includes a comprehensive assessment which can be used to identify the major goals of care. This can be used later to respond to the changing needs of the patient and thereby insures the provision of continuity of care. Saltz (1992) further mentions that the social worker is most likely to focus on social, environmental, and economic resources and observation in other areas especially the emotional and mental health needs of the patient. The initial assessment provides the linkage to the team that enhances the team's capacity for ongoing attention to the patient's long-term rehabilitation process.

Burack-Weiss (1995) points out that the importance that social workers attach to family interaction and support is crucial in enhancing the patient's informal support system. Caregiver strain has been noted in the literature and Burack-Weiss cites that despite a variety of respite services, support groups, and day care alternatives, easing the stress of the caregiver is still in its infancy. As noted in this chapter, the initial assessment of the team in providing a complete rehabilitation plan was lacking and the problems that ensued afterward were hard to correct. For example, while patient advocacy and responsibility are important parts of the strengths perspective, patients and families need help in preparing their adaptation plans. In the chapter, this is depicted in Reenie's conference with Jack. She misinterprets the real reason for his visit. She focuses on his concern about plumbing changes rather than the emotional adaptation these changes require. Although she is aware theoretically about the difficulties families have accepting permanent deficits and changes, she does not offer Jack a way to cope or even address his concerns. She is too focused on the concrete task rather than the process of rehabilitation. This mirrors the team as a whole as task- rather than process-oriented. There is no overall pattern to guide team members in using a complete psychosocial-biological assessment and, as noted earlier, this must occur at the beginning of the rehabilitation process.

While the team as a small group operates in an organizational context, Saltz (1992) notes that norms govern team behavior and affect such areas as leadership, conflict resolution, communication patterns, and decision making. When issues of professional survival and allegiance become paramount, as depicted in the behavior of the team in this narrative, the team effectiveness breaks down. Although the team leader is a physician, his role is assumed rather than active. Mizrahi and Abramson (1985) and Roberts (1989) point out that social workers must deal with physicians' assumed role of leadership on the team by acknowledging that it is part of their training, while at the same time dealing with them as human beings who can make changes in leadership roles when appropriate. There is no question that teamwork in the hospital has been greatly affected by the pressure from prospective payment systems to control health care costs by reducing hospital stays and eliminating services that are not necessary.

According to Cowles and Lefcowitz (1995) this has increased the tendency for social work referrals to be restricted to concrete services such as discharge planning and resource linkage activities to the neglect of the psychosocial component of discharge planning and other aspects of health problems. Additionally, high-risk screening systems have not been very effective or efficient in targeting patients who need social services, and social work departments have not had enough staff to serve those who have been identified. This can distort the team's effort to emphasize the unique contribution of professional roles and also the leadership process as well. The extreme of the situation is depicted in the narrative as both the lack of leadership on the team and the lack of time to thoroughly work out a rehabilitation plan for the patient. Role blurring can occur as a response to this situation, and patients and their families do not receive the benefits and preparation needed for the physical and psychological adaptation skills they need. A survey by Cowles and Lefcowitz (1992; 1995) of hospital physicians, nurses, and social workers found that social workers' view of the counseling role was a central component of their role preference whereas other professionals expected the social worker to provide more concrete services. Social workers, but not other team members, expected to equally share the emotional components of care; other team members did not view these tasks as primarily within the social workers' roles. Nurses tended to view counseling tasks for social workers to be centered around families of patients rather than the patients themselves. In addition to feeling pressured to work in concrete service delivery by both managed care organizations and their colleagues, social workers felt misunderstood in terms of their professional growth in areas such as counseling, psychotherapy, or emotional and behavioral therapies. However, the pressure of cost containment still requires social workers to expand their skills in using quality of care indices and database measurement. The emphasis on outcome data, cost savings, and evidence-based approaches is not only affecting social work practice but medicine as well.

According to Ringle (1996) managed care organizations are exerting enormous pressure to reduce the cost of medical care, and neurologists need information that will enhance their ability to identify all cost-effective treatment strategies for patients who need specialty care such as stroke patients. A national study of Medicare claims data on the costs and outcome of acute stroke patients by Mitchell, Ballard, Whisnant, Ammering, Samsa, and Matchar (1996) showed that stroke patients treated by neurologists compared to those treated by other physician specialties had better outcomes in terms of mortality, but their treatment was more expensive. Only 11.3 percent of stroke patients in this study had a neurologist listed as the attending physician. Ringle (1996) questions why there was such a low rate of care by neurologists if the care they provide is so valuable. With increasing restrictions on referral of patients to specialists, he stresses the importance of using and interpreting information that can be used in the best interest of the patient. He emphasizes that medical educators as well as practitioners need to start using evidence-based approaches and cost-effective analyses to help them become better problem solvers and to convince payers that they are managing the day-to-day care of patients with both quality and fiscal measures in mind. Developing these skills takes time and resources, but they can assist payers in an accurate identification of cost-effective management of stroke patients. In turn, this will increase the value of the services being sought.

In the narrative, there are at least two instances in which Dr. Oliviero refuses to participate in any database collection system because he feels it is an insult to his integrity as a physician. The major question is how can professionals distinguish between contemporary needs for evidence-based medicine, critical pathways, and practice guidelines from the collection and use of data that is restrictive to patients' needs? As Ringle and Hughes (1996) note, "Like it or not the neurologist's world is changing. To be competitive in today's managed care environment, programs must show in addition to cost reduction strategies that medical services are appropriate and result in high quality outcomes and satisfied patients" (867). Physicians' acceptance, they note, had been slow because of the lack of familiarity with the terms used, the analytical tools needed, the conflictual data that has been reported, and the distrust of "cookbook" or formula-driven medicine. The critical pathway, however, can optimize efficiency as it is a management plan that improves usual care by identifying the ideal sequences and timing of staff actions and allows ways to minimize testing, treatment, and length of stay while at the same time begins the rehabilitation and discharge planning immediately. While neurologists are familiar with traditional outcome measures of quality of care such as mortality, infection, cardiovascular stability, and functional status, they are less accustomed to considering serial surveys that assess patient satisfaction with care and patient-reported health status measures such as the Medical Outcome study, 36-item short-form Health Survey (Ringle and Hughes 1996, 868). Furthermore, these authors attest that neurologists have little experience with other databases that stratify patients using severity of illness measures. Once implemented, these clinical guidelines can show significant improvements in care although the authors report that implementation is slow because neurologists are busy and find it easier to continue with the status quo rather than to modify their practice using unfamiliar methods and data. A key component in their success is the strength of medical evidence for each treatment and there is still a myriad of differences in the way health systems collect and evaluate information, determine cost, and use valid data as a basis for action.

These concepts surfaced in the discussion Frank Pearman had with Reenie and their differences of opinion on what was considered good social work practice. Before Reenie can ever consider the value of such systems, she must be willing to acknowledge that newer techniques for evaluation and decision making can actually be of value in determining quality patient care, and she must feel comfortable in learning new assessment tools. Ringle and Hughes (1996) also suggest that the challenge to neurologists is to focus on the provision of quality health care rather than on meeting the needs of managed care systems. Guidelines are used by managed care organizations not just for cost control but because these organizations also have an ethical responsibility to provide appropriate care and a legal liability if subscribers do not receive appropriate care. The market will demand high-quality care as well as specific clinical outcomes. Both improving quality care and cost-effectiveness and attention to patient choices are part of a good health care system. They also note that administrative efforts are focused on reducing inappropriate care rather than increasing access to beneficial services. Thus, in order to expand effective therapies, neurologists will need to document and encourage their cost-effectiveness to demonstrate how they make clinical choices.

These principles of clinical guidelines are an appropriate model for all health care professionals because they are oriented toward both cost control and quality care. These concepts were introduced with a more positive patient-oriented view in Chapter 4. In the next chapter, effective change begins to happen.

Practice Skills

Client

1. Burack-Weiss (1995) suggests the use of a personal narrative in alleviating caregivers' stress. How might this technique be used to help Jack deal with his frustration following his wife's illness? What guidelines would you suggest the social worker provide to get at his identification of key issues? Could personal narrative be a useful tool for members of the interdisciplinary team? Discuss some possible uses.

Social Worker

1. Provide a social work assessment in the following areas for the patient based upon the team's use of empirical data: physical health; daily functioning; mental health; family issues; environmental issues; social needs; and perceived self (strengths and weaknesses).
2. What lessons about the importance of professional relationships and network can be learned from this social worker's dilemma of self-imposed isolation?

Team

1. Use Saltz and Schaefer's (1996) model to develop the rehabilitation treatment plan:
   a. *Team Structure.* What data should each member of the team use to provide a rehabilitation plan? How will their individual data provide a comprehensive plan? How does the information each team member brings affect the team structure?
   b. *Team Process.* How will the information each team member brings affect leadership? How can leadership roles be viewed as a peer process? What roles should each team member take in problem-solving and decision-making activities? What problems should be

prioritized? What might be sources of interdisciplinary conflict as solutions are identified?

c. *Outcomes.* What methods should the team use to evaluate its treatment plan? How can team members demonstrate accountability to the organization? How can the family contribute feedback to the team? What information would be useful?

2. Design a basic outcome evaluation system that could enhance this team's functioning and effectiveness within the managed care environment.

System

1. Describe the potential conflict in social work values presented by the challenge of being an administrator in managed care.
2. Describe Frank Pearman's philosophical reconciliation of these potential conflicts.

5

Seeking Wholeness: Hearing, Accepting, Adjusting, and Advocating

The early morning sun peeping through the blinds burned Violet's bloodshot eyes as she passed in and out of a restless sleep. When she had fallen into bed the night before, she had not cared whether she ever woke up again. But sleep had been no refuge, with vision after vision of herself trying with all her might to get somewhere and never quite arriving. The first hint of sun found her grateful to be rescued from the dreams but too frightened to look to the day ahead. She felt small and alone beneath her covers, fragile. She stayed there, suspended in time, wanting desperately to move and desperately not to move, when she was jarred by the knock at the door. She thought about just pulling the covers over her head and ignoring the intrusive noise, but she knew Steve would keep knocking until he got an answer. Or until he felt like he had to break the door down to make sure everything was okay. Jack had hated it that Steve would not use the doorbell. "New fangled things," Steve called them, complaining that you could never be sure they actually worked. Better to knock, he said, and be certain, with your own knuckles, that your arrival had been duly announced. Violet liked the knocking, especially this morning. It was sure and sound, solid, the rap of Steve's knuckles on the door. She made her way to the entry in the chair, too tired to walk.

"Top of the morning, ma'am," Steve tipped his hat as always.

"Whatever," Violet grunted as she wheeled to the kitchen in search of liquids. Her mouth felt like cotton.

Steve followed his familiar path from the front door to the master bath. He had almost completed major renovations. Mr. Mason was continuing to direct the project by phone, though these days he mostly just sighed and responded, "Whatever Violet wants," when Steve floated a proposed change. Mr. Mason was staying elsewhere and seemed to have little concern remaining regarding either cosmetics or cost. Partly Mr. Mason had come to trust him, Steve believed, knowing that the plumber would never inflate a price or cut a corner on quality. Partly though, Steve knew Mr. Mason just didn't care anymore. Steve pondered this as he worked on the bath. He was accustomed to moving in and out of people's lives and normally he did not give it a great deal of thought. This couple he wondered about. From all accounts, they seemed the perfect couple, happy as two lizards on a leaf. And yet they fell apart with the slightest change in the wind. Steve couldn't quite get his hands around it. Mrs. Mason was still the same person, he imagined. Only difference now was she didn't walk so well. Didn't seem right to Steve that a man would walk out on account of that. Of course, it was none of his business. Still, he wondered. Why? He didn't know. Maybe it reminded him somehow of his return from Vietnam. Maybe it was something else.

"Did you bring coffee today?" Violet's query roused Steve from his meandering thoughts.

"Coffee? Yes, ma'am. Got my trusty thermos right here with me."

"Can I have some? I appear to be out."

"Yes, ma'am. Of course you can." Steve unscrewed the plastic cup from the worn and rusty thermos, wiping the rim clean with his thumb before he filled it and handed it to Violet.

Violet took a big gulp, murmuring her approval as the hot liquid warmed her throat. "This is delicious. It's from Java To Go, down the street, isn't it?"

"That is from my kitchen counter. Same coffee pot, same coffee I been using for twenty years. Nothing fancy, but you can count on it."

"Well, it is exactly what I need after the night I had." Violet was dropping hints that she wanted to talk, hoping Steve would pick up on the cue.

"Yes, ma'am." Steve was too polite to be intrusive, though he did wonder how Violet was managing on her own. He began to unload his tools as Violet drank her coffee.

"Please don't bang those tools. I don't mind telling you I have quite the hangover." Violet gave up being subtle. "I had the worst evening of my life."

"The gala was last night, right?" Steve took the opening.

"Gala. Not exactly a proper descriptor for it."

"You were looking pretty forward to it, weren't you, Mrs.?" Steve prodded without prying.

"Yes, I was," Violet answered wistfully. The tears were burning the corners of her eyes before she could stop them. "Oh, Steve, it was horrible. A disaster."

"What happened?"

"Everything went wrong, right from the start. The van service wouldn't cooperate, I fell in the elevator, I had to use my wheelchair, and take a taxi. I was exhausted by the time I got there."

"I'm sorry, Mrs. M. I could have given you a ride if I had known."

"The worst part was the way they looked at me. Rather, the way they didn't look at me." The tears really started to flow. "Nobody even noticed when I came in. It was like I was invisible. A rolling invisible nobody. Not one soul looked at me." Violet was almost screaming.

"Mrs. M, I'm sorry . . ."

"I am the principal dancer in the company, Steve. Do you know what that means? I am accustomed to cameras, media, chorus dancers fawning over me. I float into the room and I *am* the gala. I am the ballerina." Violet slumped back into her chair with a last gasp and sob. She stared at her coffee for a long moment. "I was the ballerina, I should say."

"I remember when I came home from Nam," Steve softly remembered his own ghosts. "People would look right through me, or move to the other side of the walk like I was some sort of monster."

"That was it, Steve. They all looked right through me, or avoided any contact. Well, almost everyone did that. The absolute rock bottom came when the company director finally noticed me. Steve, he looked at me with pity. Pity!"

"I know what you're saying, Mrs. M. I do."

"Yes." Violet looked directly at Steve, sensing that he did understand. "Call me Violet, Steve. I guess that's who I am. I'm certainly not Mrs. Mason anymore. And I'm not the principal dancer. I don't know what I am now, what my role is anymore."

"You are the same person. I mean, you can't walk so good and maybe you won't be dancing Swan Lake but who you are, your insides, that hasn't changed."

"Hmm. The insides . . . who I am. I guess I have never known who that was."

"Sure you have. Maybe you just haven't put it in thoughts and words, but you know. Soon as you get in touch with that, your world will right itself."

Violet studied Steve's face, as strong and sweet as his coffee. "You know, Steve, I'll tell you another secret from last night. I tried to pick up a man in a bar."

"Hey!"

"Violet."

"Violet. You be careful now. That's not a safe thing to do."

"Unfortunately, I could not have been safer. He asked me to dance before he noticed the wheelchair. Once he saw it, he could not get away fast enough. I was perfectly safe all right."

"Mrs. Violet, I don't pretend to understand affairs of the heart. But I do know a great lady when I see one, and I guarantee, when you're ready, your dance card will be full again, chair or no chair."

"Thanks, Steve. That helps my headache almost as much as this coffee." Violet drained the cup.

"No problem. Glad to help." Steve smiled shyly, handed Violet his thermos, and set about his work.

• • • • •

"A toast, everybody. We need a toast," Reenie called out as she served punch at the little party the hospital put together to bid farewell to Josh.

"I'll do the honors," Carolyn said, quickly raising her cup. "To Josh, you rat!" Everybody laughed. "Seriously, to Josh. PrimeStaff's gain, our team's loss."

"Don't start toasting those, we'll be here all night," Reenie answered, only half joking.

"Hey, I'm going to miss you guys. It's been fun," Josh acknowledged the toast.

"Any idea who's taking your place, son?" Dr. Oliviera got to the business at hand.

"No, sir. They're asking for approval of contract therapists, I believe."

"I knew it," Carolyn responded. "I'm sure they've frozen the position, Josh, as usual, and will pay four times your salary to someone while they analyze staffing needs. Then they will finally hire someone, but only after we've oriented a half dozen different contract therapists who we'll never see again."

"Yeah, it's a great country, isn't it folks?" Josh tried to lighten the mood.

"Wouldn't have it any other way." Reenie followed suit, sending signals to Carolyn and Dr. Oliviera to do the same. It was, after all, a going-away party for Josh, not a wake for the team. Though, Reenie thought to herself, that should be scheduled as soon as possible. She was still reeling from the news that Frank Pearman was a social worker. Something had gone horribly wrong in his training, she was certain. She believed he was selling out in the worst possible way and imagined that he expected the same from his staff. At least that's partially what she thought. She couldn't quite shake his words. What was he talking about? Reenie knew he had issued a challenge, and there was a gnawing thought that she would have to rise to the occasion. She just couldn't immediately imagine, given the things Pearman had done, what good could come of trying to understand his frame of reference. And yet, his words nagged at her, clouding her once-clear vision. Reenie remembered with a start that there was a party going on around her. She shook her head, trying to shake off the cobwebs gathering in her brain, and rejoined, at least on the surface, the merriment of her colleagues.

• • • • •

The group members settled in slowly, but surely, exchanging now-familiar greetings. Reenie was proud of how Mrs. Luber, Mr. Shaw, Ms. Brown, Mr. Marshall, Mrs. Spelling, and Mrs. Mason had melded together, overcoming differences to support each other in the face of enormous life challenges. She worried, however, that they were just now revealing their sadness and anger, still in the initial phases of identifying their losses. There was much grieving still to do, and yet there was not time. The group members had only one more session and then they would be on their own. Reenie knew after her encounter with Pearman in the team conference that he would not be open to the possibility of extending the group. In fact, if anything, he would probably tell her to skip the final meeting.

Reenie realized with a start that the group had taken off without her, and Violet held the floor.

". . . couldn't pick me up because I didn't call a day in advance. I was stranded. What was I supposed to do?"

"Did you talk to a supervisor?" Mrs. Luber asked.

"Ask for the director—go straight to the top!" Mr. Shaw advised.

"I would have been so angry I wouldn't have been able to speak. They take advantage of us because we can't fight back. We have to take whatever they tell us and just live with it because we're handicapped." Ms. Brown had grown weary of fighting the system.

"So, you didn't get to go to your gala?" Reenie surmised. "Such a shame! How did that make you feel?"

"Oh, I went to the gala all right," Violet corrected.

"How in the world did you get there?" Mrs. Spelling was stumped.

"Took a taxi. I got in my wheelchair and wheeled myself down and hailed a taxi. Well, first I tried walking but decided to go back for my chair after I fell in the elevator and that nice couple from the third floor picked me up."

"You fell in the elevator? Violet, you must be careful," Reenie admonished.

"Yes, I fell. But you know what? At least I was trying. You told us that rehabilitation means taking what we have and learning how to make the best use of it, how to compensate for what we have lost. You told us the first week that recovery was going to force us to come up with creative solutions to problems. I was just following your advice."

"Yes, but you must be cautious and safe."

"If I had been cautious I would still be sitting in my apartment wallowing in pity because I was at the mercy of a bureaucratic bus system for gimps because my husband high-tailed out of my life the second I wasn't his perfect little princess anymore," Violet was on a roll now, and the group was nodding in concert with her. "If I were cautious I wouldn't have made it to the miserable gala for the worst night of my life, I wouldn't have gotten drunk as a sailor in a cheap bar where I tried to pick up a man who almost died of cardiac arrest on the spot when he noticed my wheelchair."

"Oh my, you didn't!" Mrs. Luber was astounded at Violet's boldness.

"Yes, I did. And that's the point, folks. I did a lot of things wrong but I *did* something. And I learned a lot that night that made me take stock, like Reenie has tried to tell us all along. First, I've taken a look at what I have left, not just what I've lost. And I've started to work on thinking creatively about the future, not just pitifully about the past. I'm going to live again, by golly, and life will be good again. If I can live through that miserable night, I can do anything."

Reenie was the first to break the silence after Violet finished speaking. She began slowly clapping her hands, amazed at the growth in Violet. The rest of the group joined in the applause and everyone began to talk animatedly about Violet's experience. As the din swelled, Reenie continued to hear her own words echoing in Violet's voice. And she knew that, student having surpassed the master, Violet's repetition of Reenie's words of wisdom were a powerful lesson for the social worker and the professional challenges she faced.

• • • • •

Reenie sat in front of the blinking screen of her computer once more, determined that this time it would not get the best of her. She reviewed the fresh set of instructions from the computer help center, took a deep breath, and started to type. To her amazement, she was given safe passage into the system on her first try. She was a bit intimidated by the jumble of colorful graphics that announced her arrival, but determined to go forward. She had been challenged by Frank Pearman to do a better job and reminded by her client Violet Mason to not only mourn her losses but look to the future with a sense of the assets she retained and the courage to make necessary changes. Reenie knew the time had come to move forward. She could not hang on to a system that was now outmoded. It was time to make some peace with the changing scene of health care. And Reenie knew that to do that she would need information. Up-to-date, professional social work educational data about effective practice and models of treatment. She hoped that information would be waiting for her somewhere in the far reaches of the Internet. She referred to her notes and forged ahead. After more than one false start and many deadends, Reenie began to gather some important resources. And much to her great surprise, what she found was not only helpful, but somehow exciting. She printed out possible references and dashed off to the hospital librarian for help.

• • • • •

Carolyn and Reenie met at the nursing station, both hurrying to accomplish a few more things before the beginning of team conference. Reenie was filling Carolyn in, with some exuberance, on the information she had been turning up. "Carolyn, the articles on brief treatment are really interesting. Some of the studies show that the outcomes for clients in brief treatment, like six to eight sessions, are just as good as for those in traditional long-term therapy. They make a good point that the average number of sessions people come for therapy is six to eight anyway, and really challenge therapists in private practice to adapt their models to this reality."

"Yes, but you don't get six to eight sessions with patients now, do you?"

"No, but the idea works in the hospital, too. Brief treatment is very directive, with a clear agreement right from the start between the patient and the social worker about what the goals are. Reviewing these articles reminded me that contracting with patients is one of the key components of intervention. I think I've been trying to follow my own agenda and forgetting that the patients can make their own decisions about what to work on. I've been as paternalistic as the medical model I've complained about."

"What's your complaint about me, now?" Dr. Oliviero teased cheerfully as he entered the nursing station area.

"No complaints, doc. Just telling Carolyn about some of the research I've been doing."

"How are you, Dr. O? You seem as upbeat as Reenie this morning. I don't know what has happened to the two of you." Carolyn continued the light mood.

"I just came from a very heartening meeting," Dr. Oliviero shared his own news. "Group of doctors getting together to form our own network. We negotiate as a group with managed care plans. We take on more of the financial risk, but in return, we set our own practice parameters. I like the idea. It is giving me an inkling of hope about this whole mess that I haven't had in a long time. At least I feel like perhaps there is something I can do besides sit on my thumbs while some bureaucrat sells my patients down the river for a bigger share of the profit."

"I was just saying that I'm more hopeful than I have been in a while, too, Dr. Oliviero," Reenie shared the physician's relief. "This system is still a mess, but there are some things I can do to help patients. And, I guess if I am perfectly frank, I have not been a part of any better solution."

"I understand precisely, Reenie. We're going to have to take the bull by the horns and . . ."

"Uh, excuse me. I'm a contract therapist from PrimeStaff. I'm assigned to this rehab unit for the day. Anybody know what I am supposed to do?" A voice asked timidly from across the nurse's station. Carolyn, Reenie, and Dr. Oliviero all whirled around at the same time, not believing their ears.

"Joshua. You came back to us!" Carolyn was delighted.

"You've got to be kidding me! You are our contract therapist?" Reenie was struck by the irony.

"Yes, I'm it. As soon as they realized you all were requesting someone they sent me over. Funny, isn't it?"

"I don't find it particularly amusing. This system may be more messed up than we even realize, Reenie." Dr. Oliviero was troubled by a model of care that encouraged competent therapists to work like migrant farm workers, moving to the ripest orchard. It was an effective model for harvesting fruit, but Dr. Oliviero did not like how it worked for patients in need of acute attention.

"Don't forget your meeting, Dr. Oliviero. There is hope."

"Yes, yes, I suppose you are right," Dr. Oliviero shook off his momentary relapse into despair. "Come along, young man. We are about to start team meeting. We'll do our best to show you the ropes." The reconstituted team moved toward their conference room, stepping a little more quickly and with a renewed commitment to making things work to the betterment of their clients.

• • • • •

Steve was packing his tools in Violet's bath for the last time. He had finally completed all the changes she could think of, and the room was completely accessible and safe for her. Violet could hear him cleaning up from the kitchen, where she was determined to prepare lunch for the two of them. The two had begun to share lunchtime together when Steve was working. He would eat his junk food while she nibbled at a salad delivered by the deli downstairs. Violet had come to look forward to those lunches, for she and Steve had become fast friends. He listened to her as no one in her life had ever done. And Violet had been surprised to find that he carried tremendous wisdom. She was ashamed now to admit that before the stroke, she would have sniffed her nose at Steve, disapproving of his worn clothing and feeling superior in response to his polite deference. How sad that it had taken her illness to make her slow down and take stock of the people around her. Jack was a shiny penny, one snatched off the sidewalk and carried in one's pocketbook for good luck. Steve was a rumpled dollar bill, not nearly so likely to catch one's eye at first, but clearly of more substance and value for the long run. Violet thought of Steve often these days, and more and more in comparison to Jack. She did not want their lunches or the occasions when she made Steve take her on an errand to end. So today, in celebration of the completion of the master bath, which was truly a masterpiece now, she was attempting to prepare something interesting for Steve. She decided on chicken salad to go with the bread she had ordered from the bakery the night before. She was moving quietly, hoping to surprise Steve, but it was not easy. Violet had enjoyed cooking when she first began to live alone, trying to eke by on a ballerina's salary. She had not cooked since she and Jack married, though, he had made such fun of her and she was finding it difficult to get the hang of it again now. She managed to get the precooked chicken into the bowl with her good han and added some of the other ingredients. She was having a devil of time trying to stir, however. She regretted not participating in the OT's kitchen training when she was in the hospital. Perhaps she could have picked up a tip or two that would have helped her now. Instead, she had to figure it out on her own. She tried to hold the bowl steady against her waist as she stirred with her good hand, but the bowl kept slipping. She pushed against it once more, trying to speed things up as she heard Steve whistling toward the front door. She gave the chicken salad a good stir and as she did, the bowl twisted away from her and went hurtling off the edge of the counter, leaving her helplessly whisking her spoon in the air. The ear-shattering crash brought Steve running from the foyer.

"Violet! Violet, are you okay?" Steve dashed into the kitchen looking scared out of his wits. He stopped short when he encountered the mess on the floor. He looked up to ask Violet what had happened but was surprised to find her in tears.

"Oh, Steve. I wanted to make lunch for you. I wanted to make you something healthy and delicious. Instead, I've just made a huge mess."

Steve stepped carefully over the broken glass and put his arm around Violet's shoulder, comforting her."From what I can see, it looks like it was going to be unbelievably good." Violet caught Steve's eye and began to giggle.

"It is a delectable looking disaster, isn't it?"

"Positively mouth watering. If it weren't for the glass, I think I would just sit right down on the floor with a fork and dig in." The two were laughing together now, the kind of laughter that surpasses what started it, leaving you uncertain of what is so amusing, yet unable to stop laughing. When they finally began to catch their breath, Steve asked what exactly had happened to his lunch.

"I was trying to stir, but I only have the one good arm and hand, and the bowl scooted right off the counter."

"Where's your bowl grip thing?"

"What bowl grip thing?"

"Didn't they give you one in the hospital? I've seen them before. A contraption that holds the bowl for you?"

"No, I didn't get anything like that. But then again, I did skip the home economics electives in my rehab stay," Violet laughed.

"You have another bowl?"

"Yes, but I don't want to overdo the glass. It has a tendency to blunt the taste of the chicken."

"You are so funny! I think I can fix a bowl to a board for you so it won't get away from you next time. I'll be right back."

Violet retrieved another bowl from the cabinet while Steve ran down to his truck. He returned with a hot glue gun and a square board.

"Steve, you practically have an entire hardware store right there in that truck."

"Never know what you're going to need in my line of work. It's good to have tools. Got to be ready for anything."

"Including rescuing chicken salad in distress?"

"Especially rescuing chicken salad in distress." Steve went to work, gluing the bowl to the board. "Here, put something in this and try stirring it."

Violet searched the refrigerator and came up with eggs. "Here, we'll have an omelet." She picked up an egg, then immediately recognized a new problem. She wished she had mastered the one-handed egg-breaking technique before her stroke. She had admired chefs who had the talent, but had never had a need to do anything other than a two-handed break. Now, she definitely had a need. She decided to give it a try. She cracked the egg against the side of the bowl and moved it immediately to the center. The egg splashed out of the shell into the bowl, followed quickly by half the shell. Violet glanced at Steve to see if he was watching. He was. They both began to giggle again.

"How many eggs do you have?"

"A dozen."

"Enough to practice." Steve picked up the bowl and dumped the egg and shell in the sink. Violet picked up another egg and tried again, with similar results. Again, Steve dumped the contents of the bowl and set it back down in front of Violet for her to try again. By the fourth egg she was improving and by the sixth she had perfected the technique.

"I did it! Do you see that? I did it. It is all in how you hold the egg as you strike the edge of the bowl. You have to have it positioned so that you can hold on to the two halves of the shell as it breaks."

"Excellent job. I knew you could do it," Steve was truly impressed. "Now, before you put any more eggs in there, let's see if that board holds the bowl while you stir." Violet got her whisk and began to beat the egg vigorously. The bowl and board held steady for a moment, then slid a little. As Violet and Steve both dove for it, it went crashing off the edge of the counter, the shattered fragments joining the mess on the floor that they were already stepping around. Violet stared at Steve.

"Got another bowl?" Steve asked. Violet was in hysterics again, taking Steve with her. When they recovered, Steve explained his oversight. "I forgot that the contraptions I've seen have a gripper to attach the board to the counter. Get another bowl and I'll be right back." Violet retrieved another bowl and Steve returned triumphantly bearing a small vise.

"See, we can clamp the board down with this." Steve tightened the clamp attaching the board temporarily to the counter. He glued the new bowl to the board. "Now try another egg." Violet performed the newly acquired one-handed egg-breaking feat again, and tried once more to whisk the egg. This time it went off without a hitch.

"Excellent. That is terrific, Steve. How about an omelet? A small omelet. I'm down to my last two eggs!"

"That sounds wonderful, Violet. Let me help."

Steve and Violet prepared the lunch together, as they animatedly discussed adaptations that would make the kitchen truly accessible for Violet once again.

"You know your way around the kitchen, Steve," Violet observed as Steve worked along side her.

"I like being in the kitchen. It's relaxing to cook, when there is someone to talk to," Steve replied. "We make a good team," he added a little shyly.

"Yes, we do," Violet did not try to control the pleasure in her voice. "You know, I wish I could take that kitchen training now."

"Seems like it would be good to have some of that after you get back home and into your own area," Steve agreed. Suddenly an idea struck him.

"Hey, Violet, wouldn't a video be helpful? A do-it-yourself kind of guide for how to adapt your work in the kitchen?"

"Yes, it would. Do you suppose there is such a video?"

"I don't know. Your social worker should know. And if there isn't one," Steve was becoming excited at the prospect, "I think you should make one."

"Steve, that's a great idea." Violet found herself excited about something for the first time in a long time. She picked up the phone immediately and left a message for Reenie. She then turned to Steve and gave him a quick kiss on the cheek before returning to her omelets. Steve smiled broadly at her and began to clean the mess from the kitchen floor.

• • • • •

Reenie, Steve, and Violet watched as the video technician put the last editing touch on the video. Reenie had moved quickly once Violet had approached her about the need for a tape demonstrating kitchen adaptation for patients with disabilities. She sought help from experts at NASW to draft a proposal. She discussed it at length with Frank Pearman, then revised and revised again. Next, it was taken before the hospital board where Reenie and Frank sold the idea on terms the board could understand: marketing and revenue. Finally, approval was given to move ahead with planning, and the hospital had hammered out a contractual agreement with Violet to make and distribute the video.

"And, it's a wrap," the technician announced. The three participants let out a whoop and there were high fives all around.

"This is just amazing. What do you say we go to *LaMadeleine*™ for a celebratory dinner?" Reenie was elated with the final product.

"That sounds great," Violet seconded the idea.

"Good time for us to tell you about all our other ideas, Reenie," Steve added.

"You two are absolutely wonderful. Let's go brainstorm over pasta." Reenie led the way out of the studio and through the hospital. The group encountered Josh and Carolyn in the hallway.

"How did it go?" Carolyn asked.

"Couldn't have been better. A star is born," Reenie reported, bowing to Violet.

"It was great fun. I can't wait to get the first official videotape, with the hospital's logo and everything," Violet was truly excited.

"Well, that may get slowed down a bit while we await the new logo. The merger is definitely going through. I heard it announced on the news in a patient's room."

"Merger?" Steve was not certain what Josh was talking about.

"Our hospital is joining with HealthOne," Reenie explained.

"We got the word in the nursing department meeting this afternoon. They are already 'challenging' us to think of massive nursing redesign." Carolyn added.

Dr. Oliviero spotted the gathering from down the hall and made his way to the group. "Good evening, folks. Is the video complete?"

"It's a wrap, ready to print," Reenie filled him in.

"I need a case or two for the physician's group. We're going to buy some to distribute free to our patients."

"That is so good to hear. That was our main reason for doing this, Dr. Oliviero. I hope it is helpful." Violet was pleased.

"You have heard about the merger?" Dr. Oliviero questioned his team quietly.

"Yes, the word is definitely out." Reenie confirmed.

"We've got lots of work ahead of us. This is where the rubber meets the road, folks. We have to be ready to shape this system, to lead the way in restructuring," Dr. Oliviero was the cheerleader once more. He was encouraged by the success of the physician's network and anxious to formulate concrete suggestions for guiding the pending merger. "Time for us to put into motion every idea we have for improving the system."

"Good, patient input is important to us. Good thinking," Frank Pearman pointed out as he asked to join the group.

"I have some ideas of my own for how to improve the system, having watched Violet go through her recovery," Steve spoke up.

"You know what? We are on our way to dinner at *LaMadeleine*™ to celebrate the video. It would be a great time to discuss our ideas for the system. I think it would be really helpful for us to hear Violet and Steve's point of view, and get feedback on our ideas. And a great time to brainstorm together. Can you all join us?"

"Who's paying?" Josh piped up. "Just kidding. I'm in—I've seen lots of different approaches in this contract position and I've got some ideas about how to improve things."

"I might as well get to work on redesign as soon as possible. I'll be there," Carolyn committed.

"Got room for a social worker who practices managed care philosophy?" Frank asked.

"I would love to get your input on what you're looking for from physicians, as well as the rest of the health care system. I'll meet you there." Dr. Oliviero made it unanimous.

"Great. Let's go!" Reenie was excited and hopeful. Together this group of folks just might come up with a system that would work, not just from a business standpoint, but from a service standpoint. Reenie hurried to her car, her expectations high as she headed toward the restaurant.

Analysis

In Chapter 5 we see the process of change. Violet acknowledges to Steve she had the worst evening of her life. The gala verified for her in very concrete terms that she *was* and not *is* the principal dancer of the Metropolitan Ballet Company. She reveals to Steve the humiliating feeling of being "looked through and pitied" made even more unbearable because this is in direct opposition of her former role. In her recognition of not being the principal dancer anymore, she tells Steve to call her Violet as that is who she is and what she is left with. Steve sees this as a positive step in her rehabilitation and tells her with much empathy that her insides are the same and one day she will be able to put her whole self back together again. His words and manner give her a sense of identity and purpose.

Reenie has also had an opportunity to review her role. While her role crisis was not as dramatic as Violet's, the effect is similar. She seriously begins to examine ways in which her perception of herself is stagnant and nonfunctional. She begins to evaluate the accusations of Frank Pearman, a catalyst who issued a challenge to Reenie to reexamine herself in relation to her role in patient advocacy. Although Frank Pearman's approach was different from Steve's and certainly less supportive, he made Reenie confront change as a positive step with a place for renewed commitment of her skills. The contrast between the personalities of Steve and Frank demonstrate that the initiative to change comes from both supporters as well as detractors. And it is by no coincidence that Steve's personality, his sense of caring and empathy, and his ability to mobilize Violet are the same characteristics usually associated with social workers.

In the group meeting, Reenie notices that Violet has been able to "hold the floor" and verbalize to the group her anger at the difficulties she is experiencing because she is disabled. However, she does not give in to these difficulties but rather boldly confronts the group with the meaning of active rehabilitation. She reminds them that rehabilitation is an active process and that people need to be forceful in learning how to make the best of situations in order to compensate for losses. She eschews the notions of caution and safety as a model even though her actions lead her to experience head-on "one of the most difficult and humiliating nights of her life." She points out the paradox. She wasn't cautious, which lead to her actions, and these actions caused misery. Yet, she persevered and learned about the importance of taking action. She used the skills she had been taught in her support group to enable her to reexamine her life structure and examine possibilities for future adjustment. Violet makes the following points about acceptance of change:

1. Think of being active even if it leads to mistakes.
2. Examine what is left, not what is lost.
3. Think creatively about the future; don't let pity drive behavior.
4. Accept that life will be good again even though it's different.

How is this analysis appropriate to Reenie's struggle over health care system changes? Reenie uses a similar approach to enable working through her needs for professional development. She accepts being challenged to do a better job even though she will make mistakes in finding ways to be effective and accountable. She won't view her past professional functioning as the only way to provide morally responsible and high-quality patient care. She retains her assets that will be useful and worth retaining in the future and examines and evaluates newer problem-solving approaches. She makes a tentative peace with the changing health care system and begins to use information, not lose it as a defense against change.

Up-to-date models about effective practice and models of treatment within the changing health care environment are first emerging in the professional social work literature. In order to utilize this information, social workers also need skills in evaluating their effectiveness, their efficiency, and their attention to important professional values which emphasize responsible and moral patient care. As Reenie discovers in this chapter, it might be necessary for social workers to "reach into the far reaches of the Internet." This means that there is a growing body of technical resources that have become the handmaiden of many professional groups and social workers must begin to use these technologies in order to be more effective. While there is no blueprint about how or where to find all the information that is needed, the most important step is to feel "excited" by the quest for information. Reenie's initial return on the investment of her time on the Internet gave her a way of looking at the benefits of brief treatment with an outcomes-based approach, and the decisions for brief treatment also reflect a clear agreement between the patient and social worker. This is in keeping with the mandate of health care reform in which the inclusion of patients in their own treatment needs is a major measure of outcome because it avoids noncompliance and is a deterrent to paternalistic practice.

Positive change is echoed by other members of the team as well. Dr. Oliviero is excited at the idea of a group of doctors getting together to form their own network. This network can then negotiate with managed care plans. Although some financial risk is involved, Dr. Oliviero likes the idea that physicians would have some autonomy in setting their own practice parameters. He appears hopeful because he sees his involvement as active; he is shaping and creating a system that can help patients receive quality treatment and meet the needs for professionals to set these goals. He recognizes that this approach, while not totally safe, is better than his past behavior which was dictated by inaction and distancing himself from the problem. He is at least working toward a better solution. These steps for the team do not insure that the system will change or even work better. Organizing goals is still one small part of effecting change in health care systems. However, it is the necessary first step in addressing change. Dr. Oliviero does not expect such issues as the use of contract workers which has become common in managed health care plans to change overnight. He does recognize, however, that this type of professional service excludes attention to broader issues of patient care. If he wishes to effect changes in this area, he knows that he must provide outcome data to justify his proposed changes.

The last part of the chapter focuses on personal growth. Violet's interpersonal relations are affected by her role changes. She responds with insight and perception to people around her. The context of how she lives begins to take on different meanings. It is not only an internal adjustment that takes place but an altered perception of environmental cues and how these cues are perceived. A simple activity such as making a meal becomes an enormous difficulty. The relationships of bowl to counter, of hands to implement, of object to floor have to be relearned in order to do a simple task of daily living.

She ponders why she did not take OT kitchen training while she was in the hospital. Her reaction at the time was understandable. She did not perceive a need for it and there was nothing in her previous environment that would have cued her to the significance of using mixing bowls. In addition, her professional identify was formed by mastering space and using it and controlling it. Thus, no system of rehabilitation can make patients face or anticipate all of the things they might need to reevaluate. However, a good treatment plan includes an assessment of what outcomes are of significance to the patient and which the patient should most likely concentrate and focus on. Using past and present strengths in a comprehensive treatment plan may enable a patient-oriented approach to rehabilitation. In the case of Violet, she uses her ability to relate to an audience coupled with a need to adapt to her present disability and conceives a new role for herself. While making a video for the disabled is not the same as being a principal dancer, it fulfills a need for her to return to a career. This outcome should ideally begin at the hospital and be part of the rehabilitation process because it reflects both instrumental as well as functional needs of the patient. As the hospital in the narrative begins to make plans to merge with a major managed care organization, the health care team now takes a personal interest in shaping the system and becoming actively involved in restructuring and putting into motion some of their ideas for patient care.

Raderstorf, Hein, and Jencsen (1984) note the benefits of the team approach in rehabilitation efforts with stroke patients, especially the coordinated approach, which enables each patient to return to his or her previous capabilities. Little is known, however, about the needs of younger stroke patients, especially those under the age of 40. These authors provide an analysis of the literature of young stroke patients who return to work, which they use as an indicator of a successful outcome in the rehabilitation. Their review showed that the percent of return to work is low, about 20 to 30 percent. Although the literature is scant, they conclude that the perceived chances of returning to work for stroke patients, especially those with aphasia, are low and therefore this aspect of rehabilitation has been neglected among professionals. There is some indication that present attitudes toward vocational potential are likely to reflect a negative attitude even among professionals. These authors stress the importance of examining the interplay of psychosocial factors in returning a patient to work. Through the use of a case history of a 31-year-old married male machinist who had a stroke, they examine the necessary steps to enable returning to the worksite.

Their plan includes a site visit by the rehabilitation team, a visit to the patient's employer, and a commitment from the patient to work through the difficult times. Of prime concern to the patient in the case study was how his coworkers would accept him in light of his physical and communicative deficits. Once the team members had made the site visit, they were able to prepare the patient for specific duties and prepare him for his coworkers' responses. His therapy goals were defined to focus on returning to work as the major outcome because this was of prime importance to the patient. Part of the therapeutic plan included a team visit with the patient's employer in order to discuss certain accommodations to the work schedule. Returning to work uncovered some unanticipated problems and called for continuing accommodations on the part of the patient. But the necessary changes were made to the work site and the patient's coworkers provided encouragement. This was a key factor in rebuilding the patient's self-confidence and aided in other personal development as well. Overall, by establishing his identity as a productive worker, the patient was able to build confidence and assume other responsibilities in his life.

This chapter emphasizes the importance of the work role in forming a person's sense of identity and worth. The patient in this narrative is forced to plan her own rehabilitation of that role since there is no set model from which she can learn. Violet actually provides the model in front of her support group. She teaches Reenie the lesson of using an action plan as a guide to rehabilitation. Reenie may then use this information to help her formulate rehabilitation plans for other patients as well. Glassman (1991) notes the humanistic values social group work has in enabling the norms of democratic interactions and a mutual aid system. These norms provide the framework of equality of objectives that makes social group work a distinct healing form. These norms allow clients to experience role transitions in a more enabling perspective. This is of particular importance for the chronically ill who must make major adaptations to life patterns. Glassman lists nine norms of group work that enable these role transitions (205–210):

Inherent Worth of the Individual. This emphasizes the individual as a being with an energy of his or her own and every member must own the events that brought them to the medical setting.

Individuals' Responsibility for One Another. Responsibility and need for others counteracts isolation, fear, and despair during illness, and mutual aid helps people build support and linkages that connect members to their group.

Right to Belong and to Be Included. Those in crisis can feel stigmatized by illness. Acceptance of differences allows participation by all types of members with varying responses to illness.

Right to Be Heard and to Take Part. Everyone is expected to participate; people learn to listen to each other for a cohesive and egalitarian group to emerge.

Right to Self-Determination. Powerlessness and lack of control often accompany chronic illness despite the patient's right to self-worth and dignity. Members should be encouraged to vocalize concerns to the institution that serves them about their routines and programs in the hospital.

Worker's Accountability to the Group. The social worker is expected to be a member of the group but to have skills that differentiate him or her from other group members. The group can hold the worker accountable for his or her actions and behaviors which gives members an opportunity to provide feedback to a professional in authority. This encourages members to react to the worker's behaviors and the medical structure and regulations.

Right to Freedom of Speech and Freedom of Expression. This norm requires a broadening of communication skills across group members so that all members experience the emotions and expressions of the group. Everyone makes the effort to participate with others.

Enrichment through Difference. Difference should be fostered because it has the therapeutic value of showing how diversity can lead members to find support and newer adaptive modes. The worker allows and protects the member who is different in affect, ideas, culture, race, class, gender, or age and the group learns to connect those members' affective modes.

Freedom of Choice. To feel responsible for one's destiny, members must experience the right of free choice in their group environment. This norm protects the member's right to choose what and how to change or not change. The worker clarifies the risk and experimentation aspects of the change process and identifies the member's free choice to change. The norm allows the value of freedom of choice in that a flexible role repertoire is permitted in the group and the worker can point out when members have changed or when the group has failed to acknowledge change.

These principles of group interaction were displayed in the patient support group as well as in the team meeting in this chapter. Although surprised, Reenie acknowledges Violet's painful risks and recognizes her choices in determining how the process of adaptation challenged her to action. In turn, the members of the group feel energized and encouraged by Violet's ability to share her painful and humiliating experiences and demonstration that she willingly took these actions. The team members' abilities to convey to each other their weaknesses and lack of initiatives in making action plans were received with encouragement and acceptance. Dr. Oliviero uses the term *reconstituted team* to describe a revitalized concept of the team's identity. Purtilo (1994) points out that understanding the team's moral and functional roles is important in evaluating the demands of health care reform. Professional ethics, she maintains, require that the moral function of the team includes respect for patients and the protection of their dignity. Some aspects of doing what is morally right is the consistent and responsible sharing of information so that team attempts to frame a comprehensive treatment plan are sensitive to patient's needs and preferences and provide reassurance to the patients and their families that the desire to show respect is a full expression of viewing the patient as a person. While not all teams are concerned about moral functions, for example, those who are more interested in providing functional tasks (i.e., cardiovascular technology), the ultimate goal is to provide quality patient care. This includes full expression of the patient's needs in the assessment of health care services. If too much emphasis by managed health care systems is placed on the functional roles of teams, the moral responsibility to patient care and well-being might be ignored. The heavy emphasis on measuring quality according to outcome data may be conducive to cost savings and efficiency but may not enable the patient to be assessed by internal criteria of well-being that instrumental tasks focus on. Despite this concern, there are arguments in the social work literature that more attention needs to focus on understanding the relevance of a systems approach that includes outcome assessments.

Raymond (1977) notes that social work education must respond to the changing environmental demands of the health care system so that social workers learn more about concepts of accountability. The "belt tightening" philosophy of the 1960s and 1970s was in large part directed at social welfare programs. There was a need "to show with facts and figures that we are actually helping people in the ways we claim" (430). Accountability, he argues, does not mean describing what we do. Documentation of cases, describing services offered, and hours spent offering services to clients cannot justify a departmental budget. "We cannot say we 'do good' and expect such descriptions of our activities and processes to provide sufficient proof of this assertion. We must demonstrate what good is" (430). He suggests that being accountable means to prove that a program (one social workers are offering) is the best means of responding to a problem. Thus, accountability involves determining what is the most appropriate, effective, and efficient way of achieving a particular objective. To be truly accountable, the social worker in the health care delivery system must determine and make known the needs of the client population, actively engage in developing policies that respond to those needs, and provide factual evidence that he or she is implementing these programs as mandated. This also means developing empirical evidence that can demonstrate whether these programs are accomplishing their objectives. Raymond notes that schools of social work have failed to provide adequate content to enable social workers to make and demonstrate significant contributions in the health care field. He cites, for example, the need for case load management evaluation, statistical and narrative reporting methods, and short- and long-term program development planning to name a few. He believes that schools should provide students with more training in identifying and analyzing social problems and setting goals and objectives to develop effective programs. This should be done at both the micro and macro levels. Program relevance is tied to good evaluation as well.

Raymond (1977) views this approach as starting with the problem and then defining the goal. Once the goal is defined, alternative ways to achieve the goal can be identified. The agency then chooses the alternative way that is most effective, efficient, and encompasses its professional values. This approach is a significant shift from the traditional way of operating because social workers usually address every kind of individual or social problem with either case work, group work, or community organization or some combination of each. While some solutions have worked, others have not. A systems approach demands that social workers start not with the method but with the problem and then discover the method most appropriate. Social workers in health care settings utilizing systems approaches would determine not only the best means but best mix of techniques to achieve goals. This may require certain aspects of a social work program that are not highly effective or are too costly to be removed. This tug of war between the functional and moral requirements of patient care affects decisions of the treatment team. On one hand, as described in Chapter 5, there is a need to upgrade knowledge about outcome data in order to be effective in today's complex health care system. At the same time, patient care issues are not easily discernable. They may take weeks or months to be evident to the patient, and as noted through the struggles of Violet, sometimes it takes some experience in the real world in order to be able to articulate a holistic approach to recovery. For a social worker like Reenie, it would be counterproductive to see her invest all her energies in becoming part of a system that was not compatible with her moral or instrumental responsibilities to her patients.

The more functional needs, however, take less time to plan and are more amenable to a clearer measurement of outcome. Think for example how Violet's problem of finding the right kind of bathroom fixtures was solved (via telephone call) compared to her need to redefine her personal worth. Yet both of these are aspects of well-being and adaptation. These tasks, as Reenie has noted, are difficult to measure in terms of cost analysis. The challenge to the student in examining issues of managed care system needs is to develop a vision of a social service model that is both patient-driven and morally responsible, yet effective and accountable. This must also be accomplished within a changing health care system that is driven by cost savings and community rather than hospital-based services. The final chapter examines an approach that might accomplish these goals.

Practice Skills

Client

1. Using Glassman's (1991) nine norm requirements for an effective approach to rehabilitation of the chronically ill (pages 161–163 of this text), develop a model for Reenie's support group so that the patients are enabled to make an action plan that will approach change and return them to productivity. Include in this model attention to both moral and functional aspects of rehabilitation.
2. How does Violet begin to resolve her role crisis? How has her view of change been altered? What part does risk taking play in the resolution?

Social Worker

1. How does the social worker begin to resolve her role crisis? How has her view of change been altered? What part does risk taking play in the resolution?

Team

1. How does the team begin to resolve its role crisis? How has its view of change been altered? What part does risk taking play in the resolution?

2. Using the case example of the 31-year-old machinist described by Raderstorf, Hein, and Jencsen (1984), what creative approaches might this team formulate for assisting Violet and her family?
3. After you have developed your approach, discuss ways you could operationalize and measure success. What indicators would demonstrate that your approach was efficient and morally acceptable in terms of defining quality of care?

System

1. What impact do the preceding changes on the part of the client, the social worker, and the team have on system responsiveness to client needs?

6

Compromise: Good But Not Perfect

"A toast to Violet," Reenie called above the din, raising her glass of fresh-squeezed orange juice. "A woman who has stared change straight in the eye and laughed in its face."

"I second the motion," Frank Pearman raised his glass as Carolyn, Josh, Dr. Oliviero, and Steve clinked in tribute to the blushing Violet.

"I don't think 'laugh' would be quite accurate," Violet protested. "I have come a long way, though. I will grant that."

"I can't wait for you all to see the video," Reenie gushed. "Violet was great. And the food was delicious, too, I might add. I would put the meal she prepared with just one functional arm up against that of any two-armed, five-star chef in the city."

"How did you learn to adapt so quickly, Violet?" Josh asked. "Did you have occupational therapy at home?"

"Occupational therapy at home was not a covered benefit for her," Reenie responded automatically, as if she were in team meeting.

"I had Steve," Violet smiled shyly. "That is a rare benefit indeed."

"You showed her how to cook?" Josh asked.

"She showed herself." Steve answered.

"You are an amazing woman," Carolyn admired her former patient.

"No, I'm not. It is like the song Steve played for me one day right after I got home. Remember?"

"Which one? I played every piece of music I had trying to keep you out of my hair so I could finish that bathroom," Steve teased.

Violet hummed a little before singing softly,

There is a woman I know, her body is weak.
And on a good day, she walks with a cane.
She lives with her pain everyday.
But somehow she awakes each morning and faces the day.
And she tries to be happy.

They say that she's brave, but she says what choice do I have?
I cannot hide in bed and cry.
I'm an ordinary woman, in an extraordinary world.

We all have something, some challenge or grief.
I see in your eyes, how you cope with your fate.
We all live with our pain every day.
But somehow we awake each morning and face the day.
And we try to be happy. And we try to be happy.
We're all ordinary people, in an extraordinary world.
(Written by Dawn Arnold 1995. Used by permission.)

"That says it all for me. I didn't want to change. But I didn't want to die either. Given a choice I would take my life as 'Violet Mason, principal dancer of the Metropolitan Ballet and wife of Jack Mason.' But I don't have a choice. In order to survive, I have to find some way to go on. Something extraordinary happened to me, and I responded as any ordinary person would. And I don't really believe that going back would be best for me, it would just be familiar. Change came to me uninvited. I had to decide whether I wanted to hide in bed or embrace change as an adventure leading me to other riches. Steve taught me that."

It was Steve's turn to blush. "When I came back from Nam I knew life would never be the same. I hated the changes but I knew I had to chop my way through them or spend the rest of my life fighting a war that ended in a jungle back in '73."

"Well, congratulations to you both on very impressive outcomes in the face of change," Frank responded.

"Violet had the funding she needed, fortunately," Reenie observed quickly, rolling her eyes at Frank's rose-colored administrative glasses. "Other patients in managed care are not so lucky."

"We're fighting a war of sorts in health care," Carolyn added. "Insurance companies call all of the shots," she explained to Violet and Steve.

"You exaggerate a bit," Frank countered.

"The way case managers for insurance companies micromanage, they might as well grab a scalpel and do the surgery themselves," Dr. Oliviero bristled.

"Doc, you gotta do what I had to do," Steve looked the physician in the eye. "Chop your way through or waste your time fighting a war that is over."

"Come on, guys. I see what Steve is saying," Reenie sat up a little straighter. "Managed care is here to stay. That is a done deal. All we can control now is what we do with it."

"Maybe it is like stroke rehab," Josh offered. "You work to develop compensatory strategies to deal with functional deficits while you wait for the body to heal."

"You maximize what you have and become very creative about what you don't have," Violet agreed.

"And researchers work feverishly for a cure," Dr. Oliviero laughed.

"Good point, doctor," Frank surprised the physician by concurring. "The challenge for you, for us as a health care team, is twofold: develop effective compensatory strategies to deal with the functional deficits of managed care and search feverishly for a better way. The system can change, too. Managed care is not here to stay. That's not healthy. Change is good. Managed care is here to change and grow."

"Okay, then, let's be creative," Reenie's brain was churning. "Let's make a game out of it. Health care is now managed care. How do we maximize what is left and what can we creatively do to compensate for what is missing or gone?"

"What should the program look like under managed care?" Carolyn considered the question.

"Right. If we could design the system, what would it look like?"

"Okay, so . . . ," Dr. Oliviero sighed heavily and reluctantly entered the fray, ". . . we've been spinning our wheels fighting managed care. We should be thinking instead of our vision for a better system that fits the managed care construct."

"Exactly!" Frank toasted the team gleefully. "I like this. Finally."

"Yeah, well, you haven't heard what we've come up with yet—you might not be so pleased." Reenie jabbed.

"Let's hear it! Let's get to work on some creative innovations to the system," Frank hunkered down over a napkin, ready to take notes.

Reenie joined the others in a deep quiet indicative of intense thought before beginning to think out loud. "It seems to me that part of what we have lost is art. Every thriving civilization embraces and nurtures art. Managed care has killed the art of medicine, the art of social work."

"So what can you do to uncover the art of medicine in managed care?" Frank asked.

"Impossible." Dr. Oliviero answered quickly.

"Only if you think it is," Frank pushed the envelope. "Come on, people, think. What does art need to thrive?"

"Freedom. Intelligence. A peer community. Financial support," Carolyn began to brainstorm.

"So find a way to build those into your system," Frank directed.

"That is the primary purpose of the physician network," Dr. Oliviero reflected. "We are taking on the financial risk—and responsibility—so that we can have the freedom to practice our art."

"Absolutely. It is a great idea." Frank offered.

"I wonder if social workers could form networks, incorporate perhaps, contracting to take cases on a capitated basis? That way we take on the financial risk and retain the freedom to practice our art."

"Why not?" Frank shrugged his shoulders, believing anything to be possible.

"It is harder for nurses. We basically follow orders."

"Your creativity may come in how you follow those orders, though. What level of personnel is at the bedside, what level does paperwork, that sort of thing," Frank helped Carolyn think through the nursing dilemma.

"I don't think it is possible to change how things are done in nursing. There are so many laws, regulations, standards." Carolyn was struggling to find a way to adapt to the changes foisted on her profession.

"You have to think outside the box," Frank encouraged.

"What box?" Carolyn was drawing a blank.

"I can't say much, since I'm not part of your hospital there," Steve cleared his throat awkwardly.

"Oh, please, say whatever comes to mind. You are an important part of the team." Frank reassured.

"Seems to me, ma'am, that you may have to retrain your nursing staff based on what you're saying. It's like remodeling a bathroom to make it accessible."

"Box, bathroom—I'm lost, guys," Carolyn was growing more confused.

"Well, ma'am, I can't really talk, but I know that just because I adapt a bathroom, it doesn't mean the person who owns it is going to adapt to using it. Both things have to happen before it becomes functional."

"Okay, I'm starting to see," Carolyn was nodding her head. "Nurses may need training to adapt to the new system, whatever it is, before it becomes functional for them. I need to design with that in mind."

"Precisely!" Frank Pearman was positively beaming.

"What about you, Violet? What does the patient need from the health care system?"

"That is hard for me to answer. I know what might have been helpful for me, but the same thing would not necessarily have been important to others. Every member of my support group, for example, needed something different. But I also think patients should voice discontent. I should write to someone, probably my HMO, to voice my complaints about the poor rehab program it offered instead of taking the easy way out and paying for it."

"Boy, isn't that the truth," Reenie agreed. "How in the world do we design a system that meets all of those needs? It is impossible."

"As the man said, impossible only if we allow it to be," Dr. Oliviero subtly gave Frank Pearman his stamp of approval for the first time. "We have to build a system that can adapt to the variable needs of clients."

"Oh, you know what just popped into my head?" Carolyn was getting in to the spirit of the discussion. "We need to offer services similar to the way Human Resources offers our benefits. They give us a dollar amount to spend, and the list of possible benefits. We get to decide how to allocate our available dollars—health insurance, life insurance, days off, day care, etcetera."

"Oh, I like it," Reenie shared Carolyn's excitement. "We develop a wide range of services from which the patient can choose?"

"I don't think I was informed enough to know what to choose, though," Violet was dubious. "I also want to know when doctors think my care is inferior to standards they set."

"We would have to build in sufficient consultation and professional support for patients. But it might work, Violet. If we told you, you have *X* dollars to spend and these thirty services available, say, then you could work with the team to decide how to allocate your resources to best meet the needs in your life." Reenie tried to think through how "cafeteria-style" health care might work. Perhaps videos are a good way to inform the public.

"It could work, Violet," Steve followed Reenie's train of thought. "Just like when I modified your bathroom. I had a budget, a set figure given to me by the insurance and by your ex. I knew what all the possibilities for changes were, what I could do. I discussed it with your ex and with you and we decided what changes made the most sense and fit within the given budget. You were willing to give up your imported faucet in order to get handles you could turn more easily. Another person might want to keep the handles, but change the height of the sink or something."

"Yes, I see. That could work." Violet supported the concept.

"These are terrific ideas. I would just like to throw out that your system design needs to include a method of evaluating effectiveness," Frank cautioned. "That will partially address Violet's concern that she wouldn't have enough information to select services on her own. It would also give us the ammunition we need to make certain insurance companies allow sufficient budgets for a diagnosis. We need to develop useful information about which of our services is effective, and in what situation. It is the blending of this science with your art that will offer the most for clients."

"I can see that," Dr. Oliviero agreed.

"So, these are great ideas. How do I advocate for change to take place?" Reenie addressed Frank directly.

"Don't advocate, Reenie. *Do.* We need action, not talking about the need for action. You have to apply science to your art to determine effectiveness, and then sell your product to the payer. Preparation is the key."

"Yes, sir," Steve threw in. "Got to prepare. Can't go throwing your eggs in the fry pot before the grease is hot."

"Will you work with us?" Carolyn looked for a commitment from the administrator. "We are talking about developing professional networks that may contract with the hospital system, setting up cafeteria-style services that are patient-driven, measuring outcomes to evaluate effectiveness, and retraining our professionals to know how to use a new system. We are going to need help!"

"How about a meeting Monday morning, 8 A.M.? My office. We'll get to work on it right away," Frank offered.

"I'll be there," Dr. Oliviero was the first to commit, followed quickly by the other team members.

"Violet, Steve, you are welcome to join us," Frank included the couple in his planning team.

"Might have to set up a conference call on that one, boss," Steve responded. "By Monday morning we'll be at our house trying to turn that old barn into a dance studio."

"A dance studio?" Josh was intrigued.

"Yes, sir. Violet is going to do some teaching, has an idea for choreographing a wheelchair ballet, right, ballerina? She wants to teach dance to other patients. Give them some art in their lives. She's also in my life, too. I can't believe I've ended up with a ballerina," Steve added proudly.

"Right, and no mercy to you. I'm lots of hard work. I can't do Swan Lake with the Metropolitan, but I will be involved in dance again. I can't wait."

"What a wonderful gift to give, Violet," Reenie was excited to hear of the plans. "Not perfect, I know. You can't rejoin the ballet like you wanted, but maybe this will be good enough."

"You're exactly right, Reenie. My life is not perfect, but it is definitely good enough," Violet smiled knowingly at Steve.

Frank raised his glass to toast again. "Here's to Violet. May the system we design be as wonderful as her life—good, but not perfect. A lofty goal indeed."

Analysis

The final chapter demonstrates the conceptual framework of the book. In the final meeting of the patient and the team, an approach to a *good but not perfect* ending (or beginning?) is depicted. Adaptation, creativity, integration of relationships, and role enhancement is contrasted with the first chapter that depicted denial, refusal, isolation, and role stagnation. Violet comments that it wasn't just the treatment that enabled her to adapt to and create a new view of her capacities and talents, it was the human relationships and interactions with Steve that allowed her to reach into herself for her unique, if not different, potential. This relationship with mutual regard and warmth is a representation of the ideal of interdisciplinary practice. Violet and Steve are very different, yet despite their different philosophies, training, and sensitivities, their interactions with each other displayed understanding and respect. Violet learned determination and resolve from Steve and Steve learned to express himself, a trait he had buried following the Vietnam War. These individuals are key characters because they demonstrate how diversity can create synthesis and give individuals a level of confidence to enable them to try new ideas and approach skill development as a natural occurrence rather than a chore. The road to this level of functioning was not depicted as easy, as adaptation and growth requires both despair and hope. Violet so aptly states, "Given a choice, I didn't want to change. But I don't have a choice." Change came to Violet uninvited but finally not unwelcome. The uninvited change becomes a metaphor for the changes in the health care system. Does managed care stay as an uninvited guest or is it an adventure that requires new leadership? Steve echoes the sentiments that form the final analysis of the book. "The war is over." Managed care is the result of a tangle of complex issues that resulted from years of growth in the health care industry and the consumer demands and cost inflation that came with rapid technology. True, as Reenie says "managed care is here to stay," but the broader question the reader must ask is for how long and in what form and with what changes. On a similar vein, can managed care adapt to managed care system changes? What new faces will managed care have in the next ten years or more?

Frank Pearman, the social worker turned managed care administrator, offers a better way of looking at the system, "Develop effective compensatory strategies to deal with the functional deficits of managed care and search feverishly for a better way." (Consider why he was not identified as a social worker at the beginning of the book.) And so the team members begin to consider how a better system or a managed care system with new regulations might be designed. Whether their points are on target, predictive, or futuristic is not as important as their attempt to empower themselves as health professionals in taking an active role in contributing their ideas and strategies for change to the system. This practice leads to goal development and communication within their professional groups the way denial and anger led to stagnation in the initial chapters. The team members are now able to envision a system that might work with them as they resume their professional power of influence and competence.

Reenie wants to regain the lost art of practice. Carolyn uses such words as *freedom, intelligence,* and *peer community* to describe a better system. The team members reinforce each other, each person's suggestions are respected and listened to. They acknowledge that change can be small yet significant and that change requires a lot of work, not just criticism. The words of the team are positive, supportive. Actual reflective listening is taking place. This, too, provides the empowerment necessary to form a team self-concept and to use this concept to interact with other levels of the organization. "Thinking outside the box" is what Frank Pearman suggests. Steve gives the analogy by showing that building something one person thinks is wonderful doesn't insure the person who owns it will think it's wonderful (the bathtub he built, for example, for Violet was not viewed this way by her initially). This is how managed care philosophy separated practitioners from administrators. Each had different views of the structure. Until Violet saw the bathtub as useful and knew she could work with it, the change had no significance for her. It is not only the structure that must be adapted to but the person behind the structure, the builder, the engineer. Thus, the best designs and plans begin in the mind and require more than adaptation to a structure to make them acceptable and finally usable. They require a relationship with the designer of the structure. This requires listening to the people who use the structure, the consumers, and as such, the patient-oriented system means the patient's voice is heard.

As the team develops ideas for a new system, certain elements appear. The team formulates a cafeteria plan of services in which patient input is an important element in the design. Frank suggests that evaluating effectiveness should be an important part of the system while Violet expresses concern that patients wouldn't have enough information to select services on their own. Frank sees the blending of science with art as offering the most effective system for clients. Frank tells Reenie that advocating for change (the traditional social work approach) won't help. "Don't advocate, Reenie, *Do,*" he suggests. Carolyn suggests developing professional networks that may contract with hospital systems and retrain current staff. The team as well as Violet and Steve are invited to join Frank for a Monday morning planning meeting. The team views the system and life as good but not perfect. A system that lacks perfection is always open for improvement.

In addition to what was demonstrated in the final chapter, managed care systems are already undergoing changes. You may wonder whether managed care is really here to stay or if it will be here but in an entirely new form or if this new form will be called managed care. Following are some recent developments. On August 21, 1997, President Clinton signed into law the Kassenbaum-Kennedy 1996 Health Insurance Portability and Accountability Act. According to Kuttner's (1997a) analysis, currently two-thirds of Americans are insured through their employers and a loss of a job has often meant the loss of a health plan. With the rise of medical underwriting and denial of new insurance to people with preexisting conditions, the loss could be permanent. Thus, people were deemed uninsurable because they changed jobs. Therefore, some people remained with jobs because they would be uninsurable if they left. Kuttner noted that a detailed study prepared for Senator Kassenbaum by the General Accounting Office found that 18 percent of people seeking new individual policies were flatly turned down because of their health status and that insurers often charged two or three times the standard rate to subscribers they considered medical risks and excluded from coverage particular conditions that they knew affected the person seeking insurance. As such, in his analysis of the Health Insurance Portability and Accounting Act, he maintains that its collection of limitations "sheds useful light on how a fragmented health insurance system resists fixing. The messy blend of federal and state regulations mirrors the fragmentation of the insurance system itself and compounds the complexity" (64).

The Health Insurance Portability and Accountability Act establishes federal standards for individual, small-group, and large-group insurance plans. The law will be phased in as the states implement its provisions between July 1, 1997, and July 1, 1998. The new standards generally prohibit discrimination against applicants on the basis of their health status and require that insurance be renewable except when premiums are not paid. Employers may not drop coverage or charge higher prices to employees or their dependents because of health conditions. Persons, however, may not take along their current insurance if they change jobs, and if the candidate has had insurance for at least eighteen months, no exclusions can be imposed for preexisting conditions nor can insurance plans deny coverage. If a person was insurable under one carrier, then that should be good enough for the second. However, Kuttner (1997a) states that coverage may be inferior and a person's doctor may not be on the plan; if there is a period of lapse or unemployment or if a job does not offer group insurance, the new law is more ambiguous and less effective. To qualify for protection under the Act, a person has had to have had insurance before, although the Health Insurance Portability and Accountability Act allows people whose COBRA plans have been exhausted to convert to new insurance coverage.

Jerome Kassirer, editor of *The New England Journal of Medicine*, criticizes the recently announced "Putting Patients First" initiative of the American Association of Health Plans (AAHP), the principal organization that represents managed care. He believes this initiative is "little more than a thinly veiled attempt to ward off state and federal legislative actions to curb the abuses of managed care" (Kassirer 1997, 338). The AAHP has approximately one thousand member health maintenance organizations (HMOs) and preferred provider organizations in forty-eight states and represents more than 90 percent of all health care plans in the country. The plans represented by the AAHP insure 140 million people. For-profit plans constitute approximately two-thirds of the total numbers (Kassirer 1997). He notes that since the failure of the Clinton health plan, managed care has been the object of considerable public scrutiny. In this period of enormous growth, it has been accused of many things: denial of care, gagging of physicians, callous treatment of women after childbirth and mastectomy, disproportionate attention to profit, and refusal to accept responsibility for medical teaching and research (338). To respond to these allegations, he names at last count some 1,000 bills to control health plan practices that have been introduced in thirty-nine states and approximately one hundred have been introduced to Congress. He points to a recent survey by a public relations firm who examined 589 citations in newspapers, magazines, and transcripts of television news programs which found five unfavorable stories for every favorable one on managed care. In a recent national poll that asked people to rate twelve industries according to how good a job they were doing for consumers, health insurance companies were ranked second and third from the bottom just above the tobacco industry.

Kassirer (1997) believes that managed care responded to criticism by enacting the AAHP's "Putting Patients First" initiative. The initiative has several components, all of which involve physicians in their development and implementation. It includes a quality assessment program to detect any patterns of underservice or overservice. A clinical-guideline program aims to provide current information and decision support to practitioners. A utilization-management program is designed to determine coverage by evaluating the appropriateness of health care services, and a drug-formulary program is aimed at deciding which drugs to offer on the basis of current medical practice and pharmacoeconomic information. He notes added elements are still in development.

Kassirer (1997) criticizes this initiative on the basis of a paucity of clear, strong standards and the absence of rigorous enforcement since most of the standards are in the form of recommendations, not requirements, and the language is "replete with shoulds, not musts" (338). Additionally, what he sees as more problematic is that informing health plan enrollees about utilization, rules, drug-formulary rules, the process the plan uses to determine coverage of experimental procedures, and financial incentives for physicians is available only if the patient requests the information. Members do not have to release specific details of physicians' financial arrangements, and compliance with AAHP guidelines is strictly voluntary. When applying for or renewing membership, a plan has only to attest to its adherence to the principles and practices of "Putting Patients First." Additionally, the AAHP will not release information about the number and types of complaints against a particular plan. AAHP opposes legislation that bans gag rules which prevent physicians from disclosing coverage options and the incentives under which they are paid, and AAHP opposes legislation that would allow lenient definitions of emergency room coverage. Kassirer concludes that AAHP is trying to protect its members' ability to hold down costs and avert external constraints on their practices.

Last, Kassirer (1997) concludes the initiative is not accountable to the public and he believes it is a ploy to stave off governmental involvement in protecting the public against the excesses of managed care. Rather, he believes that AAHP, as the organization that speaks for the industry, will be credible only if it explains *the real rationale for its public positions.* "To truly put patients first, it will have to strengthen the standards of its new program substantially and introduce rigorous compliance procedures" (338).

On the patient level, challenging existing assumptions about identity and self-concept and role capability is an essential element of stroke rehabilitation. Glass and Maddox (1992) view stroke as a type of event that initiates a psychosocial transition which calls upon an individual to make important and potentially lasting adjustments in their assumptions about the world they know and their interpretations of the past and expectations for the future. The challenge is acceptance and realization that the relationship between self and significant other is no longer the same; thus, there is a shift in social roles and identity. Stroke calls on the individual to bring into alignment his or her assumptive world with the newly modified life space. The effectiveness or necessary realignment constitutes effective coping and adaptation. Glass and Maddox (1992) note that the occurrence of a stroke may be described as a potentially useful and instructive event for studying psychosocial transitions because of its profound and potentially lasting impact on the life space and assumptive world of the individual. "Stroke takes place over a relatively short period and often strikes without warning and it alters the individual's capacity for social role function and functional independence" (1250). Patients must adjust to new definitions of self and new limitations in physical, psychological, and social capacity including cognitive deficits, disturbances in affect, limitation in mobility, or any combination of such factors. These impairments in vital capacities affect the patient's perception of competency, efficacy, and self-concept. Stroke patients have a demanding rehabilitation challenge. The challenge is to reestablish function and independence while incorporating residual deficits into a new personal identity and assumptive world. Thus, successful rehabilitation appears to require the construction of a new assumptive world which includes a sense of "mastery despite deficit" (1252). Additionally, McBroom (1978) points out that for social work students, the opportunity to observe the stabilization of chronic illness allows them time to come to grips with catastrophic conditions. This allows them to view the stressful reality of the patient and to understand the experience from the patient's point of view, which is many times different from what social work students might have assumed or expected.

This description of the adaptation to stroke describes not only the patient process but the process of adaptation to the health care system. The managed care crisis reflects the growing concern among professionals and the public over the changes in financing, ownership, access, administration, and professional practice that have altered the way health care is delivered in the United States. Until very recently, the comments in many professional journals have echoed such statements as "managed care is here to stay." More recently, the enormous assault on the system has changed the statement to "managed care's time has come." While the level of governmental monitoring and professional concern is growing, many individuals are again experiencing changes in their "assumptive worlds." Adaptation to the many anticipated changes causes a lot of anxiety and concern about the future of health care. As the Glassman and Maddox (1992) model theorizes, the change process entails a reorganization of thinking and feeling which makes the acceptance of change a slow but inevitable process.

Berkman (1996) notes that as the cost of health care approaches $1 trillion a year, 15 percent of the gross national product, the acute-care hospital, once the central institution of health care delivery, is responding by decentralizing and emphasizing community care. The number of services performed at out-of-hospital sites has accelerated and this has resulted in cost savings. The social work profession, she notes, has had to respond to this decentralized effect by examining how in the new health care paradigm of chronic complex illness episodes of care will be handled. Under the acute-care model, the role of the social worker was primarily to discharge patients and reduce rehospitalization and length of stay through the provision of necessary posthospital care services and resources. The social worker must be involved throughout this continuum. More and more services will be required by patients in ambulatory care including nonmedical and community-based services, such as home health care, physical therapy, occupational therapy, financial services, daycare, meals, and transportation. This suggests that social worker roles will expand into more autonomous outpatient settings and include a wide array of interventions and strategies ranging from discharge planning, adaptation to illness educational supports, risk management interventions for those dissatisfied with care, as well as consultation with other providers. The challenge in this newer system, which requires continuous interactions between health care systems, is to manage large, multiply complex issues of chronic illness that require a continuum of care and treatment from multiple professions through various services. Interdisciplinary collaboration with agencies and other providers will be essential for optimal practice. Social workers with this array of skills must be cost-effective because the present system is not adequately prepared to handle the demands and complexity of the psychosocial health care needs of the increasing number of chronically ill ambulatory patients. The goals of maintaining patients in the community is dependent on better standardized screening tools that use predictive factors to yield standardized scores which lead to an assessment of at-risk patients' social health care needs (544).

Berkman (1996) notes that increasing social workers' roles in outpatient settings to include identifying those in need of psychosocial help is necessary to change negative behaviors and stop the progression of disability that makes clients vulnerable to poor functioning. Additionally, addressing the multiple needs of patients serves the efficiency promoted in the managed care environment. When social workers are efficient in an interdisciplinary environment, the time of other team members is freed to provide therapeutic services. Clancy (1994) describes patient-focused care as a system that is patient-centered and clinically driven from preadmission through posthospitalization and includes decentralization of services, the use of clinical pathways (practice protocols), multiskilled workers, and cross-training. Understanding the roles and functions of other team members demands good communication skills and technical expertise which includes using electronic data resources and computers.

The critical path is a conceptual outline or protocol of the sequence of events and outcomes to be achieved by the patient during the episode of care. Critical paths are formal treatment plans that are prewritten in time intervals appropriate for each phase of treatment and include the process of interdisciplinary care (Bejciy-Spring, Neutzling, and Newton 1994). Critical paths for patient care becomes the cornerstone of the multidimensional needs of patients who have been hospitalized with chronic debilitating illness. Thus, as used in the nursing literature, according to these authors "it is an abridged version of the case management plan which is the detailed protocol of interdisciplinary care" (70). The critical path is then developed through the interdisciplinary process in which the outline for care is written down and reflects interdisciplinary efforts in an organized, predictable, time-managed plan. The practice patterns of the interdisciplinary team are incorporated into these tools specifying the responsibilities of nurses, physicians, therapists, dietitians, social workers, and other health care providers, and individual outcomes are integrated into the plan of care. These tools promote and strengthen collaboration and teamwork because of mutually agreed upon outcomes, time frames, processes, and responsibilities. Critical paths also enable early identification of deviations (variances) from the plan of care because they take into account factors of the patient-caregiver system that affect (positively or negatively) outcomes for the patient. This type of variance tracking helps in quality assessment and improvement factors. This variance data also indicates when there are problems at the patient, system, or personnel level and may suggest the need for practice or system change. With variance tracking, the case management process has an inherent check and balance system for the early detection and resolution of problems on a concurrent case-by-case basis (71). Additionally, client participation is noted by the nursing case manager in working with the interdisciplinary team when the course of treatment is charted and expected outcomes and time frames are planned.

The nurse case manager must recognize and work with differences that occur between the expectations of the treatment team and those of the patient. Bejciy-Spring, Neutzling, and Newton (1994) offer a case management plan for spinal cord injury. There are three components: the Patient Problem, the Discharge Goals/Expected Outcome, and the Interdisciplinary Process.

The Discharge Goals/Expected Outcome are mutually set with patient and/or family. The outcomes are listed with concurrent input from the interdisciplinary team, and the Interdisciplinary Process denotes who on the team is responsible for the resolution of individually identified outcomes (72). The complex physical and psychosocial care needs and the complex learning and discharge needs demand the attention and expertise of many health care professionals. The journey from intensive care through acute care to rehabilitation to community discharge requires careful planning for continuity of care to be maintained and optimal outcomes to be achieved. The case management process requires a collaboration effort guided by standards of care, interactive interdisciplinary team meetings, and consultation for shared planning and decision making. The ultimate goal is achieving optimal clinical, functional, and financial outcomes.

Both Berkman (1996) and Bejciy-Spring, Neutzling, and Newton (1994) concur that expanded case management is the crucial part of functional practice in a complex health care environment with its emphasis on ambulatory coordinated community-based care. The recognition of case management, clinical pathways, and interdisciplinary processes is evident in both the field of social work and nursing. There are advantages to each profession in the use of such protocols. Clancy (1994) notes "care to patients is delivered and standardized according to set protocols and recording of information is accomplished by exception-based charting. Such charting frees the average nurse form approximately two hours per day spent documenting" (4). Clancy also notes that enabling patient-focused care involves the use of computers, and therefore retraining of staff and team building is necessary. The implementation of patient-focused care also means including what patients want in their care.

Another view of the future of interdisciplinary practice is offered by Cyphert and Cunningham (1987). The traditional interprofessional medical team consists of six to ten members, represents five to seven professions, functions as an evaluation and treatment group, and deals with social and medical pathologies, usually though not always for situations of crisis. These teams meet face to face for one and a half hours and make decisions more or less by consensus. They also operate without strongly defined or sustained leadership. Cyphert and Cunningham propose over the next few years that many new models of interprofessional practice will emerge. One might be a basic team of three to four members who are joined by other professionals on an *as-needed* basis. This promotes efficiency in that all potential team members do not attend every meeting. A second arrangement could be labeled "two-tier" teams consisting of several groups that deal with differing aspects of the problem and report to a decision-making group, which synthesizes recommendations and reacts accordingly. This may be good for dealing with especially complex problems. A third form is the multiple-entry model, which may be used outside the health arena. This team exists only to deal with one problem. It is a team in the sense that there is some coordination of effort, usually by a case manager, minister, or social worker who draws on and communicates with needed professionals and maintains a common record and is capable of reaching consensus on decisions. This may be a realistic model for many situations when both economics and geography prevent constant face-to-face contact with the entire group. In each model, conclusions and solutions are broadened to include all or most of the areas that are under the realm of team practice including treatment, diagnosis, education, research, prevention, and policy making (154). Teams of the future must be flexible in order to deal with myriad communication networks and gather and disseminate information efficiently.

Berkman (1996) and Kadushin and Egan (1997) stress the importance of educating social work students and practitioners in health care to meet the challenges of the changing environment. In a recent study of course curriculum for graduate-level health care practice courses from fifty-three accredited schools, Kadushin and Egan (1997) emphasize that for the move from hospital-based care, the for-profit system of managed care, the emphasis on cost containment and the importance of understanding illness as a psychological transition makes the case management system the cornerstone of efficient and ethical practice. The fifty-three schools that participated in the study reported offering basic foundation content adapted to health care practice; the following represented the most frequent content, ranked in order: collaboration and teamwork, 77 percent; ethical issues, 64 percent; practice processes, 60 percent; theoretical frameworks, 55 percent; and financing of health care, 54 percent. The authors concluded that while there was some degree of consensus among schools about the basic foundation requirements necessary to teach initial health care practice, the content related to the changing health care environment and the impact of that environment on social work practice was included less frequently, and readings related to managed care were omitted from 85 percent of course outlines in practice courses (although they may have been covered in health care policy). Kadushin and Egan note that managed care issues need to be developed to include practice evaluation, short-term treatment models, financing and its impact on service, and ethical issues raised by managed care. They also suggest course content on discharge planning; coordination and case management for HIV/AIDS cases; and content on aging, long-term care, and chronic illness as well as more content on providing support to family caregivers.

Essential to the future of social work is the notion that health care system change is an expectation, not a response to crisis, and that alternative models of interprofessional practice are workable in different situations. The need for education in interdisciplinary settings is continuous and although it is difficult and complex it will require a commitment of high energy and reeducation. This book has attempted to demonstrate the slow but rewarding process of self-growth, the burdens of role changes, as well as the belief that psychosocial transitions are a meaningful part of life. View this book as a primer for hope, a vision for patient and professional involvement, for a system that is good—never perfect, but always striving.

Practice Skills

1. Describe your vision for an effective model of service delivery within managed care.
2. Design the implementation of your vision.
3. Implement your vision!

References

Abramson, M. 1984. Collective responsibility in interdisciplinary collaboration: An ethical perspective for social workers. *Social Work in Health Care,* 10(1): 35–43.

Abramson, M., and T. Mizrahi. 1986. Strategies for enhancing collaboration between social workers and physicians. *Social Work in Health Care,* 12(1): 1–21.

Abramson, J. S., and T. Mizrahi. 1996. When social workers and physicians collaborate: Positive and negative interdisciplinary experiences. *Social Work,* 41(3): 270–281.

Bejciy-Spring, S. M., E. Neutzling, and C. Newton. 1994. Nursing case management: Enhanced interdisciplinary care of the spinal cord injured patient. *SCI Nursing: A Publication of the American Association of Spinal Cord Injury Nurses,* 11(3): 70–73.

Berger, C. S., J. Cayner, G. Jensen, T. Mizrahi, A. Scesny, and J. Trachtenberg. 1996. The changing scene of social work in hospitals: A report of a national study by The Society for Social Work Administrators in Health Care and NASW. *Health and Social Work,* 21(3): 167–177.

Bergthold, L. A., and L. S. Solomon. 1997. Group purchasing in the managed care marketplace. In *Competitive managed care. The emerging health care system,* edited by J. D. Wilkerson, K. J. Devers, and R. S. Given. San Francisco: Jossey-Bass, Inc.

Berkman, B. 1996. The emerging health care world: Implications for social work practice and education. *Social Work,* 41(5): 541–551.

Biller, J. 1994. Spontaneous intracerebral hemorrhage. In *Stroke in children and young adults,* edited by J. Biller, K. D. Mathews, and B. B. Love. Newton, MA: Butterwork-Heineman.

Billups, J. O. 1987. Interprofessional team process. *Theory Into Practice,* 26(2): 146–152.

Blumenthal, D. 1996. Effects of market reforms on doctors and their patients. *Health Affairs,* 159(2): 170–184.

Brody, B. A. 1997. Ethical issues raised by managed care. *Texas Medicine,* 93(2): 43–45.

Burns, D. 1989. *The feeling good handbook.* New York: William Morrow and Company, Inc.

Burack-Weiss, A. 1995. The caregiver's memoir: A new look at family support. *Social Work,* 40(3): 391–396.

Castillo, C. S., S. K. Schultz, and R. G. Robinson. 1995. Clinical correlates of early-onset and late-onset post-stroke generalized anxiety. *American Journal of Psychiatry,* 152(8): 1174–1179.

Clancy, C. 1994. Patient-focused care: Part I. Danger or opportunity. *Social Work Administration,* 20(4): 2–6.

Cornelius, D. S. 1994. Managed care and social work: Constructing a context and a response. *Social Work in Health Care,* 20(1): 47–63.

Council on Ethical and Judicial Affairs. Ethical issues in managed care. American Medical Association. 1995. *Journal of the American Medical Association,* 273(4): 330–335.

Cowles, L. A., and M. J. Lefcowitz. 1992. Interdisciplinary expectations of the medical social worker in the hospital setting. *Health and Social Work,* 17(1): 57–65.

Cowles, L. A., and M. J. Lefcowitz. 1995. Interdisciplinary expectations of the medical social worker in the hospital setting: Part 2. *Health and Social Work,* 20(4): 279–286.

Cummings, N. A. 1995. Impact of managed care on employment and training: A primer for survival. *Professional Psychology: Research and Practice,* 26(1): 10–15.

Cyphert, F. R., and L. L. Cunningham. 1987. Interprofessional educational practice: A future agenda. *Theory in Practice,* 26(2): 153–156.

Dane, B. O., and B. L. Simon. 1991. Resident guests: Social workers in host settings. *Social Work,* 36(3): 208–213.

Davidson, J. R., and T. Davidson. 1996. Confidentiality and managed care: Ethical and legal concerns. *Health and Social Work,* 21(3): 208–215.

Davidson, K. W. 1990. Role blurring and the hospital social worker's search for a clear domain. *Health and Social Work,* 15(3): 228–234.

Davidson, T., and J. R. Davidson. 1995. Cost-containment, computers and confidentiality. *Clinical Social Work Journal,* 23(4): 453–464.

Emanuel, E. J., and N. N. Dubler. 1995. Preserving the physician-patient relationship in the era of managed care. *The Journal of the American Medical Association,* 273(4): 323–329.

Fraser, J. S. 1996. All that glitters is not always gold: Medical offset effects and managed care behavioral health care. *Professional Psychology: Research and Practice,* 27(4): 335–344.

Ginzberg, E., and M. Ostrow. 1997. Managed care: A look back and a look ahead. *The New England Journal of Medicine,* 336(14): 1018–1020.

Glass, T. A., and G. L. Maddox. 1992. The quality and quantity of social support: Stroke recovery as psychosocial transition. *Social Science and Medicine,* 34(11): 1249–1261.

Glassman, U. 1991. The social work group and its distinct healing qualities in the health care setting. *Health and Social Work,* 16(3): 203–211.

Gold, M., M. Sparer, and K. Chu. 1996. Medicaid managed care: Lessons from five states. *Health Affairs,* 15(3): 153–166.

Gold, M. R., R. Hurley, T. Lake, T. Ensor, and R. Beronson. 1995. A national survey of the arrangements managed-care plans make with physicians. *The New England Journal of Medicine,* 333(25): 1678–1683.

Halamka, J. D., P. Szolovits, D. Rind, and C. Safran. 1997. A WWW implementation of national recommendations for protecting electronic health information. *Journal of the American Medical Informatics Association,* 4(6): 458–464.

Hersch, L. 1995. Adapting to health care reform and managed care: Three strategies for survival and growth. *Professional Psychology: Research and Practice,* 26(1): 16–26.

Howell, E. M. 1996. Medicaid managed care encounter data: What, why and where next? *Health Care Financing Review,* 17(4): 87–95.

Huntt, D. C., and B. S. Growick. 1997. Managed care for people with disabilities. *The Journal of Rehabilitation,* 63(3): 10–14.

Inglehart, J. K. 1994a. Physicians and the growth of managed care. *The New England Journal of Medicine,* 331(17): 1167–1171.

Inglehart, J. K. 1994b. The struggle between managed care and fee-for-service practice. *The New England Journal of Medicine,* 331(1): 63–68.

Inglehart, J. K. 1996. Managed care and mental health. *The New England Journal of Medicine,* 334(2): 131–135.

Jackson, V. H. 1995. *A brief look at managed mental health care.* Washington, DC: NASW.

Johnson, L. A., and R. W. Derlet. 1996. Conflicts between managed care organizations and emergency departments in California. *Western Journal of Medicine,* 164(2): 137–142.

Jones, T. L. 1997. Managed care under fire. *Texas Medicine,* 93(3): 40–44.

Kadushin, G., and M. Egan. 1997. Educating students for a changing health care environment: An examination of health care practice course content. *Health and Social Work,* 22(3): 211–222.

Karon, B. P. 1995. Provision of psychotherapy under managed health care: A growing crisis and national nightmare. *Professional Psychology: Research and Practice,* 26(1): 5–9.

Kassirer, J. P. 1996. Mergers and acquisitions: Who benefits? Who loses? *The New England Journal of Medicine,* 334(11): 722–723.

Kassirer, J. P. 1997. Managing managed care's tarnished image. *The New England Journal of Medicine,* 337(5): 338–339.

Katz, L. A., and M. W. Cropp. 1994. Life of the HMO physician. In *The physician's guide to managed care,* edited by D. B. Nash. Gaithersburg, MD: Aspen Publisher, Inc.

Kern, S. 1995. Physician control of health care delivery in the managed care environment. *New Jersey Medicine: The Journal of the Medical Society of New Jersey,* 92(5): 318–320.

Kuttner, R. 1997a. The Kasembaum-Kennedy Bill: The limits of incrementalism. *The New England Journal of Medicine,* 337(1): 64–67.

Kuttner, R. 1997b. Physician-operated networks and the new antitrust guides. *The New England Journal of Medicine,* 336(5): 386–391.

La Pluma, J., and D. Schidermayer. 1994. Ethical issues in managed care and managed competition: Problems and promises. In *The physician's guide to managed care,* edited by D. B. Nash. Gaithersburg, MD: Aspen Publishers, Inc.

Lee, S. 1980. Interdisciplinary teaming in primary care: A process of evaluation and resolution. *Social Work in Health Care,* 5(3): 237–244.

Levit, K. R., H. C. Lazenby, B. R. Braden, and The National Health Accounts Team. 1998. National Health Spending Trends in 1996. *Health Affairs,* 17(1): 35–51.

Love, B. B., A. J. Orencia, and J. Biller. 1994. Stroke in children and young adults: Overview, risk factors, and prognosis. In *Stroke in children and young adults,* edited by J. Biller, K. D. Mathews, and B. B. Love. Newton, MA: Butterwork-Heineman.

Mackelprang, R. W. and R. O. Salsgiver. 1996. People with disabilities and social work: Historical and contemporary issues. *Social Work,* 41(1): 7–14.

Marmor, T., and J. Oberlander. 1998. Rethinking Medicare reform. *Health Affairs,* 17(1): 52–68.

McBroom, E. 1978. Interdisciplinary learning in the rehabilitation hospital. *Social Work in Health Care,* 3(4): 385–394.

Mellor, M. J., and R. Solomon. 1992. The interdisciplinary geriatric-gerontological team in the academic setting: Hot air or energizer? *Journal of Gerontological Social Work,* 18(3/4): 203–215.

Miller, I. J. 1996. Managed care is harmful to out-patient mental health services: A call for accountability. *Professional Psychology: Research and Practice,* 27(4): 349–363.

Miller, R. H., and H. S. Luft. 1994. Managed care plans performance since 1980. *Journal of the American Medical Association,* 271(19): 1512–1519.

Mitchell, J. B., D. J. Ballard, J. P. Whisnant, C. J. Ammering, G. P. Samsa, and D. B. Matchar. 1996. What role do neurologists play in determining the cost and outcome of stroke patients? *Stroke,* 27(11): 1937–1943.

Mitchell, K., K. C. Uehlinger, and J. Owen. 1996. The synergistic relationship between ethics and quality improvement: Thriving in managed care. *Journal of Nursing Care Quality,* 11(1): 9–21.

Mizrahi, T. 1993. Managed care and managed competition: A primer for social work. *Health and Social Work,* 18(2): 86–91.

Mizrahi, T., and J. Abramson. 1985. Sources of strain between physicians and social workers: Implications for social workers in health care settings. *Social Work in Health Care,* 10(3): 33–51.

Mukand, J., M. Kaplan, R. G. Senno, and D. S. Bishop. 1996. Pathological crying and laughing: Treatment with sertraline. *Archives of Physical Medicine and Rehabilitation,* 77: 1309–1311.

National Association of Social Workers. 1996. *NASW code of ethics.* Washington, DC: Author.

O'Neil, E., and L. J. Finocchio. 1997. The future of the health professions under managed care. In *Competitive managed care: The emerging health care system,* edited by J. D. Wilkerson, K. J. Devers, and R. S. Given. San Francisco: Jossey-Bass, Inc.

Parisi, L. 1997. What is influencing performance improvement in managed care? *Journal of Nursing Care Quality,* 11(4): 43–52.

Perloff, J. D. 1996. Medicaid managed care and urban poor people: Implications for social work. *Health and Social Work,* 21(3): 189–195.

Poole, D. L. 1996. Keeping managed care in balance. *Health and Social Work,* 21(3): 163–166.

Purtilo, R. B. 1994. Interdisciplinary health care teams and health care reform. *The Journal of Law, Medicine, and Ethics,* 22(2): 121–126.

Raderstorf, M., D. M. Hein, and C. S. Jencsen. 1984. A young stroke patient with severe aphasia returns to work: A team approach. *Journal of Rehabilitation,* February/March, 23–26.

Raymond, F. B. 1977. Social work education for health care practice. *Social Work in Health Care,* 2(4): 429–438.

Reamer, F. G. 1998. The evolution of social work ethics. *Social Work,* 43(6): 488–500.

Richardson, M. 1994. What health system reform means for Texas. *Texas Medicine,* 90(1): 15–20.

Ringle, S. P. 1996. The neurologist's role in stroke management. *Stroke,* 27(11): 1935–1936.

Ringle, S. P., and R. L. Hughes. 1996. Evidence-based medicine, critical pathways, practice guidelines and managed care. *Archives of Neurology,* 53: 867–871.

Rivera, V. M. 1985. Stroke: A guide to differential diagnosis and prevention. *Postgraduate Medicine,* 77(4): 81–88.

Roberts, C. S. 1989. Conflicting professional values in social work and medicine. *Health and Social Work,* 211–218.

Saltz, C. C. 1992. The interdisciplinary team in geriatric rehabilitation. *Journal of Gerontological Social Work,* 18(3/4): 133–142.

Saltz, C. C., and T. Schaefer. 1996. Interdisciplinary teams in health care: Integration of family caregivers. *Social Work in Health Care,* 22(3): 59–70.

Sands, R. G. 1989. The social worker joins the team: A look at the socialization process. *Social Work in Health Care,* 14(2): 1–14.

Sands, R. G., J. Stafford, and M. McClelland. 1990. I beg to differ: Conflict in the interdisciplinary team. *Social Work in Health Care,* 14(3): 55–72.

Shapiro, J. 1995. The downside of managed mental health care. *Clinical Social Work Journal,* 23(4): 441–451.

Smith, W. R., J. J. Cotter, and L. F. Rossiter. 1996. System change: Quality assessment and improvement for Medicaid managed care. *Health Care Financing Review,* 17(4): 97–108.

Society for Social Work Administrators in Health Care. 1994. *Special report of the managed care task force.* Chicago, Illinois: American Hospital Association.

Solomon, R., and M. J. Mellor. 1992. Interdisciplinary geriatric education: The new kid on the block. *Journal of Gerontological Social Work,* 18(3/4): 175–186.

Sparer, M. S. 1997. Managing the managed care revolution: States and the new Medicaid. In *Competitive managed care: The emerging health care system,* edited by J. D. Wilkerson, K. J. Devers, and R. S. Given. San Francisco: Jossey-Bass, Inc.

Strom-Gottfriend, K. 1997. The implications of managed care for social work education. *Journal of Social Work Education,* 33(1): 7–18.

Taccetta-Chapnick, M. 1996. Transformal leadership. *Nursing Administration Quarterly,* 21(1): 60–66.

Thomas, M. D., and T. L. Morrison. 1977. Interdisciplinary team communications: TA as a tool. *Clinical Social Work Journal,* 5(2): 118–131.

Thomasma, D. C.. 1996. The ethics of managed care: Challenges to the principles of relationship-centered care. *Journal of Allied Health,* Summer, 233–246.

Tuckman, B. W. 1965. Developmental sequence in small groups. *Psychological Bulletin,* 63(6): 384–399.

Verrilli, D. K., and S. Zuckerman. 1996. Preferred provider organizations and physicians fees. *Health Care Financing Review,* 17(3): 161–170.

Vitberg, A. K. 1996. *Marketing health care into the twenty-first century. The changing dynamic.* New York, London: The Haworth Press.

Warren, R. V. 1994. Merging managed care and Medicaid: Private regulation of public health. *NASW Social Work Practice Update.* Washington, DC: NASW.
Weil, T. P. 1996. How health networks and HMOs could result in public utility regulation. *Hospital and Health Service Administration,* 41(2): Summer, 266–280.
Weiner, J. P. 1994. Forecasting the effects of health reform on U.S. physician workforce requirement. *The Journal of the American Medical Association,* 272(3): 222–230.
Wilkerson, J. D. 1997. Messing with Medicare: Markets and politics in the 104th Congress. Edited by J. D. Wilkerson, K. J. Devers, and R. S. Given. *Competitive managed care: The emerging health care system.* San Francisco: Jossey-Bass, Inc.
Wilkerson, J. D., K. S. Devers, and R. S. Given. 1997. Understanding competitive managed care: The emerging competitive managed care market place. In *Competitive managed care: The emerging health care system,* edited by J. D. Wilkerson, K. J. Devers, and R. S. Given. San Francisco: Jossey-Bass, Inc.
Woolhandler, S., D. U. Himmelstein, and J. P. Lewontin. 1993. Administrative costs in U.S. hospitals. *The New England Journal of Medicine,* 329(6): 400–403.
Zwanziger, J., and G. A. Melnick. 1996. Can managed care plans control health care costs? *Health Affairs,* 15(2): Summer, 185–199.

Index